Competitive Strategy For Dummies®

Cheat Sheet

8 Secrets of Providing Exceptional Service

- ✔ Check that you know how quickly, well and completely your organisation is serving customers and clients.
- ✔ Ensure that you have all points of access – including the Internet – open and available when customers need and want to use them.
- ✔ If you have customer complaints, make sure that you find out what happened – and put it right regardless of the answer you discover.
- ✔ Remind your staff that they're expected to serve customers and clients – fully, pleasantly, positively, expertly and to the best of their ability.
- ✔ Always deliver what you promise.
- ✔ Never make promises that you can't keep.
- ✔ Remember: a satisfied customer tells nobody of his or her satisfaction; a dissatisfied customer tells everyone.
- ✔ Always look for ways of improving your customer service.

9 Strategies for Exerting Your Expertise

- ✔ Your expertise includes having, fostering and developing the right attitudes.
- ✔ Set the standards that you expect from all your staff and enforce them.
- ✔ If you want people to work in particular ways, then train them.
- ✔ If something is wrong, put it right.
- ✔ If you lack particular expertise, go out and find it.
- ✔ Make sure that you always have a fresh flow of expertise and ideas coming into your organisation.
- ✔ When staff and others come to you with new ideas, listen to them and evaluate them.
- ✔ Encourage everyone to continue to learn and develop at all times.
- ✔ Ensure that everyone takes up some part of staff training and development programmes.

8 Ways of Achieving Great Returns on Investment

- ✔ Always know and understand what you're investing in, and what returns are available.
- ✔ If you want returns of a particular percentage, you must go into areas in which these returns are available.
- ✔ If you want to work in a particular sector, you must accept the returns on offer.
- ✔ If you're calculating returns on investment, remember to include everything (staff, technology, premises and equipment as well as money) that you're investing.
- ✔ Things can change, and you may not get the returns that you seek. As the UK financial services authorities always say 'The value of your investment can go down, as well as up.' It applies to everyone!
- ✔ In many cases, people invest in things they *want* (rather than *need*), and then seek the reasons for doing so afterwards – which is always wrong.
- ✔ Check everything in which you're investing and inspect for risks and flaws (see Chapters 20 and 21).
- ✔ When you go into partnership with anyone, remember that the others have the right to expect returns as well.

For Dummies: Bestselling Book Series for Beginners

Competitive Strategy For Dummies®

Cheat Sheet

9 Things to Do before You Go Global . . .

✔ Ask yourself if you're really global – or do you just have a website?

✔ Know why you're going into particular locations and areas – and make sure that it's not just for fun or excitement!

✔ If you do go into new locations, make sure that you know and understand everything about them so that they're as familiar to you as your own backyard.

✔ Acquire the finance to support everything that you want to do, as well as to underwrite things that can and do go wrong.

✔ Ensure that your technology, communication lines, transport and infrastructure networks can support your expansion.

✔ Avoid simply chasing riches. A global venture must contribute to the overall development and wellbeing of the new location.

✔ Changes in energy, transport and infrastructure costs can make something that once looked attractive, subsequently very expensive.

✔ Present a clear view of how you're going to treat customers, clients and your staff in the new locality.

✔ Know and understand what kind of reputation you want in the new locality – and do everything you can to ensure that it comes about.

10 Essential Rules for Managing Risk

✔ Make sure that you know everything that can possibly go wrong in your organisation – and make sure that everyone else knows too.

✔ Concentrate on setting standards as high as possible.

✔ Ensure that you always follow up on breaches of security.

✔ Keep a constant vigil for bullying, victimisation, discrimination and harassment.

✔ If money goes missing, always find out why.

✔ Ask lots of questions about any new laws and regulations so you can identify all the inherent risks involved.

✔ If you're ever taken to court and lose, decide that you're going to learn from the mistakes – and then never make them again!

✔ Draft and enforce health and safety policies that truly prevent accidents and disasters from happening in the first place.

✔ Make sure that you always follow up on staff complaints.

✔ Always follow up on customer complaints. You never know how angry a customer actually is or how valid the complaint may be until you examine the situation fully.

For Dummies: Bestselling Book Series for Beginners

Competitive Strategy

FOR

DUMMIES®

by Richard Pettinger, MBA

WILEY

A John Wiley and Sons, Ltd, Publication

Competitive Strategy For Dummies®

Published by
John Wiley & Sons, Ltd
The Atrium
Southern Gate
Chichester
West Sussex
PO19 8SQ
England

E-mail (for orders and customer service enquires): cs-books@wiley.co.uk

Visit our Home Page on www.wiley.com

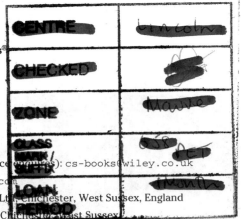

For general information on our other products and services, please contact our Customer Care Department within the U.S. at 800-762-2974, outside the U.S. at 317-572-3993, or fax 317-572-4002.

For technical support, please visit www.wiley.com/techsupport.

Wiley also publishes its books in a variety of electronic formats. Some content that appears in print may not be available in electronic books.

British Library Cataloguing in Publication Data: A catalogue record for this book is available from the British Library

ISBN: 978-0-470-77930-9

Printed and bound in Great Britain by Bell & Bain Ltd, Glasgow

10 9 8 7 6 5 4 3 2 1

WILEY

About the Author

Richard Pettinger has taught at University College London, where he is a senior lecturer in management, since 1989. He is the course director for the undergraduate Information Management for Business programme, which is especially concerned with ensuring that the next generation of managers and leaders are entrepreneurial, expert and competitive!

Richard teaches on foundation, undergraduate and postgraduate courses relating to general management, strategy, finance and marketing. He works also as a consultant, where he advises especially on different aspects of strategy, marketing, finance and investment – especially on the real pressures that have to be faced when struggling to stay competitive and remain effective.

Richard is the author of over 30 books on these different aspects of management and business and organisational practice. He has produced two other books for the *For Dummies* series – *Managing For Dummies* and *Weekend MBA For Dummies*. He has produced numerous journal articles and conference and study papers.

Acknowledgements

This is to acknowledge the efforts that everyone concerned has put in to make this book something that we can all be proud of. I am especially grateful to Anthony Impey for getting me the gig in the first place! As always, I have also had wonderful support all the way through! Thanks are especially due to Peter Antonioni, Jennifer Bingham, Roger Cartwright, Hasna Chakir, Kelvin Cheatle, Peter Clark, Steve Edwards, Paul Griseri, Frances Kelly, Jacek Klich, Brian Kramer, Anne O'Rorke and Helen Heyes – all of whom have played their part in making this project into something that we can all be really proud of. Finally, I would like as always to dedicate the book to my wife Rebecca, without whom nothing is possible.

Publisher's Acknowledgements

We're proud of this book; please send us your comments through our Dummies online registration form located at www.dummies.com/register/.

Some of the people who helped bring this book to market include the following:

Acquisitions, Editorial, and Media Development

Project Editor: Steve Edwards

Development Editor: Brian Kramer

Content Editor: Jo Theedom

Commissioning Editor: Samantha Spickernell

Publishing Assistant: Jennifer Prytherch

Copy Editor: Anne O'Rorke

Proofreader: Helen Heyes

Technical Editor: Peter Clark

Executive Editor: Samantha Spickernell

Executive Project Editor: Daniel Mersey

Cover Photos: ©Martin Poole/GettyImages

Cartoons: Ed McLachlan

Composition Services

Project Coordinator: Lynsey Stanford

Layout and Graphics: Samantha K. Allen, Reuben W. Davis, Christin Swinford

Proofreader: Jessica Kramer

Indexer: Christine Karpeles

Brand Reviewer: Jennifer Bingham

Contents at a Glance

Table of Contents

Part III: Putting Strategic Management into Action 101

Introduction

· ·

*O*n a personal level, everyone today seems to want instant success, fame, glamour and prosperity. And the same is true in business – every company and organisation is striving for that magical formula that guarantees amazing profits and enables all employees and backers to live happily (and wealthily) ever after.

Over the past 20 years or so, this drive has led many people to try to find prescriptions and recipes that guarantee success. And so such varied consultancy enterprises as Six Sigma, Total Quality Management (TQM), Business Process Re-engineering (BPR) and many other techniques and philosophies have emerged, claiming to provide orderly and assured paths to salvation and success.

Invariably, people using these approaches found that, like medical prescriptions, the best that you can hope for is that they cure a problem; they don't, in themselves, give you enduring health.

However, where all these prescriptions do have a point is that, in order to use them or follow them, you have to know what you're doing – and you have to be prepared to work hard and discipline yourself when following what's prescribed. Unfortunately, people frequently miss these bits!

- Large organisations hire consultants to bring in a prescription programme and then sit back, confidently expecting that all their problems are solved.

- People attend business seminars on a host of subjects in the (often forlorn) hope that they'll discover by chance the secrets of enduring success.

Of course, life isn't like that because business and management aren't so orderly. Whatever you do, whoever you bring in to advise you, however you look at things – everything boils down to one or two very straightforward propositions:

- You must know what you're doing – as well as when, where, how, why and for whom.

- You must know where your strengths lie – and then play to them.

- You must understand that, because you're not the only organisation in the world, you have to compete with others for business.

In a nutshell, this is all that competitive strategy is – except for the hard work that goes with making sure that you do indeed follow all the points above, concentrating your resources where they're needed and producing and delivering your products and services to the standards and quality that your customers expect.

So, clearly, an easy option it is not! But if you want success for yourself and your company or organisation, working towards a clear plan for progress – your competitive strategy and position – is going to give you the best possible chance of achieving your goals.

This is where *Competitive Strategy For Dummies* comes in. I strip away all the floss that surrounds so much of today's business practice. I start by defining what competition and strategy are and then go on to break them down into some clear component parts and processes. I then look at the pressures and constraints within which everyone works. Next, I examine how to set and maintain standards – and how to recognise the things that can, and do, go wrong. And finally, I explore how to spot and take advantage of all the opportunities out there, both in your own backyard and everywhere in the world.

So this book is for anyone coming to the subject for the first time. After all, 'competitive strategy' is one of those things that everyone in business is supposed to know about, but in practice very few do. This book is also here for anyone needing or wanting a top-up or a fresh look at what they already know. And it's hopefully a good read in any case!

From whatever point of view you're coming, this book is a call to action! Each of the areas that comprise competitive strategy requires people to do things. For example:

- ✔ Customers and clients don't come to you. *You* must persuade them that doing so is in their interests.

- ✔ Risks don't sort themselves out. *You* must make sure that things don't go wrong.

- ✔ Standards don't set themselves. *You* must make sure that they exist and that you enforce them.

Everything I cover in this book represents part of the expertise that you need in order to be a successful and effective leader, director or manager in today's business world.

About This Book

Everything you need to know about competitive strategy is in here! A world of difference exists between what people say is competitive strategy and what it actually is. Why? I contend this difference comes from the fact that 'competitive strategy' is one of those phrases that all too easily rolls off the tongue, particularly of people in positions of authority, business analysts and commentators.

Therefore, this book gets straight into what is truly important in today's world. And what is important is your *expertise* – your capability, knowledge, understanding and execution of those things that you need to do in order to make your company (and yourself) successful and effective, not just immediately but also over a lifetime.

I cover all the main areas of competitive strategy that you need to know about. I lay out the material in manageable and digestible chunks so that you can see how things are built up.

However you go through this book, the purpose is to make you think. Because thinking is one of the things that the next generation of top executives, business leaders and managers is going to have to do very much better than in the past. *Critical thinking* – the ability to use your own expertise to form, argue and, where necessary, defend your expert point of view – depends on your expertise in the field!

In addition to enhancing your expertise, the purpose of this book is to give you a good overall coverage of what you need to know in order to compete effectively in the world of business as it is at present and as it is likely to unfold. All the way through, I provide extensive examples of real organisations. As you come across these, have a think about why things went well or badly, and what the main lessons are that everyone ought to learn.

How This Book Is Organised

Competitive Strategy For Dummies is organised into six parts. The chapters in Parts I to V cover specific topic areas in detail, making finding the topic that you need simple and straightforward. Part VI provides some recommended reading, plus techniques, questions and a checklist for further guidance.

Part 1: Laying the Foundations of Competitive Strategy

In this part, I establish the basics that you need in order to give yourself the best possible chance of becoming and remaining competitive. I cover the nature of competitive strategy, the context of strategy and how to get to know and understand competitive environments. I also discuss how to lead and become an expert (as well as enjoying some of the rewards of being an expert).

Part II: Being Competitive

I explain what competition is and how to set yourself up to compete effectively, successfully – and profitably. I introduce the forces of competition and examine how they operate within the constraints of your competitive environment. You take an in-depth look at what leadership is, particularly the need for expert and committed people at the top of every successful company.

Part III: Putting Strategic Management into Action

Here, I look at how competitive action is generated and how competition works in practice, in the real world. I probe deeper into topics of finances and investment, as well as products, services and market inaction. You find out how markets (and customers and clients) behave, how to act and react to different initiatives, where the best opportunities exist and how to spot them for yourself.

Part IV: Enhancing Your Competitive Strategy

In this part, I look at how to make and sustain progress. You need always to be mindful of changing needs and wants so you can create and develop an organisation that remains competitive, manages risk effectively and sets and maintains standards of appropriate work and behaviour.

Part V: Looking Towards Your Future

I share with you all the things that strategic business leaders need to be aware of in today's world. I look at expansion, outsourcing and the opportunities of new markets and globalisation. You also find out about project work and the changing nature of public services, including the opportunities that these developments bring to strategic organisations.

Part VI: The Part of Tens

Every *For Dummies* book wraps up with a part of tens, a quick and concise look at the things that are, and remain, important. So here, we give you ten top books to read on competing and strategy (who doesn't love a good story?), ten techniques for managing risk, ten essential questions to ask about any investment and a ten-point checklist for action when you're contemplating a merger, acquisition or takeover.

Icons Used in This Book

I use icons next to blocks of text to draw your attention to particular nuggets of information throughout the book.

The bull's eye highlights a good idea that can save you time and trouble.

This icon draws your attention to pieces of information about competition and strategy that you shouldn't forget.

Real companies and organisations go through all the things I discuss in this book. These ripped-from-the-headlines examples can get you thinking.

Look for these techniques and processes that can help you do new things or do things better.

This information can help you avoid disasters – both personal and professional!

Where to Go from Here

For Dummies books are easy to access because they break up a big subject into easily identifiable and manageable chunks. This book is structured so that whatever you want, you can find it easily. *For Dummies* books are designed so that you can start anywhere you like. If you're new to business management, aiming for a top job or wanting to know how companies work when at their best, you may want to start at the beginning and work your way through to the end. A wealth of information and practical advice awaits you. Simply turn the page and begin.

If you already have plenty of experience, you may want to turn to a particular topic or question, such as understanding a competitive environment or defining what leadership is. You can go straight to the section or chapter that seems of interest to you by using the table of contents or the index.

And if you have any questions at all, do please get in touch. It will be lovely to hear from you. Please write to r.pettinger@ucl.ac.uk.

Part I
Laying the Foundations of Competitive Strategy

In this part . . .

I establish the basis that you need in order to give yourself and your organisation the best possible chance of becoming, and remaining, competitive. I explore the nature of competitive strategy, competition, the context of strategy and ways to understand your competitive environment. Along the way, I highlight how you can become an expert, along with the rewards of developing expertise.

Chapter 1

Gearing Up to Get Competitive

- -

- -

*W*hatever your walk of life, you need a purpose, something to strive for and something to propel you onto the next level. Nothing and nobody stands still – everything changes and advances. People are always looking for new things to do, new interests, fresh challenges and adventures.

All companies and organisations – including yours – have a drive for purpose and challenge. Organisations don't exist in isolation, nor do they exist without human contributions. They need to make progress, stay vibrant and do things better and differently. The people who work for organisations expect progress, as do their customers and clients. And, in any case, things like technology, competition, the actions of managers and the demands of shareholders and backers force change and development on organisations.

Successful individuals and organisations decide what they're going to do – and why, when, where and how they're going to do things. In other words, they form and develop *strategies* – patterns and processes by which they make progress and advance in pursuit of goals and objectives.

You can wish for anything; this is a part of human behaviour. But unless you then determine to put in the hard work to back up your wishes, all you're doing is daydreaming – and this is no use to anyone but yourself. Strategy is about laying the foundations for hard work and making sure that your dreams do indeed come to fruition. Strategy isn't merely about thinking – it's about action!

Strategy – along with the interconnected ideas of competition and priorities – is the focus of this chapter. In the following sections, I show you how to establish the foundations for hard work and make sure that your dreams come to fruition.

Defining Strategy

Though you may have just opened this book, you probably have a good idea of what strategy is, the bits and pieces that you need to add to give a strategy life and some ways to make a strategy effective.

Strategy is about having goals, aims and objectives – and then creating the patterns of activities and behaviour that you need in order to aspire to and eventually meet these aims and objectives. Strategy is about having the processes in place that make everyone's life as easy and as productive as possible as you strive for your goals.

Who actually *needs* a strategy? Well, the answer is pretty much everyone! In every walk of life, you must know what you are doing – as well as why, for whom, where the profit is coming from and who you are competing against for work.

Although strategy is a pretty simple concept, having a good strategy for your organisation is actually complex. The following sections can help you lay the groundwork necessary to give yourself the best possible chance of enduring commercial and competitive success. If you consider all the aspects I address in the following sections, you may still not succeed, but at least you can track back and figure out where and why you failed. (And even in failure, you can succeed in a sense. Even the best strategies contain weak points. If you identify your weakness, your revised strategy becomes that much better.)

If you don't go through the processes I discuss in this chapter and book and yet you do succeed, you'll have no idea *why* you succeeded – and if you fail, crucially, you'll have no idea why this happened either.

Being effective

A key characteristic of any strategy is that it's *effective*. In the case of an organisation's strategy, being effective means:

- ✔ You make and deliver products and services that people need and want from you – at prices that they're willing and able to pay.
- ✔ You look to make progress, to change, to advance and develop, to do things better than before.
- ✔ You have the resources (finance, technology, expertise and so on) at your disposal so you can do what you want and need to do.
- ✔ You achieve results by engaging your staff's commitment and their expertise.

✔ You do everything at the right time for everyone involved.

Your timing has to be right. Right for any stage of the economic cycle, right for your team and people, right for your customers and – most importantly – right for your company or organisation.

Of course, the preceding list sounds great, but how many 'important business initiatives' have you encountered or been part of that actually resulted in less getting done, more slowly, more expensively, by more people, at greater cost? If you're truthful – probably quite a few!

Or how about the many good new ideas that have been introduced and failed because people didn't know quite what they were doing and why. Or something that was a really good idea, but what with one thing and another it came in two years too late and failed utterly.

Clarifying every detail

Another top priority for any strategy is clarity – of purpose, priorities, conduct, behaviour and performance. Without these things, you immediately limit your effectiveness and your ability to compete.

You must get your strategy clear at the outset of any project, initiative or effort. Your strategy is, after all, going to be the cornerstone or basis of everything that you do, how you do it and for whom you do it. If you don't make yourself clear at this point, you're always going to struggle to get your message across in the future.

Begin planning any strategy by making it absolutely clear to everyone what you're setting out to do – as well as how, why and for whom. And 'everyone' here means everyone – your staff, your backers and shareholders, your suppliers, your customers and clients, as well as the markets, locations that you serve and the communities in which you operate. (Yes, I just threw out a lot of terms. So in order to make myself completely clear about what I mean, turn to Chapter 9 to find out more about customers and clients; turn to Chapter 4 for markets and locations.)

Clarity is the basis of what eventually becomes your competitive strategy. By getting it as clear as possible, you are:

✔ Sorting out where your priorities truly lie (see the section 'Establishing Your Priorities' later in this chapter).

✔ Figuring out how you're going to create your own order and structure.

✔ Determining how you're going to conduct yourself as you pursue your business.

Clarity is important early on because you need to establish yourself and your activities so that everyone knows what you do and for whom; and that you say what you mean, and mean what you say. You're setting out the standards and attitudes that you're going to adopt towards your customers and clients – those on whom you ultimately depend for your very survival.

Clarity also involves the basis of the ways in which you interact with others, including:

- ✔ The attitudes that you adopt towards your staff. How are you going to communicate to inspire your people?
- ✔ The attitudes that you adopt towards your suppliers. For example, are you going to exploit and drive them into the ground, or are you going to work in partnership and collaborate with them to the benefit of you both?
- ✔ The attitudes that you adopt towards the communities in which you're going to be working. Remember that these communities not only serve as an important customer base – they're also where many of your employees are going to come from.
- ✔ The attitudes that you're going to adopt towards people who put money and resources into your company and your activities. How are you going to spend what is, after all, their money? How are you going to invest to generate the returns that they seek and that they are entitled to?

Change, progress and development

One of your main priorities as a competitive, strategic individual and leader of an organisation is to change, progress and develop.

Now, this is hardly news! Yet so many companies and organisations introduce developments that actually don't change, progress or develop. Many changes, unfortunately, result in things being done less quickly, more expensively, for fewer customers and clients, with declining results.

- ✔ Ever been involved in a mega-computer or technology project that was to revolutionise the way in which data was processed – only to find that you then had to wait ages for something that used to be available at the tip of your fingers?

- ✔ Ever waited patiently for the next games console, only to find that it was so full of glitches that it had to go straight back to the makers?

- ✔ Ever seen a one-time charge on a Balance Sheet that is a testament to an ill-starred corporate adventure into the unknown – and which everyone now must pay for?

Look carefully and critically at any proposed change, innovation, enhancement or development from the point of view of improving everything – not of getting in the way of progress! (For how to do this successfully, see Chapter 9.)

Here's the important question. How do you want to be known by all the preceding people? Because know you they will! So make sure that you establish your relationships right and open in your own terms, from the very beginning of any endeavour. Asking and answering this question invariably serves as a reality check for many organisations and their top managers – many of whom never considered what people may think about them!

You need to make these considerations at the outset of any venture because people like to know where they stand with everyone and everything that they come into contact with. People gravitate towards other people who they know, trust and understand, and away from those of whom they're not so sure.

And if after considering how you want to be known, you determine that you do really want to be known as hard, exploitative, overbearing – then at least have the courage to say so up front, rather than leaving this realisation to the local gossip and grapevine.

Finding purpose and direction

Another essential aspect of any strategy is a statement of your purpose, direction and priorities. Being as clear as possible about your purpose and direction helps to reinforce people's confidence in you. And you're going to need this confidence in every quarter:

- ✔ **Your staff** need and want to know what you're like as an employer.
- ✔ **Your suppliers** (of raw materials and components, data, technology and transport) need and want to know that you're a good company with which to do business.
- ✔ **Your customers** need and want to know that your products and services are of the quality and value that they seek, and that you charge fair prices and fees.

By getting your purpose and direction clear at the start, you build the confidence that everyone needs to have in you.

You're also refining and steering everything that you do – because you have to! You have to change every time one of your competitors does something to which you have to respond. You have to change every time you develop something new or introduce a new product or service. You have to change every time you discover a new group of buyers for your products and services. And you have to be able to respond every time the external pressures in the environment change. (For more on these pressures, go to Chapter 5).

So by extension, your competitive strategy can't be static. It has to be the basis of your active (not passive) involvement in everything that you do. It must be flexible and responsive to demands, needs, wants and opportunities.

You can't know what these demands and opportunities are unless you're first clear in your own mind about how you operate and how you compete. What you do and how you do it are important of course; but *why* you do things – your purpose – is the most vital element. Whatever you do, you have to be able to explain and justify, and very often defend. So make sure that you've worked out clearly why you do things in particular ways and at particular times.

Figuring out your purpose and direction gives you a secure foundation from which to operate. You need this base because as organisations progress and advance, they can lose sight of where their strengths truly lie, which can lead to all sorts of trouble. For example:

- **Leeds United Football Club** forgot that it was a very successful domestic and regional club and spent £93 million pursuing the illusion that it was one of the world's top clubs. This illusion arose at the club because its management thought that it was unbeatable after just one spectacular season!

- **McDonalds** lost focus and experienced considerable turnover of staff when, in response to criticism that it was fuelling an obesity crisis, it introduced 'healthy' food ranges and reduced its standard menus. Although the intention may have been superficially laudable, offering healthier food options did not (and does not) alter the fact that people don't immediately think of McDonalds as being a health food restaurant.

As you progress and advance, your strategic and competitive position must act as an anchor and as a reference point. Only change your core position when it clearly is no longer delivering what it should.

What strategy is not

While you're spending time and exerting effort to figure out what your strategy is, you also need to be clear about what strategy is not! Strategy is not any, or all, of the following:

- A wish list or daydream.

- A perfect plan with everything laid out neatly and nothing without a place in the structure of things. People mistake plans for strategy all the time. You can't plan for anything with certainty; you have to be aware of all the forces that can and do affect things.

- An exotic but impossible and buzz-word filled description of a fantasy future, bought in from high-priced management consultants.

- A set of bland statements which mean nothing at all. Recent examples of these sorts of statements include: 'Seeking opportunities wherever they may be' (Laing) and 'We are well placed to take advantage of the upturn' (Cable and Wireless). These statements are actually counterproductive because people can see that they're filled with blandness or bromide – truly indicative of a lack of energy and commitment. (And both Laing and Cable and Wireless have lived to regret their approaches.)

✔ A statement that is totally boastful or fanciful. Notable examples include: 'To be the world's top provider of last minute goods, solutions and gifts' (lastminute.com, shortly before it was taken over by Thomas Cook) and 'From the world's best energy company, to the world's best company' (Enron, shortly before it went bankrupt).

✔ A positive notion that is ultimately lifeless or meaningless. For example, 'We're going to advance and win the war' is not a strategy – unless you then go on to describe the detail by which you're going to do this.

✔ A goal that you describe in general terms but then don't resource properly. This is a besetting sin of many public services as well as commercial organisations. For example, the UK NHS is held to be the model for all healthcare providers to follow, and yet its hospital wards are not kept clean due to under-resourcing.

✔ A goal that you simply ignore. For example, in the US, Eastman Kodak long described itself as a digital photography company whilst still emphasising traditional film cameras and photographic paper.

✔ An ideal that operates in isolation from what the company actually does in practice. For instance, many companies state that they're global players, but they actually carry out their main activities in one or two areas only.

✔ A lofty ambition that's impossible to achieve. Telling people that your only purpose in life is to go to Mars (for example) is a lovely idea, but it's not at all feasible, at least at present.

✔ A replication of someone else's ideas and approaches. Whereas you can indeed learn lessons from the best and most successful, you're never going to be able to repeat how they do things, the expertise or activities that they themselves conduct or how they behave in their own particular domains.

Make up your mind *now* that you'll avoid all the preceding misguided definitions of 'strategy' – at least not without adding lots of detail to them. And if you're not yet senior enough to be doing things as you'd choose, you must know and understand now that you're always going to have problems if you're faced with implementing or trying to work towards any of the preceding.

Defining Competition

In organisational terms any strategy has to be *competitive*. The structure of markets and the behaviour of customers and clients mean that, if people buy particular goods, products and services from one outlet or organisation, they don't buy from others.

Some call this situation a *zero sum game* because you have to be prepared to fight your corner! If you don't fight, others simply take from you.

Here then you are forming a *competitive position* – the basis on which you're going to compete with others and prevent them from simply taking from you. The foundations of forming an effective competitive position arise from the clarity of your strategy (see the section 'Clarifying every detail' earlier). If you set yourself and your organisation out clearly and simply, people know what you stand for and you then have the best possible start to developing a fully effective competitive position. If you can't state a clear strategy, you can't expect people to know what you stand for and what you can and can't do for them; so they won't come to you, but they'll go to others who have set things out clearly from the beginning.

I introduce the basic drivers of competition – the forces of competition – in Chapter 3. You also need to understand what competition is not, which is harder to grasp than may first appear (see the sidebar 'What competition is not' for details).

What competition is not

Deciding how to compete can lead some people into the illusion that rules of strategy and competition exist. The unwary can easily be led to believe that they need to do something because:

- Someone else in the sector is doing it.

- The CEO of a rival organisation is doing it.

- Your organisation won't be fashionable if it doesn't.

Of course, any of these examples may be worth following, but your justification is vital. If you choose to follow someone else's path you must still be able to ask and answer, 'But why is my organisation doing this?' Be prepared to provide support and if necessary defend your decision to follow in another organisation's footsteps.

In the past, people have envisioned their competitive plans metaphorically, with mixed success. For example:

- Some try to plan their commercial futures on the basis of the assurance of a military campaign. This approach is fine, as long as you also follow the rules of successful military campaigns – and don't start mistaking this process for moving pieces neatly around maps from the comfort of your office. Clever illustrations may be lovely and look very neat – but they miss the point! Competition is rough and tough and messy and hard work; competition is not orderly or predictable.

- Others try to look at competition and competitive strategy as a game of chess – and this is even worse! Apart from anything else, the chess metaphor assumes that only two players exist and that only one moves at a time. And competition as a game of chess also assumes that you accept defeat gracefully if that's how things pan out. Wrong, wrong, wrong! In business and commercial competition, if things go against you, you have to fight back with whatever you have at your disposal. So if you're losing at chess, you may need to throw your pieces around and then go and find a cricket bat or a rugby ball or a swimming costume – anything rather than slump to defeat without a fight!

Don't be led down these paths. Make sure that you compete from the position of your own strengths and impose these on those who compete with you.

Surveying Different Types of Strategy and Competition

You can rarely summarise your strategy and competition position in a crisp one-sentence statement – or even an elegantly worded paragraph. Often, an organisation needs a toolkit of strategies to respond to current competitive pressures. The following sections explore these various types of strategy that you need to become familiar with and develop for your own organisation.

Grand strategy

Your *grand strategy* is the position that you define as the core or hub of all your activities. Normally you base your grand strategy on cost advantage, brand advantage or something else that's of value to the customers you seek to serve. Whatever your grand strategy, you must provide value and benefits for which your customers are prepared to do business with you and pay the prices and charges that you make. (See Chapter 2 for more on identifying your grand strategy).

Your grand strategy also defines the kind of organisation that you run.

- ✔ **If you seek cost advantages**, you normally concentrate as many of your resources as possible on front-line activities.

  For example, if you're a manufacturing operation, you may have all your resources directed to your factories rather than your head office facilities.

  One reason for the lack of success in many public services is that few allot enough resources at the front line and direct considerable resources towards office, administrative and other non-service functions.

- ✔ **If you seek quality or brand advantages**, you normally place your primary effort on building and supporting the brand.

- ✔ **If you seek something else**, you concentrate as many of your resources as you have to, in order to make sure that people never forget the 'something else' that you stand for.

Sub strategies

You need sub strategies in all areas of activity. Your *sub strategies* support and reinforce everything that you set out to do. The important thing about sub strategies is that you integrate them as fully as possible with your grand strategy (see the preceding section) and the basis on which you're competing.

Specific sub strategies that you need include:

- **Marketing strategies**, to present your products and services to the best advantage in terms of how you serve your markets, customers and clients.

- **HR strategies**, to ensure that you treat your staff properly and you parcel up work in the most effective ways possible.

- **Reward strategies**, to ensure that everyone shares in the organisation's successes; and to make sure also that you attract and keep the best possible staff.

- **Production and output strategies**, so that you have the resources necessary to deliver your products and services at the quality and volume that you need and want.

- **Product and service strategies**, to ensure that your customers and clients know and understand where they're buying your goods and services from, and how they can make contact with you when they need assistance or additional products and services.

- **Service delivery strategies**, so that your customers get the best possible service from you and that you put right problems and complaints as quickly as possible.

- **Financial strategies**, so that you deliver returns to your shareholders and backers – and yourself, of course!

- **Investment and capital management and appraisal strategies**, so that you have a good sound basis for delivering your products and services for the future.

- **Product and service development and innovation strategies**, so that you continue to satisfy your customers and clients far into the future.

Incremental strategies

The great beauty of *incremental strategies* is that you take small steps forward. So if you make a mistake, you can withdraw early and adjust without too much loss. And if you're successful, you can take lots of small steps very quickly – and people see steady progress.

The trouble with incremental strategies is that they're not exciting! And they don't always sit comfortably in an age when everyone expects excitement and glamour and can travel the world on company business, making highly profitable interventions all over the place.

Even when you do take small and considered steps, they still have to be in support of your grand strategy and priorities. Otherwise incremental strategies amount to nothing more than a random series of small actions which may or may not work as you thought and expected. (And if you don't have at least some idea of a grand strategy, you're never going to be quite sure whether your incremental strategies were good moves or not.)

Radical strategies and transformation

Radical strategies are those which set out to change the whole world – or at least an organisation's position in it!

Radical strategies create excitement of course. These are the types of strategies that everyone wants to be involved in! Everyone sees the excitement that's attached to doing something that they've never done before; they see glamorous and exciting figures from the world of business make incredible transformations and then go on to great fame and fortune – and they want to be a part of this!

Of course, life is never so simple! In practice, most of these great adventures fail. And those that succeed do so because the leader or director actually approaches the radical transformation with very great caution, so that they don't foul up at all. For example:

- ✔ When he first went into the air travel industry, Richard Branson sought advice from everywhere about the pitfalls that he would encounter. He set out to gain a foothold on the UK–USA routes, some of the most profitable in the world. And he succeeded by making sure that he learned and understood at least as much as anyone else about these routes and he surrounded himself with experts in air travel.

- ✔ When he opened his chain of fitness clubs, Duncan Bannatyne ensured that his clubs included a full range of leisure as well as fitness facilities, including swimming pools, bars and restaurants – because he knew that these facilities were what his target clients actually wanted.

- ✔ However, when the first mobile phone technologies were being pioneered, BT, the original protagonist, faced opposition from naysayers who didn't see the use of mobile phones. After all, telephones were universal, and anyone could use one at any time! And here was BT, the great landline provider, looking at changing everything! In this case though, having pioneered the mobile phone, BT was unable to cash in, as others moved faster; and BT's interests in mobile phones were later hived off and became O2. The lesson? Regardless of how great and dominant your company is in its present markets, you still must be able to support radical transformation into other activities.

Establishing Your Priorities

From all your consideration of strategy and competition, you eventually establish the priorities necessary to secure your competitive position and the basis on which you serve your customers and deliver your products and services.

Centre your *priorities* on producing and delivering the goods and services that your customers and clients seek and expect from you. Nothing else will do! Anything that does not serve this aim is wasteful and expensive!

If you're determined to dominate a particular market, you must concentrate everything that you can on establishing a position that indeed dominates. If you're determined to be a global player, you need the resources to be able to operate effectively in hundreds of different countries and to adapt those strategies to the different demands of each country in which you operate.

Identifying your priorities is only a start! You must then go on and work out the full details for each priority. For example, if you're determined to be the best tunnelling company in the world, your top priority is to know and understand everything about how to build tunnels. Your next priority is that you target people with whom you want to do business and serve anyone who wants a tunnel built, based on your standards as the best tunnelling company in the world. Your third priority is to establish a series of prices and charges that reflect your status as the best (if you want the best, you have to pay, of course; and if your customer expects the best, he expects to pay, as well).

The preceding may sound simple, but what you're actually doing when you take this kind of approach is setting out a position of consistency and clarity (see 'Clarifying every detail' earlier). People who come to you already have a good idea of what you can do for them and how you're going to do it. If you're not consistent and clear in your priorities, people wonder exactly what you do and how you do it – and as a result they gravitate away from you and towards those who do have consistency and clarity.

What priorities are not

If you set the wrong priorities, you're likely to find yourself pursuing things that look smart and fashionable – but which get in the way of progress and ultimately hurt the performance of your company. For example, in times of difficulty, you can easily prioritise things like layoffs, product withdrawals, outsourcing and re-branding when you should instead concentrate on developing what your organisation does have going for it. These actions and activities look and sound tough and decisive, but you're simply re-prioritising to do the wrong things instead of the right ones!

Going for it – or not!

Having spent a number of the preceding pages preaching discipline and rigour, I now have to pull the punch a little! One of your priorities also needs to be the capability and flexibility to seek opportunities as and when they arise, to recognise them for what they are and to take advantage of them when they arise. This means that you must have the expertise to know what an opportunity is for you and your organisation. If your specific definition of an opportunity is clear, you can also have the strength of character to walk away when something's just not right for you.

The best leaders, managers, executives and entrepreneurs do indeed have this combination of clarity, order, discipline and flexibility – all of which they combine with their expertise and attitudes that say very quickly whether something is truly an opportunity to them. If it is, they do everything they can to grasp it with both hands. If it isn't, they forget it and go on looking around.

Knowing Whether You're Willing

When you figure out your competitive position and develop all your various strategies and priorities, you give yourself the best possible chance of success. (And as I state earlier, if things do go wrong, you can at least backtrack to establish why.) You've proved your capability; now you must prove your willingness.

Determining whether you're truly willing to pursue your strategy is important because in addition to being able to do something, you must also *want to do it.* However trite this may sound, you need to make sure that:

- ✔ You want to do it.
- ✔ Your colleagues want to do it.
- ✔ Your backers want you to do it.

If any or all these groups don't see the value of the endeavour, or can't be bothered, you'll have problems. Collective as well as individual commitment and motivation is vital. You want all groups behind you, supporting you – not dragging their feet (or indifferent, which is nearly as bad).

Figuring Out What Matters

And so to a key question: how do all the topics I cover in this chapter matter to you? After all, you're surely aware of organisations where products turn out to be awful, where the service is appalling, where companies charge high prices for poor quality products and services – and yet these companies seem to go on from strength to strength, success to success.

Many of those who argue against having a competitive strategy and the kind of detailed approach that I outline in this chapter state that a competitive strategy restricts you, preventing you from having the flexibility and responsiveness that you need in order to move fast and take advantage of opportunities when they do arise.

I counter that whatever your chosen approach, you must know what you're doing and why. So you have to have all the detail and the structured approach in place in order to be able to recognise and know what an opportunity actually is. Otherwise you're simply choosing to go into things at random. You need the kind of structure and order that competitive strategy brings in order to actually understand what advantages are available and how you can maximise them.

So why does competitive strategy matter? Well, part of the answer is – it matters to you. You want to do the best for yourself and everyone around you. You want a reputation that you can be proud of. You want to be able to point to your achievements. You don't want to be one of those people for whom, when the subject of jobs comes up at a dinner party and you tell people who you work for, everything goes quiet and then people start talking all at once!

Another part of the answer is – your competitive strategy matters in the future. When resources are neither scarce nor expensive, your ability to compete can always be at least partly addressed by throwing resources at a problem. Now, whatever the circumstances, this is actually a very expensive way of remaining profitable, and you should avoid this approach if at all possible. In practice, you are simply wasting the resources that you have, and which you are certain to need for the future, on something that you can avoid if you do the job properly first time around.

Competitive strategy really does matter when the crunch comes! Whenever credit and consumer crises hit, the first organisations to suffer are those that don't have a clear position. Suddenly, people have to look very hard at the cash that they have and the cash that they spend. And so they turn to those companies that provide products and services that they can be sure of – those that they know to be good value and good quality, or those that they know to have some distinctive benefit (such as clarity) for which people are still prepared to pay.

Chapter 2

Laying the Foundations of Strategy

· ·

· ·

*N*othing comes from nothing. You have to start somewhere when establishing an organisation's competitive strategies. In reality, you can't completely choose your ideal starting point. You have to start any new idea, venture or initiative from where you are at present.

And in order to start somewhere, you typically must deal with a lot of baggage including:

✔ Your organisation's history of products and services.

✔ Your staff's expectations and aspirations in terms of work, compensation and rewards.

✔ Customers' and clients' expectations in terms of quality, speed of delivery and types of products and services.

✔ Shareholders' and backers' expectations in terms of returns on their investments.

Knowing where you're starting from isn't new or revolutionary in business. Indeed, many successful leaders over the years have benefited from having a clear understanding of what their organisations do, as well as how and why they do what they do. These leaders also have specific visions of what their organisations now need to do to succeed in highly competitive marketplaces and set goals accordingly.

This chapter looks at the foundations of competitive strategy in terms of what you need know about your organisation's past and present – as well as the future you envision for it. In the following sections, I pinpoint the elements that you need to have in place if you're going to succeed in competitive business today.

Building on the Past and Present

Before you can establish an effective competitive strategy for your organisation's future, you must realise two things:

✔ You must work with what you already have.

✔ Your current situation is where you need to start.

What happened in the past is not nearly as important as what you now do. You can take your present position and make it work to the best possible advantage – for you, your customers and clients and your shareholders and backers. You have to be able to take finance, technology and expertise and use them to your best advantage in the present and unfolding future. And you need to be able to commit yourself to and support everything that you set out to do.

After you commit yourself to this position, you must make certain decisions:

✔ **You must have a core position.** Your *core position* is a summary or basis by which everyone recognises and identifies you. It is the one thing for which you are known. For example:

- Marks & Spencer is known for the quality of its products.

- Tesco is known for its huge range of products and services, and for the convenience of being able to get everything under one roof.

- Ryanair is known for its low fares.

Be clear in your own mind about what you are and want to be known for. If you cannot easily describe what you are known for, you probably need to do a bit more thinking.

Don't make up something as your core position – and don't be bland or boring! Make sure that you are known for something that is vibrant and positive – and reinforced with actions! See the following section 'Considering Core Positions' for more.

✔ **You must be selective and decide which customers, clients and markets you serve – as well as those you don't serve.** See the section 'Being clear about what you will – and will not – do' later in this chapter.

✔ **You must recognise and meet all the obligations and commitments that arise from serving your identified customers, clients and markets.** See Chapter 9 for more on this topic.

✔ **You must do everything in the context of your business or market.** Working with your business or market's *context* means you agree to work in the ways that the sector and its customers and clients expect. For example, if you want returns of 35 per cent, then you need to be in a market that can deliver these returns. And by extension, if you want to be in a particular sector (such as civil engineering), you must be prepared to accept the returns on offer in that sector.

✔ **You must invest in your own future.** Nothing happens by chance. And nothing happens just because you keep your prices down or your quality high. You have to be prepared to invest in everything that contributes to your goals over the lifetime of your company or organisation. See Chapter 15 for more.

If you do all these things, you give yourself a good start and the best possible chance of building an organisation that delivers the products and services sought by the customers and clients.

If you don't do these things, people may become unsure about the quality and value of your organisation and its products and services:

✔ Backers become uncertain about what they're investing in and what sort of returns they may get; they turn towards organisations they can be more sure of.

✔ Customers and clients become uncertain about your products, service quality and value; they too turn to those organisations whose quality and value they already trust. These customers and clients may not be easily attracted or persuaded away from their providers ever again.

Considering Core Positions

After you're clear about what you are known (and hopefully loved) for, you need to determine and set out your organisation's core position, based on your grand strategy (see Chapter 1).

Your *core position* has five aspects:

✔ **Being clear about where your organisation's true strengths lie (and playing to these strengths).**

✔ **Being clear about the customers and markets that you will (and will not) serve.** For example, the Co-operative Central Bank, through its board, limits its dealings and investments to companies that do not harm people or the environment.

✔ **Being clear about how you serve your customers and markets, including your speed of service and the prices that you charge.** For example, Pret a Manger expects to serve every customer within three minutes of his or her arrival in a shop.

✔ **Being clear about what else customers and clients can expect from you in addition to your core product or services.** These additional things can include your presentation and packaging of goods, an easy-to-use website or a phone that you answer on (or before) the first ring. For example, Amazon promises that customers will normally receive goods within two to three days of placing orders.

✔ **Being clear about what you expect of your staff in supporting, developing and conducting your business.** And if you clearly and constructively involve your staff, good workers will beat a path to your door. For example, Body Shop still has a long waiting list of potential staff because the company continues to carry the cachet of setting distinctive standards of behaviour and performance.

Whatever core position you take – cost advantage, brand advantage or some other advantage (see Chapter 1) – your core position has to be valuable enough to the customers and clients that you target that they will pay the prices, fees and charges that you establish.

Each position comes with its own distinctive set of commitments, which I examine in the following three sections.

Focusing on cost leadership and advantage

If you seek cost leadership and advantage, you set out to deliver your products and services both cheaper and more cost effectively than your competitors on an ongoing basis. To gain cost leadership and advantage, you need to be as cost effective as possible, which means:

✔ You concentrate all efforts and resources on product and service output and delivery, as well as on marketing and distribution functions which directly support these aspects.

✔ You keep administration and support functions to the absolute minimum.

✔ You invest in production and service delivery technology and equipment to help secure your cost leadership and advantage.

✔ You deliver your products and services with minimal defects in quality.

If you can do all this, you give yourself all the competitive advantages of overall cost effectiveness, thus securing several immediate and enduring operational competitive advantages:

✔ You have much more freedom than your competition to set prices for your products and services. And if you can charge higher prices, you have the power of greater operating profit margins at your fingertips.

- ✔ Because you are the most cost-effective operator, you can sustain price wars for longer than any of your competitors.

- ✔ You keep a close watch on all costs, particularly when they start to rise.

- ✔ You use your strength as cost leader to secure a market position based on the cost or price value that you deliver to your customers.

Going for cost leadership doesn't mean that you're cheap or that you're good value for money. Nor does this position mean that you cut costs and are a cheapskate! What this position means is that you ensure maximum returns on everything you invest in the organisation and you always concentrate on:

- ✔ Maximising productivity in terms of output per employee.

- ✔ Maximising machine and technology use and efficiency.

- ✔ Maximising returns on investment that you make in premises and technology.

Core position for public services

If you supply public services such as health care, education or transport, you need to seek a cost advantage position, maximising and optimising your costs. If you don't, you're using public resources for other purposes when all resources should be concentrated on serving your clients or users.

A cost advantage position is essential in public services because the 'customer' and 'demand' are already set – a specific public exists that needs to be served by a ministry or department. Your organisation must define the quality, timing, location, manner and convenience of providing its service.

This stance sounds reasonable on the surface. However, if you think for a moment about the state of real-world public finances (the budget deficits in schools, hospitals and road building programmes, for example), you quickly realise that these services are short enough of cash and resources without wasting them anywhere else. Increasingly, too, many public services now charge users additional fees (fare premiums to repay railway repairs and upgrades, charges for eye tests and dental care, university top-up fees). These situations (and others) highlight the importance of investing any available money in developing the overall service provision.

People in charge of providing public services need extremely clear priorities before allocating resources in order to ensure that they deliver what is required and demanded to as many clients and users as possible. Actually, this principle applies whether you're providing services as a public body or a private organisation.

Unfortunately, few public service providers have decided what their core purposes are, where their priorities lie and how they are going to operate in the continued best interests of their clients and service users. No wonder so many public bodies, privatised organisations and commercial contractors have such poor reputations for service performance, overcharging, waste and profligacy.

(continued)

(continued)

If you're establishing the core position for a public service provider, you need to:

✔ Determine what customers, client groups and service users actually need, want and expect from you.

✔ Decide how you're going to meet these demands, needs and wants in terms of staffing, technology, premises, locations and equipment.

✔ Maximise the number of front-line professional staff (train drivers, nurses, social workers and so on), while you minimise the number of administrative and support staff, head office workers and back office functionaries.

✔ Invest in training, developing and rewarding all workers, so you can keep the best people doing what they are good at.

Banking on brand leadership and advantage

The clear alternative to cost leadership and advantage (see the preceding section) is securing for yourself a position of brand leadership and advantage. Brand leadership is all about *differentiation* – giving your products and services a perception and appearance of difference from the competition, substitutes and alternatives.

If you choose this core position, you:

✔ Create advertising, marketing and branding campaigns so that people know and understand the quality and value that you're delivering.

✔ Engage in ongoing market research to ensure that you continue to meet people's expectations and understanding of your products and services.

✔ Produce a steady stream of product and service upgrades and developments.

✔ Produce a steady stream of real and perceived quality and value enhancements so that you continually raise – and then meet – people's expectations.

Quality is about two things: What you deliver and what your customers *think* you deliver. This is what I mean by real and perceived quality. Producing the most reliable products or services in the world is of no use to anyone if people don't know this (or don't believe it). By the same token, if you promise or indicate a particular level of quality and value in your products and services, you *must* deliver. If you do not, people quickly turn away from you and towards others who do meet their promises.

Successfully differentiated products and services have a *brand*, a consistency of logo, appearance, design, presentation, colours and images so that people can recognise them instantly and know what they stand for.

In addition to these visual elements, successfully branded products or services have brand values that customers know, understand and are prepared to pay for. *Brand values* are those things that reflect customer expectations and satisfaction – quality, value for money, durability, convenience, choice and so on. The more of these triggers that your products and services press, the greater your ability to develop these values as integral parts of your brand. For example:

- ✔ Swatch watches come with brand values of good value for money, unique designs and a sense of fun.
- ✔ BMW cars come with an assurance of full and comprehensive servicing, as well as a recognition of luxury and exclusivity.
- ✔ Nokia phones come with an assurance of reliability and connection with anyone on any network anywhere in the world.

The preceding organisations use these values to set their products apart from competitors and alternatives in their sectors.

If you can become the top brand in your sector, you can command the highest prices. For example, in the UK:

- ✔ People are willing to pay more for Coca-Cola than supermarket brand colas.
- ✔ People are willing to pay more for a British Airways plane ticket than for low-cost alternatives (such as easyJet) even though the airlines operate on the same routes.
- ✔ People are willing to pay more for a basket of groceries at Waitrose than they do at Asda.

Where you're seeking a brand advantage, you commit yourself to doing everything necessary to build and reinforce customer perceptions of your product or service's quality, value, durability and reliability. You're setting and managing people's expectations so that your customers and clients come to you with the absolute assurance that you can deliver what they expect. Maintaining a brand advantage takes constant reinforcement, so your priorities and commitments truly lie in marketing, advertising and PR. Everything that you do reinforces the strength of the brand, its values and the product and service quality that you deliver. For all these promises, your customers are prepared to pay the prices and charges that you choose.

The care and feeding of a brand

Think about the last time you saw a Coca-Cola advertisement, poster or display in a supermarket or smaller shop. You probably didn't even consciously notice this bit of promotion and had to think a bit about where and when you exactly saw it because the total promotion of the brand is so all-encompassing.

Now try to imagine going a whole week without experiencing any promotion of Coca-Cola anywhere. You would probably begin to wonder what had happened to the company.

The point is that the Coca Cola company knows that if it doesn't continually promote its product and brands, people begin to wonder about the company – and beginning to wonder is only a short step from consumers losing confidence and turning elsewhere. So if you do seek a brand advantage, make up your mind now to commit to doing everything necessary to reinforce what the brand stands for at all times.

Taking a position based on something else

If you can't command cost leadership and advantage, or brand leadership and advantage, you need something else as your core position. This something else may be:

- ✔ **A second in the field or close challenger position,** in which you adopt the position of second best brand or second lowest cost. You're not the leader, but you have advantages over everyone else but the leader in your category.

- ✔ **A single or multiple niche strategy,** in which you can still make a good living, particularly in precisely defined market niches. With this position, you satisfy *some* needs for *some* customers *some* of the time. (See the sidebar 'Nifty niches.') Note that this position can still be extremely profitable, particularly for organisations in large, open and active markets such as food, retail banking or cars.

- ✔ **A personal and/or professional knowledge, understanding and confidence position,** in which you use your own reputation, expertise and quality of products and services to target particular customer and client bases.

- ✔ **A convenience and access position,** in which you use your location, reputation, personal standing and ease of access as the basis for building your customer and client base. This is overwhelmingly the strategic position used by corner shops, local garages and services, specialist manufacturers and product and service providers. If you own or work in one of these businesses, your customers come to you because they like what you do and how you do it; or you are convenient to them for a specific set of needs and wants.

So if you're not the cost or brand leader, you still have some clear options from which to choose. But you do need to be clear about choosing any of these 'something else' positions – you are, after all, setting out the basis of your existence and activities. Your choice must reflect where you know and understand your main strength or strengths to lie.

The downsides of taking a 'something else' position include:

✔ **You appear to be all things to all people.** Nobody can be all things to all people – so don't even try to be! Besides, you can easily spread your resources too thinly in the pursuit of an ill-defined core purpose.

✔ **You take a woolly rather than clear view of where your advantages (and disadvantages) truly lie.** If you're not cost or brand leader, you can finish up with the position of 'our strategy is to muddle through'. Everyone has to do this from time to time anyway, so don't set yourself up for this from the outset!

✔ **You fall between the two stools of trying to be a cost leader and brand leader at the same time.** Of course, you need to use your resources to the best possible advantage. But if you don't make clear where your core lies, nobody else will be sure either. As a result, customers and clients turn from you to those where clear sets of expectations exist already.

✔ **You use the 'something else' position as an abdication of responsibility.** If you position your organisation as not being able to compete with Company A on price or Company B on quality, you can end up going back to sleep strategically and playing to your competitors' advantage – rather than trying to establish where your strengths do truly lie.

Nifty niches

You create a core position based on something other than cost advantage or brand advantage by choosing to serve specific niches. If you make this choice, you need to be able to state clearly the nature of the niche or niches that you will (and will not) serve. And your definition must be as precise as possible. For example:

✔ Coutts, the merchant bank, summarised its core position as 'Bankers to the royal family', which meant that they only served the very wealthy, providing exclusive and discreet service.

✔ Caterpillar, the civil engineering and earth-moving equipment company, stated that it took contracts only in excess of £100 million. This position meant that Caterpillar did not involve itself in smaller activities.

After defining your niches precisely, you need to evaluate them to see whether they're truly enduring and profitable business sectors. And performing this evaluation can be very difficult in some circumstances. The nature and demands of specific niches change, so you must change your approach to niche markets

(continued)

(continued)

or else face real difficulties. And in the preceding examples:

- Coutts has had to expand its niche to include services for sports, show-business and media personalities.

- Caterpillar found itself undercut by Komatsu, which targeted the niches that Caterpillar didn't serve. In fact, Komatsu was so successful at it that it was asked to compete for work in the niches that Caterpillar served.

Caterpillar, in turn, has had to re-evaluate its approach and even work to win back previous clients.

To effectively serve niches, you must be clear that you're meeting all the demands of the particular niche you're targeting – and that you're not laying yourself open to competitive pressures from outside. Remember, if you identify a profitable niche, others are likely to want a slice of the action themselves.

Reinforcing Your Core Position

By establishing a core position, you're setting the cornerstone of your organisation's competitive position in your marketplace. The benefits of getting your core position clear and right are:

- Staff have clear knowledge and understanding of the sort of company or organisation that they work for.

- Customers and clients know and understand what they can expect – and what they can't expect – from your organisation or company.

Whatever core position you take, you have to reinforce it in everything that you do. And organisations that remain successful in their sectors reinforce their foundational core positions over and over again. For example:

- **Ryanair.** Everything that this airline does and says reinforces the core position that it's the low-cost and good-value choice. Even its advertising quite deliberately looks cheap! And the company reinforces its promise of low fares and other discounts on other travel services by offering low-cost car hire and hotel rooms via its website. To see what I mean, just visit www.ryanair.com – everything is driven by cost and low prices!

- **BMW.** Everything that BMW says and does reinforces its brand. Its advertising and presentation is all about quality, high performance, luxury and exclusivity. Indeed, the company tag line is 'The ultimate driving machine.' The people who appear in advertising campaigns reflect the images that the consumers who buy BMW products aspire to – and for which they are prepared to pay BMW's high and exclusive prices. All this gives consumers confidence in the company and the brand, as well as in the cars themselves. To see what I mean, go to www.bmw.com where everything is beautifully designed and presented to reinforce the perceptions (and, of course, reality) of these 'ultimate driving machines.'

> ✔ **Local newsagents and corner shops.** Everything about a local news-agent or corner shop has to be based on *local reputation,* which is a combination of excellent service, a complete range of offered products and friendly, helpful human interaction. Such places additionally reinforce their local reputation by opening early and staying open late. This practice in turn bolsters the shops' commitments of convenience and service to their communities. And, in many cases, they very successfully charge higher prices than supermarket chains.

The following sections take you through several essential questions you need to answer in establishing and building up your organisation's core position.

Lessons from a country pub

The English country pub is a threatened species! Once the focus of rural and village life, it has come under attack from all sides:

✔ Beers, wines, spirits and soft drinks are now so cheaply available in supermarkets that consumers no longer need to go to the pub for a drink.

✔ Pubs that provide food (and many are excellent at this) are in direct competition with ready meals and takeaway services, as well as other restaurants.

✔ The ban on smoking in public places has affected people's perceptions of what the pub stands for and the nature of a pub visit for customers who do smoke.

✔ Pubs raise the question of responsibility and public safety because people who drive to a pub to consume alcohol (a pub's core product and service) have to drive home afterwards.

Running a pub is not all fun and games! Anyone laying the foundations for competition and competing in the pub sector must acknowledge these changes and the challenges that they bring.

Furthermore, in order to run a successful pub, you have to provide your products and service in ways that address each of the preceding points – and still make a visit to your pub worth everyone's while. You have to get to the nature of what constitutes a nice evening out for the clientele that you want to attract. And you have to gain a clientele that's large enough to provide levels of business that can sustain you and generate a profit.

Customers don't just come to your pub because they happen to be passing, and passing trade is no longer enough to support your business. You have to cultivate customers on the basis of *active attraction* – you need to ensure that the quality of service, ambience, facilities and décor, as well as the food and drink, are sufficiently high and attractive to those who seek this kind of evening out. You have to know and understand how often people are likely to visit you (including how often they actually visit, not how often they say they'll visit you).

All sectors, companies and organisations offer similar lessons. The discipline and commitment that anyone running a country pub clearly needs is a key part of managerial excellence for everyone, whoever they work for. And if you do work for a large organisation, and do know and understand the foundations of your competitive position in this kind of detail, then you'll go further than most. And that's worth raising a pint to!

Being clear about what you will – and will not – do

Being clear about what your organisation will and will not do has two faces:

- ✔ Doing the things that you need to do with the highest quality possible.

- ✔ Identifying what is right and wrong for your company in terms of ethics, morality and standards, as well as economics and finance.

If you're clear about what you do and don't do, make sure that you communicate this information to everyone and reinforce this aspect of your position at all times.

If you don't clearly delineate between what your organisation does and doesn't do, you can get into all sorts of problems – often with cost price tags. For example:

- ✔ One major motor car company discovered a fault with the tyres on one of its models. Rather than recalling the cars and replacing the tyres, the company chose to deal with customers on an individual basis when they prosecuted.

- ✔ One major chemical company took the decision to tip effluent into the local river because it calculated that the resulting fine was less than the cost of disposing of the effluent properly.

So the point is to take an active choice as to how you're going to approach and address everything that you have to face. And remember that if you choose to take the seemingly 'easy way' as in the preceding examples, you must prepare for losses in your reputation, local standing and position within your sector – as well as negative effects on your organisation's profitability.

Rules, priorities and flexibility

Just stating your core position is not an end in itself. For example:

- ✔ If you're seeking brand leadership or advantage, you must have a way of branding, packaging and presenting your goods in order to deliver both *real* and *perceived* quality to your targeted customers. Your goods and service have got to look and feel different from your competitors' in some way.

- ✔ If you're seeking cost leadership or cost advantage, you can't compromise the quality or service levels that your sector demands.

✔ If you're seeking to become a specialist and service niches as fully as possible, you have to be prepared to meet all the main demands of these niches – and that can be expensive.

After choosing your core position based on your vision, strategy and expertise, you need to develop your own rules and establish your own priorities. You can certainly take cues from others who have been (and remain) successful, but you can't simply copy their rules and priorities. You must take the time to make your own rules and set your own priorities.

Developing your own rules

The rules that you develop and set out for yourself (and you must consider them *rules*) are the basis of how you're going to work with your markets, meet your obligations and deliver your products and services to customers. Your rules affect everything that you do within your organisation.

In an ideal world, you begin developing your rules based on consideration of right and wrong, specifically:

✔ If you do something wrong or unethical, you'll be caught. Maybe not immediately, but eventually for sure.

✔ If you do something inadequately, you eventually have to do it properly.

✔ If you do get away with something (and everyone does), make sure that this situation remains an exception to the rule – rather than becoming the rule.

✔ If you can't tell the truth, at least tell no lies.

If you can do all the preceding, to a greater extent at least, you're adding a stiff dose of integrity to your core position. You'll be respected for doing so – especially if some of your competitors and alternatives aren't quite so exacting in their ethical stances. And if your competitors do behave themselves, then you, above all, don't want to gain a reputation for being the dishonest one.

After you consider right and wrong, you need to consider openness. By *openness* I mean how you face up to any challenge when it arises, dealing with every matter with respect.

Be sure that you never ever take the following attitudes:

✔ 'They will be wanting nannies next.' (Director, Townsend Thoresen, on crew ferry safety issues the week before 'The Herald of Free Enterprise' disaster.)

✔ 'People should stop moaning.' (A Railtrack senior manager after the Paddington and Potter's Bar rail crashes in which more than 40 people lost their lives.)

 ✔ 'People should wear two pullovers.' (Centrica CEO responding to peoples' worries over domestic fuel price increases.)

Your attitude needs to be positive and honest. You need to treat all your people – customers, staff, suppliers and backers – as you yourself expect to be treated.

You also need to establish rules for conduct, behaviour, performance, dealing with suppliers and customers, reporting to other stakeholders and dealing with regulatory obligations and demands – to name but a few major business aspects you need to consider. See Chapter 13 for more on ethics and rules.

Whatever your core position, you establish rules so that they make everyone's life as easy as possible, and so that as much resource as possible is concentrated on delivering your products and services in reflection of your core position.

Make sure that the rules by which you operate are as simple and straightforward as possible. A challenge, I realise, but the people you work with and for will appreciate the effort! When you build up too many rules and regulations, you start to make people uncertain. They begin to wonder what on earth they're supposed to be doing – and eventually whether they are coming or going! Over time, their commitment to you and your organisation becomes uncertain.

Never say one thing and do another. Even if you're forced into things by circumstances or competitive pressures (rather than outright dishonesty), you end up tarnishing your own reputation as someone who people can trust. Keep everything transparent and everyone informed. Deal with problems and issues quickly. Never make promises unless you're sure that you can keep them. And if (when, of course) you do have to change your mind over something, then make sure that you explain your shift in thinking.

Setting your priorities

In addition to rules, you need to determine where your priorities truly lie. And nothing signals your priorities so clearly as:

 ✔ What is rewarded in your organisation.

 ✔ Where the best jobs are in your organisation.

An often repeated managerial truth says 'what gets rewarded, gets done'. And so it goes! If you reward people for hard work, they work hard. If you reward people for excellent customer service, they serve customers to the best of their ability. If you reward people for finding fault, they find faults. And so on.

In addition to paying attention to what's rewarded, note where specifically the rewards go. For example:

- ✔ If rewards go everywhere or are evenly spread, you at least have the confidence of people knowing that they're all in it together.
- ✔ If you reward head office staff at the expense of those at the front line, good people seek head office jobs.
- ✔ If you reward people for excellent and productive service, good people will indeed stay at the front line and not seek to move away in the interests of progressing their own careers.

Your priorities are also reflected in where you allocate resources. If you have a wonderful head office but a lot of your front-line workers are short of resources, you clearly indicate that head office is the priority. If you put major resources into new ventures, at the expense of existing and steady-state activities, then your priority is clearly the excitement of the new, rather than the familiar and mundane.

Align rewards with priorities – and ensure that when priorities are met, you fully and visibly deliver rewards. This in turn reinforces everything – the strength of your strategy, the emphasis that you put on its delivery, the veracity of your rules and the esteem in which you hold your people (collectively and individually).

Maintaining flexibility

You need to establish rules and priorities for your organisation, but you must also allow yourself to be flexible.

Parable: The fiver

If at the beginning of an hour's conversation, I put a £5 note on the table and I ask you to lend me £5, which I promise to repay at the end of the conversation, would you lend the money? Probably so; you can see that you'll almost certainly get your money back.

But what if at the beginning of the same conversation, I put the £5 note on the table and ask you to lend me £150,000, which I promise, of course, to repay at some time? Will you still lend me the money?

To what extent does this made-up situation parallel the sub-prime mortgage and credit crunch crisis? To what extent does it reflect what is, in many circumstances, the difference between what you will, and will not, do as a person; and what you will, and will not, do as a company?

The answer is, of course, you will personally lend the fiver, but under no circumstances will you lend the £150,000! And yet, when you put the question in a business context, suddenly the rules are totally reversed! Most organisations won't lend the fiver, but they will lend much larger amounts – and often without taking any active steps to ensure that they're going to get their money back. Avoid this sort of madness at all costs in the future!

You cannot simply go on producing and delivering the same products and services as you always have done. In terms of quality and productivity, you will always be seeking developments, improvements and enhancements.

Although you can adjust your rules, you must never ever compromise your standing and integrity in the process. If you ever become known for being flexible with the truth, you will lose any standing that you had. And it will take ages to rebuild!

Getting specific about future priorities

The preceding sections in this chapter establish that that if you're going to be successful, you must know what you're setting out to do. By extension, you can only measure your future success against what you intend to achieve. For example:

 ✔ If you intend to increase sales by 25 per cent and you only increase them by 24 per cent, then you know you've missed your target and can then seek an explanation. But if you intend to increase sales 'significantly' and increase them by 24 per cent, you never quite know whether this increase was good or not.

 ✔ If you intend to increase sales by 25 per cent and increase them by 50 per cent, you may think that you've succeeded beyond your wildest dreams. But a more sober assessment may lead some to wonder if you actually knew what you were doing in the first place because you misjudged your performance by such a huge extent!

In any case, whatever you set out to do has to be achievable in the actual context of your organisation and market. Pie in the sky targets and aims are useless. An organisation needs to be capable of achieving any goal you set within the markets that you serve and with the available technology, staff, finance and other resources that you have at your disposal.

Avoiding Sure-Fire Failures

When you establish a core position and build on it, you maximise your chances of developing long-term success, effectiveness and profitability. If you don't take the time to plan, then you're not clear about what you are doing, and so therefore not sure about how you're going to deliver your products and services. And nobody else feels clear or sure either. Over time, these people are very likely to turn away from you and towards those organisations that are clear about what they offer and how they offer it.

Clearing up things at Sainsbury's

Clarity is everything. You lose out if you're not quite sure about where your true advantage lies. The case of J Sainsbury plc showcases the need for establishing clear core positions.

In the late 1980s, then CEO David Sainsbury dismissed the need for a core position, asserting that his company offered both superior quality and low prices, as exemplified in its slogan 'Good food costs less at Sainsbury's'. As a result, the supermarket tried to charge medium prices for good quality products. This unimpressive position yielded disappointing results. The company was squeezed on one side by

Tesco (with brand advantage) and Asda (with cost advantage). In 1986, Sainsbury's had 20 per cent of the UK grocery market; by 1999 its market share had fallen to 9 per cent.

Sainsbury's finally rebounded (reaching 14 per cent of market share in 2008) when it begin recognising its position as a near challenger to Tesco (see the section 'Taking a position based on something else'). Sainsbury's further developed this position by broadening its range of products and services; it now competes on quality and value, not on price.

The potential for failure is at its highest when any, or all, of the following conditions are present. You also need to be aware – and do everything to avoid – the following strategies for failure:

- ✔ Rising prices and static quality (such as train fares going up without improvements in the volume or reliability of services).

- ✔ Steady prices and declining quality (such as many supermarkets' own brands of food stuffs).

- ✔ Rising prices and declining access to products and services (such as some niche brand mobile phone services and alternatives to the BlackBerry personal phone/organiser).

- ✔ Pricing up those parts of the product or service that were hitherto free (such as after-sales and servicing agreements for car dealers).

- ✔ Loss or removal of a key benefit or feature (eliminating the offer of free, fitted kitchens in new houses).

- ✔ Rising prices in a captive market (increasing costs for water, gas, electricity, energy and transportation).

You must face up to the preceding conditions, whether you introduce them or whether things happen as the result of forces outside your control (rising energy prices, reductions in consumer demand, loss of a key supplier and so on).

As customers, people hate it when any of the preceding things occur. And yet when many people go to work in their own companies and organisations, they often lose sight of this simple fact.

Your customers and clients view each of the preceding situations as your organisation changing your agreements – even if market conditions are responsible for the changes. You must be careful about how you respond to any of these situations. For example:

- ✔ Faced with an inability to attract and hire contractors, Metronet, the London Underground network maintenance company, raised its fees and passed these charges on to London Regional Transport. London Regional Transport in turn passed these charges on to passengers. Unfortunately, Metronet was still unable to complete the work quickly enough; faced with political as well as economic opposition, it went bankrupt.

- ✔ Faced with pressures from low-cost competitors and alternatives, British Airways removed its full catering service from economy class on its short-haul routes. However, the airline more than compensated for the change by reducing fares substantially. The company, in this particular case, avoided falling into one of the strategies for failure.

You can tackle all the specific problems of rising costs and changes in suppliers without changing, damaging or diluting the integrity and substance of your products and services. But you need to be doing this on behalf of your customers and making this clear. You need to be aware too that if you're seen to be acting purely in your own interests, your customers turn away from you. And – as in the case of Metronet – this applies to more or less captive markets and business relationships.

Part II
Being Competitive

'The trouble is that they all want to be leaders.'

In this part . . .

1 go right to the very heart of what competition actually is and then show you how to position your organisation to compete effectively, successfully – and, yes, profitably. You encounter the forces of competition and discover how to operate within the constraints of your competitive environment. In addition, I look also at what leadership is, notably the need for expert and committed people at the top of every successful company and organisation.

Chapter 3

Feeling the Effects of the Forces of Competition

Competition exists wherever a choice exists. Given this, you need to know and understand where your own *competitive strengths* lie in terms of the choices of products and services – as well as price, quality, convenience and value – that you offer to your customers and clients.

More importantly, you need to know the forces of competition and understand how they operate in your markets and discover ways you can influence these forces so they work to your best advantage.

This chapter guides you through the process of identifying and capitalising on your organisation's competitive strengths and introduces you to the key competitive forces you need to understand and work with for strategic success. I also highlight one very important part of competition – choosing partners and companies to work with, not against!

Competing to Your Best Advantage

If you're going to compete effectively in today's marketplace, you need to do so from a position that serves your own best advantage. You need to know and understand your strength, or best advantage. (See Chapter 2 for more on identifying your advantage.)

Some things your best advantage is not

Identifying your own best advantage is the cornerstone of your ability to compete. And yet, too many top and senior managers lose focus and concentrate on things like:

- Exploiting market dominance, rather than serving it.

- Paying attention to short-term share value, rather than long-term profitability and viability.

- Driving down supply and distribution costs to a point where suppliers and distributors cannot remain financially viable.

- Reducing quality without reducing price.

- Generating hidden extras, such as expensive finance plans that look attractive but actually drive customers away.

- Adopting adversarial and conflict-based approaches to staff and contractors.

- Treating new customers and clients differently from existing customers and clients.

Although all the above may seem appropriate and even attractive in some circumstances, they're invariably wrong. For example:

- Market dominance of the grocery sector has led to high food prices and the emergence of cheaper, good-value supermarket alternatives such as Aldi and Lidl.

- Concentrating on short-term share value at the expense of enduring product and service quality was the major cause of Marconi going out of the defence electronics business (and indeed subsequently collapsing altogether).

- Many financial services companies offer better rates to new customers, causing resentment among those who have been with them for some time. As a result, Nationwide's marketing and advertising highlights how the firm treats all customers the same.

Right is right and wrong is wrong. Most people hate being wronged and yet as soon as they go into work, too many are both willing and able to treat staff, customers and clients with disdain and contempt. Everyone hates being treated in this way. Don't be an individual or part of an organisation that treats others in this manner.

Your *best advantage* is the core of what is going to enable you to survive, grow, expand and develop in good times and bad. Your best advantage is based on the strengths that you have and that you make work for you. Your job as a business leader is to decide how best to combine all your strengths so that you do everything in the best ways possible.

Your organisation's strengths likely include:

- **Your products and services,** including the ways you deliver them.

- **Your staff,** who work on your behalf to the best of their abilities.

- **Your technology, equipment and premises.**

You also need to have a clear view of how you're going to compete; your attitudes to your markets, customers and clients and your attitudes to your staff and investors.

Clearly identifying your best advantage informs the approach that you're going to take when responding to and working with the forces of competition. A clear best advantage helps:

- ✔ **Your customers and clients** know and understand why you're offering a particular combination of products and services, and the advantages over competing offers.

- ✔ **Your staff** produce excellent work, commit fully to your business and achieve top results.

- ✔ **Your investors and financial backers** have the greatest confidence that you're using their resources to the best possible effect.

Your own best advantage lies in operating your business consistently. If you always deliver the lowest prices, the highest quality, the most distinctive presentation or the most appropriate response – to name just a few best advantages – then other people know and understand what you stand for. However, if things vary on a daily or weekly basis, or if some (but not all) products and services meet expectations, then you diminish your ability to compete.

You *must* be extremely clear about your best advantage early in the process of establishing your competitive strategy. (See the sidebar 'Some things your best advantage is not' for some helpful advice.) However, if the phrase 'best advantage' or 'competitive advantage' comes to mean little more than a hollow advertising tag line, don't even bother. Customers are not fooled by pompous self promotion.

After you know and establish where your best advantage truly lies, you have a firm foundation on which to understand the forces of competition and how they operate in your sector (see the following section). If you don't know this, you can't take full advantage of opportunities that present themselves. Nor will you be able to respond to the forces of competition, no matter how well you know and understand the definitions and dynamics of these forces.

Getting to Know the Forces of Competition

After you know and understand where your own best advantage lies and what your strengths and weaknesses are, you can start to look at the competitive forces around you. You need to know the following five forces in order to understand the full context in which you are going to compete.

The five main forces of competition are:

- ✔ Rivalry with your closest competitors, as well as other more distant competitors that want to take business from you.
- ✔ Substitutes and alternatives for your products and services.
- ✔ The threat of entry into your markets and locations by new players.
- ✔ The amount of power that your buyers, consumers and customers have.
- ✔ The amount of power that your suppliers have.

Figure 3-1 graphically depicts all these forces interacting in the competitive environment. You can see how you must look at every aspect of the ways in which you conduct your business. The following sections look at each of these five forces in depth. (I also cover a few others in the later section 'Acknowledging Other Competitive Forces.')

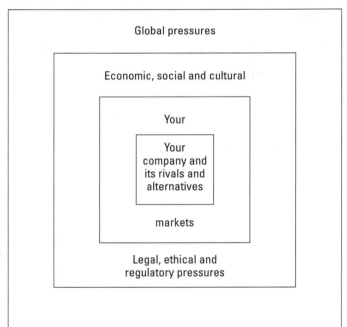

Figure 3-1: The five forces of competition.

Rivalry

Rivalry is the extent to which genuine and active competition exists in your sector. Your rivals are the people or organisations with whom you go directly into battle – those people or organisations that do their best to take your market share or positioning from you (as you do from them).

Rivalry is more than just competition between individual organisations in the same location or market. Rivalry is fuelled by a combination of seeking to deliver and sell products and services as well as the human and emotional drive to 'be the best' or 'be the biggest'.

In terms of competitive strategy, rivalry also includes:

✔ Macro-level or inter-company competition between large and international companies such as Coca-Cola and Pepsi, McDonald's and Burger King or Tesco and Asda.

✔ Competition between the top managers of these large companies in terms of building their individual reputations as well as those of their companies.

✔ The effects of large company operations on smaller companies, which can and do drive the smaller players out of business. The decisions of large companies also offer opportunities for smaller companies to make the most of their flexibility and responsiveness compared to larger, more cumbersome players.

✔ The competition between top managers within a company or organisation. The give and take of these individuals influences behaviour and activities throughout the entire company or organisation.

✔ The competition for customers' and consumers' loyalty, confidence, trust and of course their disposable income. In business, you're always setting your stall out to make sure that customers come to you and not to your rivals and close competitors.

✔ The battle for preferred sources, distributors or business partners.

Although the specifics of rivalries vary in every sector or location, rivalries typically drive marketing, advertising and sales campaigns. Rivalries lead you to persuade your customer bases that your products and services are better – and better value – than anyone else's. Rivalries encourage you to make access to product or services as easy and convenient as possible for your customers and clients, which builds a bond of trust, confidence and loyalty between you and your customers or clients.

Substitutes and alternatives

Substitutes and alternatives are products and services that you don't produce – but others do. These other products and services provide an equivalent (or greater) value to those customers who may otherwise use and consume your products and services.

Looking at substitutes and alternatives is especially important when you know that your sector offers a large degree of choice.

The degree of threat from substitutes and alternatives comes from the ability of other companies to say: 'It is true that we don't produce product or service x; but we do produce product or service y, which is better – and better value – for the following reasons.' Examples of substitutes and alternatives include:

- ✔ Butter and margarine
- ✔ Olive oil and sunflower oil
- ✔ Starbucks and Burger King

Of course, some sectors offer few substitutes and alternatives. In the UK, for example, petrol buyers have little choice but to go to one of the petrol station chains or the large supermarkets. Customers of public utilities (gas, electricity, water) have little choice in practice. Interestingly, the lack of choice in these sectors actually encourages some companies to consider how they may, at some point, choose get into these sectors.

Seemingly non-similar products can also be substitutes and alternatives – in terms of customers' disposable income. For example, a person with £5 in his pocket may consider Burger King and public transport substitutes and alternatives. How so? Well, he has two different yet appealing ways to spend a limited amount of money that afternoon.

The important thing in substitutes is the buyer's opinion. At first, telephone companies didn't think that mobile phones could ever be a substitute for phone booths and yet that is exactly what has occurred. And for some, texting on a mobile is perceived as a substitute for phoning or email – or both!

The threat of entry

You always need to be aware of competitors that may enter your market, affecting and potentially damaging your business.

Think of threat of entry this way: you have a highly successful and profitable business. Others naturally want a slice of the action. Just as you are always scanning the environment for fresh opportunities, so are others.

You need to be always on the lookout for potential entrants, and you of course need to know that they can come from anywhere in the world. And when you do identify potential entrants, you need to do a full evaluation of their strengths and weaknesses. Do everything you can to figure out what gives them their distinctive advantages. You can then determine their likely and possible effects on your business and the market as a whole if they do come in.

The Ryanair alternative: Expanding an industry

For many, Ryanair is a direct competitor to flag-carrying and branded airlines such as British Airways and Aer Lingus. And yet, Ryanair offers very few routes that are in direct competition with any other company (though London Gatwick to Dublin is a notable exception).

Originally founded as a luxury, exclusive and high-price airline, Ryanair quickly ran into difficulties. It was on the point of bankruptcy when the company owners asked its auditor Michael O'Leary to take over as chief executive. O'Leary saw immediately that consumers didn't want an exclusive service – they wanted a low-price, mass market alternative.

Yes, flying to and from 'non-standard' airports has given the company a reputation for dropping its passengers off in the middle of nowhere! But in practice, Ryanair offers an alternative – a particular and clear choice different from other airlines. Passengers can choose whether to fly with a flag carrier to and from familiar destinations; or they can fly with Ryanair on an alternative route that is (or is understood to be) equivalent but not the same.

The Ryanair alternative appeals to consumers – and has even greatly enlarged the number of people who fly. While Ryanair has grown a market of 48 million customers per year, the numbers using British Airways have not gone down, remaining at about 38 million passengers per year. Ryanair generated its very own customer base – people who would not have flown, or flown so often, until the opportunity was available within their price range.

By offering an alternative, Ryanair forced the branded and flag-carrying airlines to respond – and some have responded better than others. For example:

- British Airways has reduced its fares on domestic and short-haul routes by up to 75 per cent, especially for flyers who book early.

- Aer Lingus has engaged in cost-cutting among its support and managerial staff, in an effort to avoiding putting up its fares too steeply.

- Air France has expanded and taken over other airlines (notably KLM, the Dutch national airline) to increase its overall volume of passengers and business.

- Companies such as Qatar and Emirates have gone steeply up-market, so as to demonstrate a real choice at the top end of the market.

The effect of alternatives is similar for all organisations in all sectors. New and different ways of doing things – alternatives – are always emerging. And when these alternatives are successfully introduced, they're likely to generate their own interests and their own distinctive customer bases, just as Ryanair did.

Being first to market is sometimes but not always an advantage. For example, in the US, Kimberly-Clark's Crux was the first paper nappy, but the category was quickly overtaken by Procter and Gamble's Pampers brand. So you need always to be aware of the potential threat of entry, even if you're the current market leader or only player in a specific market.

New entrants can, and do, change the operations of markets, not just in terms of the products and services that they bring, but also in terms of production technology, employment practices, distribution and delivery networks.

Also, new entrants can, and do, destabilise your sources of raw materials, technology and expertise (see 'The power of suppliers' later in this chapter). If you have someone else buying up raw materials, supplies or production technology you have to be able to respond and look after your own interests. Additionally, if the new entrant needs staff and expertise, some of your own people may be tempted to go and work for the new entrant.

Never underestimate new entrants. If you think that they are spending their every waking hour trying to figure out how to displace you in the market, you're probably right!

And conversely, never treat potential entrants with disdain or disrespect: you may live to regret it. Remember that until the new entrant came along, you had a perfectly good business – so you must be doing many things right! Respect the new entrant, learn from the situation – and then fight back as hard as you can!

The power of buyers

The power of buyers – your customers – depends on several factors:

- ✔ Where your products or services fall into their priorities. Can people live easily without what you provide for them?

- ✔ Whether you're meeting an essential *need* (such as food and drink), or merely supplying a *want* (such as entertainment).

- ✔ The amount of choice that buyers have in purchasing your products and services. Do people have to buy from you, or are there a lot of other companies that provide a near equivalent?

- ✔ The number of other organisations or companies supplying the same, substitute or alternative products and services.

The preceding points form the basis on which you assess the power of your buyers. If a large number of alternatives exists, the power of the buyers is extremely high. On the other hand, if you're one of very few providers, your buyer's power is reduced – at least until they either find some other way to satisfy their needs and wants or until someone else enters the market and provides you with some competition!

The threat of entry – and its consequences

Not so long ago, the UK had its own thriving car and electrical goods industries.

The UK domestic car industry consisted of companies such as Hillman, Rootes, Riley and Morris; and it used to produce nearly 3 million cars per year. (This didn't include Ford and Vauxhall who were – and remain – American-owned companies manufacturing cars in the UK.) However, because these UK cars were not reliable, well made or easy to service, the big European and Japanese car companies easily came in and took over the market.

Similarly, the UK electrical goods firms of Triumph, Pye and Richards all produced goods and appliances for the domestic market. But like UK automobiles, the quality of these electrical goods was unreliable, and the standard of service variable. Sharp, Sony, Panasonic, Samsung and the rest came in and took over the entire market.

Rather than responding in terms of product and service quality, the British companies first ignored the threat, believing in error that British consumers always preferred British goods. After all, their collective wisdom was that nobody wanted Japanese goods anyway. When this approach didn't work, the UK companies cried foul, complaining that the Japanese were dumping their goods at rock-bottom prices. And when this tactic didn't work either, they complained about Japanese labour practices, Japanese government support for its industries, import barriers that prevented reciprocal trading arrangements – anything in fact rather than improving their own products and services.

The result is that Japanese and other foreign companies have now filled the UK domestic market, accounting for nearly all the car and electrical goods production in the UK.

To influence the ways in which customers respond to you, you need (as I discuss in the section 'Competing to Your Best Advantage' earlier in this chapter) to be absolutely clear about what you deliver, its value and the expected prices and charges. Never take customer understanding for granted because people's habits, perceptions, expectations and priorities are always changing. Make sure that you keep fully engaged with your customers and clients (see Chapter 9).

Never underestimate the power of customers and clients, however captive your market may appear to be or assured their loyalty appears. If people really can't do without you and your products and services, they find other ways of trying to exert their power and influence. For example:

- ✔ The British Post Office receives an average of 17 complaints per hour, all of which must be responded to.
- ✔ The NHS must deal with the 10,000 complaints it receives each day.
- ✔ In 2007, the UK water companies were fined a combined total of £47 million for a combination of poor water quality, pollution scares, leakages and service overcharges.

So you need to set yourself up so that people do not complain at all! As well as being damaging to your reputation and demoralising to your staff, continually responding to each and every dissatisfied customer is extremely expensive. Determine your reasonable standard of service and then seek out the most cost-effective way to achieve that standard.

The fact that you may have a dominant position is no guarantee that you won't go bankrupt. In recent years, Railtrack (railways), Northern Rock (personal banking and finances), Lehman Brothers (investment banking), Equitable Life (pensions and insurance services) and Safeway and Somerfield (both supermarket chains) have all either gone bankrupt or else needed bailing out. Never underestimate the power of your customers to find substitutes and alternatives for what you provide (see the preceding 'Substitutes and alternatives' section) and exert any influence that they can over you.

The power of suppliers

You have a supply side to manage, whatever your line of work. Your business's *supply side* includes raw materials and components, as well as suppliers of information, technology, facilities, expertise, staff and finance. If one or more of these elements is a dominant feature of your business or exerts influence over the ways you operate and compete, they limit your effectiveness and potential.

As you assess your supply side, take the broadest possible view. You need also to look at any shortcomings that you may have, especially:

- ✔ If you have a reputation as a bad employer, your ability to attract and retain staff diminishes. This situation only worsens if others with positive and supportive staff policies and practices come into your market or location.

- ✔ If you have a reputation as a bad payer, your suppliers only put up with your lateness until they can find others with whom to do business.

- ✔ If you need specific supplies of technology, raw materials, information or expertise, you must strike a balance between obtaining a particular resource, paying or over-paying for it and keeping your own costs as low as possible.

You've surely been a customer of an organisation that said, 'We can't deliver your goods yet because we're having difficulty getting a certain part.' You don't like hearing this sort of explanation – and neither does anyone else! So if you identify specific resources or supplies that you must have in order to avoid customer and client disappointment (and protect your own business interests), you need to take whatever steps are necessary to secure them – however expensive these efforts may seem. Protecting your business interests may mean, for example, that you carry stockpiles of certain components or pay over the odds for key sources of data.

Acknowledging Other Competitive Forces

As well as the five main competitive forces (see the preceding section), other forces exist that affect all companies and organisations in all sectors, as follows:

- The threat of regulation
- The threat of withdrawal
- The collapse of a competitor

You need to be aware of the extent to which each of these forces exists in your business's sector. Assessing the likely and potential effects that each may have on your business enables you to compete effectively. I examine these three additional forces in the following sections.

The threat of regulation

The rules of the game can change at any time for you and your business, so you have to be prepared to do anything and everything to meet this threat. In practice, you have little or no control over regulations. If governments decide to introduce new laws or compliance demands, you must comply.

Always scan the horizon for potential new rules and regulations that may affect your business. Regardless of what you may think of the regulations, if they have to be complied with, you've no choice. So keep your eyes open at all times!

Pay attention to numerous areas in terms of potential new regulations. Take some time and consider how you and your business would respond to changes in any of the following:

- Financial reporting and transparency
- Taxation changes
- Product and service compliance standards
- Marketing and advertising standards
- Employment practices
- Contract laws (especially in terms of engaging suppliers and subcontractors)
- Pollution and environmental regulation
- Rises in transport costs due to government action (such as taxation, tolls, charges and restraints)

✔ Health and safety regulations, product quality assurance and other inspection processes

You often must be prepared to comply with new regulations without any sort of grace period. You may be fortunate in some cases, but you can serve yourself much better if you take steps in advance to know what regulations may be coming along and how much they may cost you. Taking this approach, you know what you need to do and what effect the changes will have.

If you don't do your homework, a new regulation can easily create a crisis. For example:

✔ Fast food and confectionery companies have been repeatedly asked by legislators, lobbies and pressure groups not to advertise directly to children. New legislation to formally address this request is coming at some point in the not-too-distant future because the fast food and confectionery industries haven't sought to regulate themselves.

✔ The financial services sector has been asked by financial services authorities to take a more responsible attitude when making credit and loans available to those least able to afford to repay them. If these higher-risk lending practices don't stop, the companies are certain to be asked to provide detailed tracking of meetings with all customers and clients, which is likely to prove very costly for financial services firms.

✔ Road haulage and trucking companies are certain to be asked by the environmental authorities and local government to regulate their total carbon emissions. In time, the companies will have to replace their old haulage fleets or otherwise pay heavy duty and taxation premiums.

When you're faced with potential or impending regulation, you must consider the worst case scenario – that you'll have to comply eventually with some kind of regulation. Compliance is certain to cost you time, money and other resources, but by planning now, you can have a good idea of what's ahead for you.

The threat of withdrawal

A major player withdrawing from the market leads to two possible outcomes:

✔ Greater opportunities for those still in the market

✔ Destabilisation of the market

Although greater opportunity may sound like a dream come true, you still need to plan carefully. If you and the other remaining players in the market can't fill the gaps quickly and effectively, your customer and client base will become frustrated and begin to look elsewhere.

Your own active and expert knowledge of your markets helps ensure that you know who may be thinking of moving out. Seek to know your competitors' and rivals' ideas and initiatives, so you can be ready to take any actions that may present themselves if withdrawals happen.

Prepare yourself to step into the breach, if possible. If you have spare capacity, make sure that you can quickly harness it to take up opportunities when they come along. Make sure that people know you as a reliable provider of your products and services, so that they automatically think of turning to you when their main provider has gone. And if you don't have spare capacity, be aware that things may go wrong for you also in the future.

The collapse of a competitor

As with withdrawal, the collapse of a competitor can bring about great opportunities for those left behind. However, collapse can, and often does, also bring about a wider loss of confidence in the entire sector. For example:

- ✔ The collapse of Enron caused everyone to question the strength and integrity of the energy market sector.

- ✔ The collapse of Enron also brought about the demise of Arthur Andersen, Enron's auditors. And Andersen's downfall called into question the overall integrity of the entire audit sector.

- ✔ The collapse of Bradford and Bingley, and the resulting bail out of all the major players, called into question the confidence of the whole UK retail banking sector, The problem was compounded when stock market traders tried to speculate on the shares of other retail banks at the time.

So the collapse of a competitor is clearly a competitive force because it can, may – and does – affect everyone's confidence and expectations. The 2008 credit crunch and economic crisis left many industries with fewer players – and fewer, not more, opportunities for those still left in the game.

Collapses and withdrawals can lead to even wider losses of confidence. For example, if a major player withdraws, suppliers are going to want to know immediately that you and the other remaining companies and organisations are indeed going to take up the slack. You need to be able to give a quick and accurate answer. If you dither, your suppliers are going to think that you too may withdraw. And at a time when your suppliers are bound to feel anxious anyway, the last thing that they need is prevarication from you or anyone else.

You need to be scanning the horizon and your closest rivals for any signs that they may be in difficulty. In many cases, identifying threatened rivals is fairly straightforward; industry and sector insiders often know who is in trouble. But the process can be tough. Few people foresaw the collapse of the hedge fund sector, and fewer still thought that Enron would fall.

You may also find yourself in the position of having to buy up or bail out your competitors. For example, when Alitalia, the Italian state airline, filed for bankruptcy protection, its rivals jumped in to ensure that service was maintained. This action led to Air France taking a minority stake in Alitalia in order to underpin the strength and integrity of Europe's short-haul airline sector. Air France's actions also ensured that Alitalia continued to be viable until a consortium buyer emerged.

Developing Existing and New Markets

In the preceding sections, I explore how the forces of competition work out and the main things that you need to be aware of when developing your competitive position. But if you're going to compete effectively for a long period of time, you also need clear ideas on how you're going to work within these forces to develop your existing markets, as well as how you plan to get involved with new areas, locations and customer and client bases.

Expanding in your existing market

In order to develop your existing markets, you must constantly scan the environment for ideas and opportunities that you can turn profitably to good use or help you better serve your customers' existing needs and wants. For example, following the collapse of Woolworths, many department store and supermarket chains saw an opportunity to consolidate their own positions and presences by buying up Woolworths' stores.

You also need to look very hard at the specific needs, wants and demands of your customers and clients to see what else you can provide, the value that this something else can deliver and how much your customers and clients are prepared to pay. This process of *adding value* has two functions:

- ✔ To develop the market and the potential of your existing customer and client base.
- ✔ To maintain your customers' and clients' loyalty to you and prevent them from looking elsewhere for what you supply and deliver.

As you work to expand your existing market, you also need to constantly re-evaluate your pricing policies in terms of:

- ✔ What you include in an all-inclusive price
- ✔ What you charge extra for
- ✔ How you present your pricing policies in terms that are acceptable to your customers

Examples of price strategies include the following:

- ✔ Sandals, the luxury and exclusive holiday company, states clearly the high levels of its prices, almost making the prices a feature of a Sandals stay. However, these price levels are fully inclusive and cover all food and drinks, entertainment, events and activities, so you don't actually need to spend anything else at all while on a Sandals holiday.

- ✔ Ryanair continues to offer low fares (indeed, the tickets are free on some routes!), but the company adds on everything else, including regulatory and statutory taxes, costs and charges. The result is that in many cases your free flight can be quite expensive.

Business for both of the preceding companies has been successfully developed because customers and clients know all important pricing details and what to expect.

However, innovative pricing alone is not enough to be competitive over the long haul. To remain fully effective, Sandals must constantly add to its menus, drinks ranges and activities offered as part of the all-inclusive package. To remain fully effective, Ryanair must demonstrate that its ticket prices (exclusive of taxes) do indeed remain low compared to other airline options.

Developing new markets

As you seek fresh opportunities in new areas and locations and with new customer and client bases, you have to strike a balance between:

- ✔ Knowing and understanding the relative strengths, quality and value of your products and services to those new target customers.

- ✔ Recognising that these proposed markets have done perfectly well without you so far.

When you're going into new markets, always remember that what you consider to be the high points of value in your products and services may not be seen as such by the new location. (For things to consider when expanding your business internationally, see Chapter 17).

Always test and evaluate new locations before you open for business. Make sure you:

- ✔ Know and understand how the forces of competition operate in these places.

- ✔ Can operate within any regulatory constraints.

- ✔ Understand the importance of your products or services in the new location.

> ✔ Ascertain that you can deliver the value that is demanded in these locations before committing your time and resources.

If you go into new markets, you may also have to consider taking up with partners and engaging in joint ventures. Joint ventures let you take advantage of working with somebody experienced, thus minimising your risks. But you also have to be prepared to share the profits of course!

If you go into a new market, you must be clear about how and why you're entering the new market. You also need to examine all the issues around the forces of competition that are present in the new market.

If you have new and exciting ventures in the pipeline, make sure that you consider how these opportunities are going to affect your existing activities. If you sacrifice something that you are known (and hopefully loved!) for, you're taking a considerable risk. You do not want to give up one of your strengths, only to dip out on the new venture – and then lose substantially more than you may have if you stayed with what you were good at in the first place.

Getting wet: Blue and red water competition

You can divide markets into two fancifully named categories:

- ✔ **Blue water competitive markets:** They have no existing players.

- ✔ **Red water competitive markets:** They put you head-to-head with others (so the waters are red because the sharks are fighting each other!).

Fun, but also substantial. If you're going into blue water markets – sectors and locations that don't use and consume products and services like yours – you're going to have a first-mover advantage. However, you're also going to have to convince these sectors that they do indeed need and want your products and services. (After all, they've presumably gone on quite happily without them up until now). You're also going to have to convince these new customers and clients that *your business* is the right option!

If you're going into red water competition, you must convince the customers and clients of other companies and organisations that you're a better provider of these goods and services than existing players. So you're going to have to fight with the existing players to take away customers – and of course your competitors are going to fight back!

Whichever type of water you choose, you have your work cut out! Make sure that you do your market research in full. Understand the competitive forces within the market.

And never ever guess at what is important and of value to the customers and clients – get the answers from the customers and clients themselves. Remember that Virgin Cola engaged in red water competition with Coca-Cola and Pepsi because Virgin Cola always came out best in blind tasting compared to the other beverages. But Virgin Cola failed because the company assumed that customers wanted great cola taste; in fact, customers wanted the brand name and assurance of Coca-Cola and Pepsi.

Considering Alternatives to Competing

Another part of knowing and understanding how the forces of competition operate is recognising where you genuinely have to compete – and where you can engage in other profitable activities. If the main force in your section is rivalry, clearly you have to compete directly. But if a real threat of entry or substitution exists, you may choose to:

- ✓ **Collaborate,** by pooling your resources with others to create an industry or sector bloc, which makes entry more difficult for future, non-bloc competitors to enter the sector.

- ✓ **Cooperate,** by sharing information or access to specific resources. This strategy can be especially useful for managing the supply and distribution sides – or creating common customer bases (as I explain in the following section).

Most markets, sectors and activities can support a measure of cooperation and collaboration. For example:

- ✓ A quick tour around all the petrol retailers in your district shows you that they quite independently calculate their prices to within 0.01p of each other.

- ✓ Other than special offers, the price of basic foodstuffs sold by the big supermarkets varies very little.

- ✓ Nationally agreed labour rates establish costs for specific skills, knowledge, experience and professions such as teaching, medicine and the law.

Of course, you can choose to break any, or all, of these aspects – or any similarly consistent circumstance that appears in your own sector. But in practice, doing your own thing carries risks. If you try to operate independently of the rest of the market, you must be large and powerful enough to change the rules, stick to them and make others stick to them.

If you genuinely have to compete, use your resources to play to your own strengths and relate your strengths to the needs, wants and expectations of customers and clients.

In practice, however, you can't expect to impose everything on others purely to your advantage – otherwise they'll only work with you until they can find others. You're going to have to collaborate and cooperate to some extent with your suppliers and distributors.

Work to recognise where your suppliers' interests lie and accommodate these interests as much as possible if you're going to have productive and profitable relations with them. For example, supermarkets and grocery chains and stores have to be prepared to accept night-time deliveries from suppliers because travel is easiest during times when few hold-ups exist on the road networks.

Examples of cooperation and collaboration include:

- **Regularised alliances:** You find examples of these in the air travel sector between One World and Star, which provide integrated routes, ticketing and baggage and passenger transfers, so customers can book themselves (and their luggage) to a greater range of destinations.

- **Preferred contractor status:** Within many public and commercial bodies, preferred contractor status allows easier access to a range of products and services at previously agreed terms and rates. For example, local government authorities engage building and civil engineering contractors on this basis for public works, and banks and financial services companies engage computer, IT and customer service providers on this basis.

- **Joint ventures and a host of other partnership agreements and arrangements:** These can all serve multiple parties' best interests. For example, those who provide specialist services (drainage or tunnelling) to big civil engineering projects have to be confident that their contribution is going to be well rewarded. By the same token, organisations that provide specialist data management and information services to large and diverse organisations have to be recognised for their critical contribution, and again rewarded adequately. These needs, in turn, ensure that the large contracting organisations that provide these types of services can charge the prices necessary to stay in business. So everyone wins!

Chapter 4

Scanning and Analysing Your Competitive Environment

*I*n order to be successful and effective – and remain competitive – you must know and understand your *environment*: the physical and psychological space and location (or locations) in which you create your products and services and compete with others.

You must be capable and willing to take advantage of the opportunities presented by your environment, as well as to work within its economic, social, legal, political, technological and ethical constraints. Additionally, you must understand where the various demands on your costs come from and be prepared to change your way of working. Furthermore, you must do all this while recognising that most of what goes on in your environment is, to a greater or lesser extent, outside your control.

If all this sounds like a tall order, you're correct. It is. So what you need to do, whatever your line of work, is examine past events and use them to broaden your knowledge and understanding of how your environment really works. Through this examination, you can identify the things that can and do change – and how they affect the ways you conduct your affairs now and in the future.

This chapter shows you how to become an expert in making everything you do fit into your environment, in how your environment supports and accommodates you and how people compete within your environment's rules, boundaries, opportunities and constraints.

Exploring Your Environment

Your business's environment has different meanings in the context of competitive strategy. *Environment* includes:

- ✔ **The physical location** in which your activities take place and which support your organisation.

- ✔ **The competitive arena** in which you and others offer various products and services.

- ✔ **The conditions** under which you provide finance, technology, expertise and other resources to be used to conduct your business.

- ✔ **The ways** in which you organise your work and output.

- ✔ **The ever-evolving philosophical and ethical debate** that you employ (both positively and negatively) based on your actions and based on your vision of corporate and social responsibility.

You must know all these aspects of your environment in full detail in order to work profitably. The following sections offer several key strategies for getting to know and understand your environment.

Considering environmental constraints

In order to be as effective as possible, you need to know and understand the environmental constraints within which you can safely exist. These *constraints* include the political, social, economic, legal and technological forces within which you have to work.

You also need to be aware of any constraints that you may have to overcome if circumstances change. For example:

- ✔ If demand for your products and services suddenly takes off, can you command the raw materials, staff expertise and technological capacity to be able to satisfy this new level of demand? Or will you have to stand by and watch others come into the market and take advantage of all your hard work?

- ✔ If demand for your products and services suddenly drops off, what else may also drop off? Will losing demand for one or two of your products or services cause people to stop coming to you at all?

✔ What else may the market demand from you? What other needs and wants can you profitably supply? For example, if you sell cars, do you also need to profitably sell insurance packages? What about sound systems and CDs (especially considering that these items are now so cheap to buy wholesale from suppliers)?

✔ If employers in your area put up their wages and salaries, do you have to do the same in order to keep your best staff?

✔ If a competitor suddenly invents a new way of doing things that reduces costs and increases the competitor's speed and quality of production, do you have to follow suit? Can you follow suit?

To be able to answer all the preceding questions about constraints and more, you must know and understand your operating and competitive environment. The following section examines a process for discovering more about environments.

Analysing your environment: Environmental scanning

Analysing your environment gives you a detailed understanding of all the factors, elements and forces with which you have to contend in your environment.

Analysing the environment, or *environmental scanning*, means you look at your environment from a range of different points of view. Combining multiple points of view naturally builds your knowledge of your environment, highlights where different pressures are likely to come from and gives you a clearer understanding of how different bits of information are important to different people, institutions and groups.

If you don't analyse your environment, you're going to be guessing at what's happening out there. Make a commitment to becoming an expert in all aspects of the environment. All you're doing here is assessing what your operating environment may or may not support. This activity is a part of your professional management and executive discipline – and it always repays dividends.

Make sure that all your colleagues participate in environmental scanning as well. Get them committed to your company's future by having them go out and look at what competitors are doing. Encourage them to express their views on what may happen to your industry in the future. And make sure that you have the kind of organisation (or at least team) that considers these views important and useful.

You can choose between numerous environment analysis techniques. I cover several of the most useful in the following sections. Paying attention to the five competitive forces (see Chapter 3) is another way to more deeply understand your environment.

PEST analysis

PEST is an acronym that stands for Political, Economic, Social and Technological. PEST analysis first involves itemising the factors that affect your planning *within* your environment in the following categories:

- ✔ **Political:** Internal political systems, sources of power and influence, key groups of workers, key departments, key managers and executives.

- ✔ **Economic:** Financial structure, objectives and constraints at the place of work.

- ✔ **Social:** Social systems in the workplace, departmental and functional structures, work organisation and methods.

- ✔ **Technological:** The effects of the organisation's technology, the uses to which you put the technology and the technology that may become available.

PEST analysis then focuses on the strengths and influence of forces *outside* the control of your organisation, or outside the control of particular managers or supervisors:

- ✔ **Political:** Legal and statutory changes that may take place, such as legislation that limits the ways companies can advertise or legal changes to maximum and minimum work hours.

- ✔ **Economic:** The effects that prosperity and hardship have on your activities.

- ✔ **Social:** How people's habits and customs change, how these changes may affect your business or your ability to employ staff.

- ✔ **Technological:** Technological changes and advances that are being developed, whether your company needs them and the effects of other companies acquiring and using them.

Although outside your control, these factors nevertheless constitute the boundaries and pressures within which you must carry out activities. Figure 4-1 shows how PEST analysis works.

Figure 4-1 pinpoints overriding pressures and forces for several cases. However significantly outside your control things and forces may be, you still need to understand where problems and issues may come from so that you can respond as effectively as possible.

Model

POLITICAL	ECONOMIC
SOCIAL	TECHNOLOGICAL

You can investigate each of the points raised further, if required, and use the analysis to identify and evaluate the forces present in any situation – macro or micro – as follows:

a)   PEST for centralised personnel services in a large organisation (simplified)

POLITICAL

External
  • Employment law compliance
  • Identification and management of external issues
Internal
  • Need for professional advice

ECONOMIC

  • Fixed costs incurred
  • Secondary costs
  • Accommodating meetings

  • People expect a personnel or HR function in large organisations
  • Social and welfare workplace roles

  • Information systems and databases
  • Data protection regulation compliance
  • Security

SOCIAL

TECHNOLOGICAL

b)   PEST for a corner shop (simplified)

POLITICAL

  • Opening hours
  • Sales restrictions (for example, alcohol, tobacco)

ECONOMIC

  • Opening hours
  • Prices charged
  • Range of goods
  • Fixed costs

  • Convenience
  • Opening hours
  • Range of goods
  • Social roles (for example, message forwarding)
  • Meeting point

  • Reordering
  • Security
  • Accounting and charging

SOCIAL

TECHNOLOGICAL

c)   PEST for a unionised production line crew (simplified)

POLITICAL

  • Role of union
  • Legal factors
  • Need for IR specialists

ECONOMIC

  • Costs and benefits of unionisation
  • Cost of time spent on unionisation and union matters

  • Expectations of belonging to union
  • Divided loyalties (?)

  • Production process
  • Automation and alienation
  • Work and job rotation (?)

SOCIAL

TECHNOLOGICAL

Figure 4-1:
PEST
analysis
examples.

To conduct a PEST analysis:

1. **Gather your team, department, board or other group.**
2. **Brainstorm a list of all forces that you recognise under each of the PEST headings.**
3. **Use your findings to start a discussion about how each force may affect your company.**

   Begin to think of ways in which you can work within the forces you identified and itemised. For example:

   • If you recognise reductions in consumer spending as an economic force, you can start to work out ways of making sure that consumers still come to you as often as possible.

   • If you identify that the minimum wage may rise, you can work out how to get even more out of your staff.

SWOT analysis

SWOT analysis looks at specific aspects of an organisation, department, division or function and the organisation's products or services. SWOT places these elements into one of four categories:

✔ **Strengths:** Things that the organisation and its staff are good at, and for which they have a positive/strong/good reputation.

✔ **Weaknesses:** Things that the organisation and its staff are bad at, or for which they have a poor reputation.

✔ **Opportunities:** Potentially profitable directions that may be worth exploring in the future.

✔ **Threats:** Potential problems with outside competitors as well as potential internal issues such as strikes, disputes and resource or revenue constraints.

In practical application, a persistent limitation of SWOT is lack of insight. For example, many middle managers fearful of offending top management don't dare suggest that their product is viewed as second-rate by customers, even sometimes when that's exactly what is happening!

Figure 4-2 shows how SWOT analysis works.

Model

STRENGTHS	**WEAKNESSES**
OPPORTUNITIES	**THREATS**

Each of the points raised and identified can then become the subject of further investigation or evaluation, as with the PEST approach. You can then identify the overall strength or weakness of the position of whatever you're assessing in this way. Here are some examples:

a)   SWOT for a large international airline (simplified)

STRENGTHS	**WEAKNESSES**
• Name and brand • Route network • Passenger numbers • Revenue	• Costs and charges • Competition on given routes • Overheads
• Networks and alliances • Command of supply side	• Regulation • Disasters • Price wars
OPPORTUNITIES	**THREATS**

b)   SWOT for a small hospital in a country town (simplified)

STRENGTHS	**WEAKNESSES**
• Knowledge of services • Public confidence • Range of services	• Public sector costs • Range of services • Opening hours (for example, for accident and emergency) • Retaining expert staff
• Development of services • Development of community facility	• Political pressures • Health economics • Health service costings
OPPORTUNITIES	**THREATS**

c)   SWOT for a new information systems installation (simplified)

STRENGTHS	**WEAKNESSES**
• Excitement, opportunity • State of the art • Training for staff • 'Everyone else' has one	• Cost • Teething troubles • Access to advice and problem solving
• Develop expertise • Develop quality access and use of information • Develop staff • Change culture (if required)	• Costs, on-costs and hidden costs • May be at the mercy of suppliers • Staff may not like it, and will not use it
OPPORTUNITIES	**THREATS**

Figure 4-2:
SWOT
analysis
examples.

Putting on your analysis SPECTACLES

In his book *Mastering the Organisation in its Environment* (Macmillan Masters, 2000), Roger Cartwright takes a very detailed approach to environmental analysis, combining aspects of PEST and SWOT analysis. Cartwright uses a ten-point approach, summarised with the acronym SPECTACLES:

✔ **Social:** Changes in society and societal trends; demographic trends and influences.

✔ **Political:** Political processes and structures; lobbying political institutions (within the country and larger governing bodies); political pressures brought about by market regulations (such as the Social Chapter).

✔ **Economic:** Sources of finance; stock markets; inflation; interest rates; local, regional, national and global economies.

✔ **Cultural:** International, national, regional and organisational cultures; cultural clashes; culture changes; cultural pressures on business and organisational activities.

✔ **Technological:** Understanding the technological needs of a business; technological pressures; the relationship between technology and work patterns; communications; e-commerce; technology and manufacturing; technology and bio-engineering.

✔ **Aesthetic:** Communications; marketing and promotion; image; fashion; organisational body language; public relations.

✔ **Customer:** Consumerism; the importance of analysing customer bases; customer needs and wants; customer care; anticipating future customer requirements; customer behaviour.

✔ **Legal:** Sources of law; codes of practice; legal pressures; product liability; health and safety; employment law; competition legislation; European law; whistle-blowing.

✔ **Environmental:** Responsibilities to the planet; pollution; waste management; farming activities; genetic engineering; cost–benefit analyses; legal pressures.

✔ **Sectoral:** Competition; cartels and monopolies; competitive forces; cooperation within sectors; differentiation; segmentation.

Cartwright's intention is to 'widen the scope of analysis that needs to be carried out' within organisations and their environments using a precise and detailed approach. SPECTACLES analysis requires managers to take a detailed look at every aspect of their operations within their particular environment. (For a full explanation of all these factors, refer to Cartwright's book.)

Any analysis technique can yield difficult truths and questions, but SPECTACLES analysis is likely to raise precise and often uncomfortable questions that many managers (especially senior managers) may rather not address. For example, after considering cultural factors in full detail, an organisation may have to face the fact that it doesn't actually understand the effects of particular customs on buying patterns or on its ability to get staff to come and work for it. (See Chapter 17 for more on cultural concerns.)

To do a SWOT analysis, simply generate a list of everything that you can think of about the company and its products and services and then place each item under one of the four SWOT headings I list earlier in this section. After you do that, the real fun begins. Start discussions with others about how to:

- Build on strengths
- Eliminate weaknesses
- Recognise and take advantage of opportunities
- Minimise or eliminate threats

From discussions on each of the preceding topics, you gain valuable insights into what everyone else thinks about the state of your business. And most importantly, you can discover *why* they think that particular things are strengths, weaknesses, opportunities or threats.

SWOT analysis is particularly useful for understanding and addressing your weaknesses. For example, if one of your identified weaknesses is slow invoicing, which in turn negatively affects your cash flow, you can turn immediately to working out how to speed up this process.

Figure 4-2 makes SWOT analysis look easy, right? All you have to do is parcel things up, list them out – and you suddenly achieve full understanding! Actually, no. While you do (hopefully) identify lots of strengths and good things, you're also making sure that everyone knows where the problems truly lie. After you identify your problems and everyone knows that you do indeed have them, you must move on to the truly challenging job of tackling and resolving them.

SWOT analysis is also not simple because you must be able to say *why* the things that you list as strengths, weaknesses, opportunities and threats are indeed so. You can justify your categorisations by:

- Explaining how political, economic, social, technological, legal and ethical forces are going to affect your business.
- Describing the threat of entry from potential new competitors and market entrants.
- Estimating the strength of forces that drive your business and restrain any changes you may implement.

Knowing your markets

One key output of environmental scanning (see the preceding section, 'Analysing your environment: Environmental scanning') is that you come to know and understand each of your markets in full detail, including:

- Economic, social and legal pressures
- The behaviour patterns of consumers within the market
- The behaviour of competitors and alternatives within the competitive environment (see Chapter 2 for more on competition and alternatives)

    ✔ Changes in customer and client attitudes

Keep your knowledge and understanding of your existing markets right up to date by reading the business and trade press on a regular basis. But even more critically, go out and see for yourself what is happening in your sector and with commercial activities as a whole.

You must also work to become an expert in any new markets that you're considering entering *before* you open for business (see also Chapter 9). For new markets, you specifically need to know:

    ✔ Customers' buying habits – and things that cause these habits to change.

    ✔ Why customers are loyal to their present suppliers – and what may cause them to change their loyalties. (Hint: you must deliver more than just lower prices, you also have to deliver positive benefits!) See the sidebar 'More than low fares at Ryanair and easyJet' for more.

Considering technology and work practices

Another major output of environmental scanning (see the section 'Analysing your environment: Environmental scanning') relates to your ability to use technology and your workforce to best advantage.

Outside changes, inside impacts

As you become expert in your environment, you need to challenge yourself to make as many possible connections between what is happening out there and how it can conceivably affect the ways in which you do business.

Never ever take anything for granted when trying to connect outside forces to your organisation's internal responses. For example:

    ✔ You may assume that you can simply pass on the costs of rising fuel prices and interest to your customers. If you can do this, well and good – but always check! You must consider whether customers will stop using your products or services entirely,

stop using them as frequently or stop using them as soon as a lower cost alternative is available. And if you can pass on your extra costs to customers, you need to ask: for how long can I do so?

    ✔ A technological development may promise to improve quality, volume and/or cost effectiveness of output. Always check every claim that people make for their products and services, especially for any advantage that they state they can deliver. And if a product or service does seem to deliver on its promise, have you seen actually proof – or are you taking the promise on trust?

You must deliver any technology and workforce advantages to your customers, your organisation and your staff. Information technology (IT) in particular, means that people can now work from home, while they're travelling and in any location. You can serve, contact and advertise to your customers at any hour and place that you choose. You can process transactions quicker, take orders faster and more accurately and establish instant contacts.

Technological advances have led to a huge rise in non-standard patterns of work, changes in job structures and demands and a very different approach to the whole concept of the work/life balance. (I deal with all these topics in more detail in Chapter 12.)

At this point though, having thorough knowledge and understanding of your workforce means:

- Assessing what is important and of value to your staff.
- Creating patterns of work that your staff are happy with.
- Removing barriers and obstacles to effective employment practices.
- Creating the means and patterns of communication to ensure that all staff are kept fully informed of changes and progress.
- Creating and maintaining effective patterns of management and supervision.
- Becoming aware of pay and rewards that you need to offer in order to attract and retain staff.
- Identifying any barriers to work, such as public transport access and road and rail links if you require your staff to commute.

More than low fares at Ryanair and easyJet

As you analyse your markets and become really familiar with your customers, you must strive to be completely clear about what makes people sit up and take notice of you – and what doesn't.

For example, when they first started, Ryanair and easyJet forced people to take notice of their low air fares because their fares were so much lower than British Airways, Air France and the rest of the traditional airlines. If Ryanair and easyJet had simply come in a few pounds cheaper, few flyers would've changed their habits.

Because Ryanair's and easyjet's fares were so much lower, people were forced to look. They still continue to remind flyers of their low-cost advantage in their new advertising campaigns.

Nevertheless, in order to keep people's interests – and gain and develop customer bases – Ryanair and easyJet still had to put complete packages in place. These airlines had to provide services that customers considered appropriately regular, frequent, convenient and reliable, otherwise, no matter how low the fares were, people would not choose Ryanair or easyJet.

Noting Present and Future Concerns

In addition to knowing your environment, you must also be aware of the present and future concerns of everyone – including your organisation, your staff, your customers, your suppliers and your backers.

- **Present concerns** are those that you know and understand currently. They inform the ways you conduct your business at present.

- **Future concerns** are those that you know currently and understand may arise at some point. You have a range of responses ready to go if and when these matters do come to pass.

Inform your approach and attitude to present and future concerns based on what's actually going on in the real world. When you know what's happening every day in your organisation and environment, you can effectively respond to concerns. And if you are scanning the environment, as I discuss earlier in 'Analysing your environment: Environmental scanning,' you give yourself the best possible chance of genuine, detailed and expert understanding.

Present and future concerns are certain to come up on a regular basis, and of course, some are going to be more important than others. As you pursue your activities at present, you need to be especially aware of:

- **The threat of regulation and legal changes in all your organisation's practices:** You need to be aware of possible changes to employment law and financial reporting that's currently of particular concern.

- **Carbon emissions:** You'll almost certainly be asked to reduce the amount of carbon that your business generates – or to pay much more for maintaining your present level of carbon emissions.

- **Waste and effluent management:** Similar to carbon emissions, you'll be asked to pay very much more for disposing of the waste and effluent that you produce, otherwise, you'll be required (possibly by law) to engage in recycling activities.

- **Credit squeezes and the cost of finance:** At the time of publication, the availability of finance is reducing and the cost of credit is rising.

- **Fuel and energy prices:** With fuel prices and charges fluctuating greatly and energy supplies becoming scarcer overall, you need to be aware of consequences to your organisation brought on by any energy squeeze (including restraints on days and times in which energy may, or may not, be available).

  Estimating energy prices based on much higher oil prices than you're currently experiencing seems wise. Taking a cautious approach to energy matters means you are much less likely to be caught out when energy prices do indeed rise again!

When energy prices are low, people tend to stop worrying about energy and focus on other, more pressing concerns. Don't follow the herd! You must take the view that if something can happen once, it can and will happen again. Use any period of calm to figure out what you're going to do in the *next* crisis.

- **Transport hold-ups:** Transport is an enduring problem for anything that has to be physically distributed in the UK as well as in many other places. You need to know the costs of transport to your business, both in financial terms and its effect on your reputation for reliability. You must identify where hold-ups are most likely to occur and what you can do about them.

- **Access to information technology and databases:** In particular, you need to pay attention to any changes in costs and charges associated with how you use data sources.

In addition to the preceding, you also need to note the potential for natural disasters, disease epidemics and the effects of extreme weather conditions on your activities. Of course, these events are unpredictable, but all organisations need to be able to respond to them when they do occur.

Recognising and Dealing with Opportunities and Threats

Identifying the opportunities and threats among your environment concerns isn't an easy process. But if you go through a rigorous environmental scanning process (see the preceding 'Analysing your environment: Environmental scanning'), you can identify the specific challenges you need to be tackling.

When you start to tackle opportunities and threats, always keep your core position (see Chapter 2) in the front of your mind and seek to identify where your forces of competition come from (see Chapter 3).

In this section, I show you how to put *all* the results of your environmental scanning in the context of your core position and the forces of competition.

Considering context

Not all opportunities are created equal. Certain situations provide great opportunities for some people, some of the time, while the exact situations may offer quite poor opportunities for others.

Laker Airways

Once upon a time, Laker Travel Services Ltd. was an excellent air ticket sales company. It made a fortune by buying up blocks of tickets at heavily discounted rates from the world's airlines and then selling these tickets to customers at notably discounted rates.

And everyone was happy! The airlines sold blocks of tickets in advance for assured revenue rates. Customers who were able to book earlier enjoyed cheap plane tickets. Laker was highly profitable for many years.

Eventually, company founder Freddie Laker decided to extend his company's success to running its own airline and selling its own tickets. After a (very brief) period of superficial attractiveness, Laker Airways went to the wall – and nobody heard again of the company's supremely excellent business of selling discounted tickets.

Looking at business situations as Laker did can be terrifically attractive, but the organisation needed someone to pipe up and say, 'Hold on a minute. We don't actually have or own our own airline. So we don't know anything about how this machinery really works, how to maintain planes, how to acquire landing slots or how fuel costs may affect our ability to do business. We also don't have a single pilot on staff, hundreds of whom are required to actually fly these things!'

Encouraging people within an organisation to pipe up takes courage and discipline. If someone brings up a major concern involving the context of a business decision, always take the time to genuinely listen. You may save your organisation from a major blunder.

Context – the combination of a particular possibility or proposal along with your specific business and environmental circumstances – is essential for determining whether a situation presents genuine opportunity. For example:

- ✔ Excellent and effective railway station retail outlets such as Sock Shop and Tie Rack flopped when they were taken overseas.

- ✔ Successful personal and retail banks such as Abbey caught very serious colds in the financial markets when they tried to move into corporate finance and capital banking. (In particular, Abbey lost a lot of money on the Channel Tunnel project.)

In each of the preceding cases, people associated with the decisions saw opportunities *out of their contexts*. (See the sidebar 'Laker Airways' for another example.) What appeared to be opportunities weren't opportunities at all. Pondering others' decisions, however, you can easily see the lines of reasoning that led to the poor decisions.

You must have the discipline and courage to question decisions. Courage is particularly important when you have to confront dominant, powerful or strident personalities who seem to have bits between their teeth. Even if these personalities do shout down your concerns, an idea is still only an idea until you go through all the fine details and conclude that the idea may just work. For example:

- Sock Shop and Tie Rack worked in a peculiar environment – large British railway stations. Location (along with their ranges of products and services) gave them their success.

  But Sock Shop and Tie Rack needed to examine the specific role of location in much more detail. Success wasn't just about being located in railway stations themselves. At these stations, people wander about buying books, magazines, food and all the other things that they forgot to pack or else suddenly find that they need. Environmentally speaking, Sock Shop and Tie Rack got their initial leg up not just because of the locations themselves, but because stations have large numbers of people milling about. People at British stations are looking for things to do – and especially things to buy. If you just have large numbers of people rushing in and out of stations who are not also looking to buy things, you do not have a potential market.

For any failed past decision, consider whether social or behavioural aspects of the environment were part of the failure. Your decision must have seemed a good idea to start with (after all, everything starts out as a good idea), so consider whether you overlooked a social or behavioural issue.

- Abbey thought that financial expertise was an end in itself. Furthermore, the bank thought that investing in mega projects was a sure-fire winner. After all, 200 other banks were involved already in the Channel Tunnel project; they couldn't all be wrong, could they? And so, in Abbey went!

  However, as Abbey very quickly discovered, returns on investing in major building projects can (and often do) take a lifetime to achieve. Also, the other successful corporate finance companies involved in the project had other major ventures which delivered more quickly on a more assured basis.

Pinpointing the real opportunities – and passing on the illusions

The situations I describe in the preceding section – Abbey, Sock Shop and Tie Rack – as well as the sidebar 'Laker Airways' are all reminders of what can happen when you don't correctly assess your environment. To avoid falling into similar traps, you must separate out the real opportunities from the illusions.

Dotcom dreamin'

Remember the dotcom revolution of the late twentieth century? Many pundits heralded the end of retail and wholesale shopping. Whole town centres and retail parks were going to become urban wastelands. These predictions caused many to put over-large volumes of resources into Internet companies. And of course most lost their shirts as the result. As any true and detailed analysis carried out at the time accurately found, the whole premise was based on a set of *assumptions* that proved to be *illusions*. For example, many pontificated that:

✔ People would prefer to do business from home and the office rather than actually going and seeing things for themselves.

✔ Everyone in business had a computer.

✔ People would use the computer as the hub of their whole lives, rather than for just what they themselves chose.

✔ Computers were totally honest and reliable, so that whether you were offered cheap plane tickets, a Russian bride, online banking or a share of $32 million from Nigeria, these propositions were all honest, assured and guaranteed transactions.

Of course, none of the preceding came to pass. Over the past several years, these assumptions have proven to be illusions – and shattered illusions at that. The assumptions simply didn't stand up to environmental scrutiny. Indeed, the only Internet companies that survived were those that gained sufficient customer bases to cover all costs and generate profits. Just the same as everywhere else in fact!

Your first and foremost goal is to minimise your chances of failure. You can only do this by knowing and understanding all the forces present in your environment. Having good products and services is not enough! You must know your environment so you can recognise the genuine opportunities for introducing and developing your products and services.

Separating real opportunities from illusions is also important because if things do go wrong, you have a good basis to begin working out why failure happened. Your company must be able to answer the question, 'Why are we doing this?. If you don't (or can't) tackle this question, you almost certainly don't know and understand the environment in enough detail to give you a full answer and make the most of the potential opportunity.

Beware of beautiful illusions – you know how they creep in! Someone comes along with a grand idea that promises untold riches, market dominance, vast numbers of customers beating paths to your door and a website overwhelmed by thousands of hits. If something looks too good to be true, it probably is! If something looks like money for old rope, then a catch almost certainly exists. If somebody guarantees you untold riches in five years' time, run away from that person as fast as you can.

OnDigital: Everyone wants football, right?

The OnDigital venture was the ill-fated excursion by ITV into satellite and digital broadcasting. Shambolic from the start, it was based on a set of illusions:

✔ People wanted an alternative to Sky, the satellite and digital broadcasting market leader

✔ People were prepared to pay for the system setup

✔ People loved football

Now, all these statements are not illusions! They are all perfectly true. However, truth is not an end in itself:

✔ People only wanted an alternative to Sky if it was good and delivered advantages that Sky did not

✔ People would pay start-up costs, provided that the equipment worked when it was installed

✔ People do love football – especially Premiership, European and international football

Unfortunately, OnDigital provided not only an alternative service but an inferior one. The equipment was faulty and not strong enough to give an assured signal. And the final nail in the coffin came from the football: having failed to secure Premiership, European and international football, OnDigital paid £330 million for the lesser domestic competitions – the Championship and lower divisions. OnDigital soon found that nobody watched these games in the numbers necessary to turn a profit and so, in turn, they were unable to sell enough advertising and sponsorship.

Concentration on the headline issues – the excitement of digital television, the ability to compete with Sky and above all the illusions of 'football, football everywhere' – rather than analysing things, meant that the whole venture was conceived on a pattern of assumptions and illusions. Not only did the venture fail, it also caused serious damage to the lower-grade football industry, and it assured the position of Sky as the major domestic alternative to terrestrial broadcasting.

I don't mean to be a killjoy, but your job isn't chasing off on exciting adventures and using shareholders' resources just because something looks fun. If you need to shatter people's beautiful illusions of untold riches and market dominance along the way, you'll do no harm at all – only good in fact.

Assessing Environmental Factors

The great advantages of using the PEST, SWOT and SPECTACLES analysis approaches (see the preceding section 'Analysing your environment: Environmental scanning' and the sidebar 'Putting on your analysis SPECTACLES') is that they make you recognise the number and magnitude of factors that you need to know and understand.

After you identify these factors, you can examine how specific factors work and interact with each other in your environment. But you can only do this higher-level analysis if you know and understand what the factors are in your own particular area and how they interact.

Assessing the strength of factors

Get into the habit of continually assessing the ways in which environmental factors operate and which factors exert greater influence on your environment.

Of course, the relative strengths of factors change all the time, so you need to be aware of these changes as they happen (before they happen, if possible), and of actions you can take to counteract the negative impact of the factor changes. For example:

✔ If the government raises interest rates and also gives the go-ahead for fuel and energy price rises, you clearly know and understand that the resulting changes are going to have an effect on your customers' and clients' purchasing power and propensity to spend.

✔ However, what does it mean if the government reduces interest rates and orders a freeze on fuel and energy prices? Will such actions enhance your customers' and clients' confidence, leading them to spend more with you? The answer is neither yes nor no; the answer is 'it depends'! The answer depends on the customers and clients that you serve, on what is important and of value to them and how badly they've been hit in the past by squeezes and difficulties.

Take public commentaries and forecasts as your *starting* point, and then do the work for your own company, sector, industry and location.

To experience first-hand how various factors affect a purchase decision, try this thought experiment:

1. **Consider the various factors that are likely to be present next time you make a major purchase, such as buying a car.**

   When purchasing a car, without a doubt you consider price, comfort, brand and marque. You also consider fuel consumption, car tax, reputation, tax advantages or losses (if it's a company car) and financing options. And you certainly consider whether you like the vehicle!

   The relative strength of each of these factors on your final purchase decision is directly influenced by what you're thinking about at the time you're buying.

2. **Consider the various factors that are likely to be present for your own customers and clients the next time they purchase your products and services.**

   Ask yourself:

   - Which factors truly influence their behaviour and buying decisions?

   - Which are the factors that are more marginal?

   - Which should you concentrate on and prioritise? (Be honest with yourself here!)

When pondering customer behaviours, business leaders tend to look at the rational aspects of choice (price, value for money) and emphasise these as the rationale for how to deliver their products and services. Instead, you need to look at the *real* drives – the ones that you yourself have when making purchases!

Be sure to consider especially what people actually like about the process of buying and then owning your products and services. Doing so helps you to understand them better all round!

Making progress: Drives and restraints

Another aspect of working with environmental factors is understanding the drives and restraints that affect your ability to make progress.

On the face of it, *drives* – the things that you need to do to improve every aspect of your business – are easier (or more straightforward at least) to identify. Drives include:

- Improving production, sales, output, turnover and profitability.

- Maximising and optimising your use of resources.

- Knowing and understanding your customers' and clients' needs, wants and demands.

- Ensuring that you've assured your supply side as far as possible in terms of resources, data, technology, components, raw materials and expertise.

Identifying drives is the easy part; and this is where you need to concentrate your efforts and place your priorities. To make the identification process as effective as possible however, you need to know and understand the environmental forces that are present (see the earlier section 'Analysing your environment: Environmental scanning').

Identifying restraints is harder. *Restraints* are all the things that drive you to frustration – if not despair! Restraints include:

- **Equipment and technology breakdowns** that you can't fix for several days, causing you to lose production and output.
- **Website glitches and crashes,** which result in lost business, limited access and frustration to you and your customers.
- **Supply-side hold-ups** that may seem inexplicable to you (everyone knows that the roads are overcrowded – why didn't your supplier set out earlier?) still happen.

When you acknowledge the environmental factors and forces that affect your business early on, you can prepare yourself to modify your own approaches and responses to these forces, if necessary. For example, if you take supplies from an energy-intensive or transport-intensive supplier, rising fuel bills mean that their costs are rising as well. Think about how you can respond to this supplier if it comes to you for help and attempts to negotiate a different price or agreement. If you can say: 'No, we have a contract and we expect you to honour it,' various things can happen including:

- The supplier does indeed honour the contract. However, that supplier is then likely to look around for others with whom to do business – people who take a more sympathetic attitude than you.
- The supplier may break the contract, in which case you can choose to go to court, which is likely to take months (if not years) to resolve.
- The supplier may go broke, in which case you have no supplies.

Or you can choose to listen to the supplier's tales of woe and decide how best to progress, such as agreeing to a rise in their costs or extending their credit.

You don't have to accede to every hardship story that comes your way, but you should always listen and deal with each individual case on its own merits. Above all, take time to consider what the effects on your business are likely to be, depending on the outcome of any talks and negotiations.

Many large retail and wholesale chains are quite happy to invoke 24-hour contract cancellation clauses with suppliers if, for any reason, the supply doesn't match requirements and expectations. For some reason however, these same companies seldom consider the reverse effect – that of the supplier foreclosing.

You next need to be aware of the following situations. In different circumstances, they can either be drives or restraints on progress. And of course you need especially to be aware of their influences – and the opportunities and consequences for your business, company or organisation:

✔ The current capabilities of your top and senior managers and your workforce.

✔ The race to install and run the latest technology.

✔ The need for a presence in high prestige locations (central London, Berlin, Milan or Beijing) or a particular address, regardless of whether these locations are profitable.

✔ The need for international expansion, especially if you do not produce products and services that are easily exported.

✔ Expansion and growth for its own sake, rather than what's in the best interests of your company or organisation and your customers and clients.

✔ The assumption that cutting costs makes you profitable.

✔ The assumption that cutting prices brings customers flooding in through the door.

All these situations are exactly the kinds of things that companies and organisations do in response to isolated drives and restraints. You must consider how all these factors are likely to play out in the markets and wider environment before going ahead and doing them.

And if some powerful top personalities, dominant shareholders or some other knee-jerk response is pushing you into any of these decisions – particularly in response to operational difficulties – prepare for trouble, because trouble you are very likely to get. For example:

✔ The CEO of one of the UK train-operating companies ordered a 20 per cent increase in journey time for all trips. He reasoned that if journey times were made slower, trains would be more punctual.

The CEO didn't understand that punctuality was a function of the reliability of the trains and the infrastructure and the availability of terminus facilities. He didn't understand that the speed of the trains was a minor factor in their punctuality.

✔ The project director of a major engineering venture accepted calculations on delivery schedules that assumed country roads associated with the project would never be blocked or impassable, that traffic jams in small town centres didn't occur and that tractor traffic in the countryside wouldn't be encountered.

When the country roads were, indeed, impassable and blocked with tractors and other country traffic, the project got delayed and was eventually delivered five years late. The project director should have factored the true nature of the operating environment into his calculations at the outset.

✔ One government department produced cost forecasts on the basis that (in 2007) the price of oil would be $10 per barrel – without considering the other extreme that oil may be $200 or even $300 per barrel. Even worse, the department went on to accept its projections as gospel and ordered its service providers to work within these constraints. Consequently, these particular service providers found themselves with plenty of capacity to work with the government departments; they just couldn't afford to!

So if you don't look at the drives and restraints, you hinder, and sometimes destroy, your chances of any effective progress at all.

Fussing with forces: Force field analysis

Identifying and knowing the forces that affect your business is well and good, but figuring out what you can actually do to respond to these forces is much more useful. Figure 4-3 shows the idea that some basic forces exist that businesses must contend with, including forces that drive progress and forces that hinder it.

Figure 4-4 takes this basic situation and adds some life and detail. A more fully fleshed-out diagram like Figure 4-4 enables you to see the problems you need to tackle.

DRIVING FORCES
→
→
→

RESTRAINING FORCES
←
←
←

Figure 4-3:
Force field
analysis.

You parcel up the forces driving progress, and those restraining progress, so that you can see what you're up against.

Figure 4-4:
Force field
analysis:
Illustration.

DRIVING FORCES
You need a new product
You can develop people's careers
The company has an opportunity
to progress

RESTRAINING FORCES
The CEO doesn't want it
The staff are happy where they are
The company has been prosperous
for many years

You must decide where you're going to start – which of the forces you're going to tackle first. Your answer is very much up to you. A variety of answers can be correct, as long as you support yours with your own expert judgement and line of reasoning.

For example, you may decide that unless the CEO changes his mind, your organisation has no hope of progress, and so you concentrate everything on changing his mind. Or you may decide that if you tackle everything else first and show progress, then the CEO will have to change his mind (and that he may even do so quite happily, especially if you convince him that the change was all his idea).

Working within present and envisaged constraints

Even if you know and understand your present set of constraints like the back of your hand (see the preceding section 'Considering environmental constraints') and you question everything, you may find yourself back to square one. You may feel you've accomplished nothing, whereas you've actually done yourself a whole lot of good: you're now taking an active rather than passive interest in everything that goes on.

Taking an active interest in your environment means that you're much more likely to spot early any new constraints when they arise. And you can start to develop active, informed and expert opinion about how you can tackle these constraints.

Envisaged constraints – those that you know and understand may arise – are harder to tackle. You know the sorts of things that can and do happen at any time – you can identify some preventative actions (see the preceding section 'Making progress: Drives and restraints'). Concentrate your efforts on prevention rather than response. That way, you're better able to keep everything on an even keel for much longer than if you constantly find yourself responding to emergencies.

Some envisaged constraints occur with great frequency. You can be more or less certain that all the following are going to rise:

- Energy and fuel prices and charges
- Water, gas and electricity charges
- Local business taxes
- Fees related to waste and effluent disposal, environmental management and exhausts and emissions

You also need to look at those constraints that aren't immediately apparent. This process requires you to cultivate an informed and enlightened view of what can conceivably go wrong at any time, especially regarding the difference between the impossible and the unlikely.

For example, a large company such as Nissan may seem highly unlikely to come into your area to set up a production facility – but what if it does? What are the likely and possible effects on:

- ✔ Your own access and egress?
- ✔ Your ability to attract and retain staff?
- ✔ Your ability to command local sources of supply, transport and distribution?
- ✔ Your ability to expand your operations if you want to do so in the future?

Obviously, you do have a good range of things to address. And the same is true in reverse. What if a large local player closes? Where does this leave your business? How do your duties and obligations to the area change? How does this change in your environment affect your moral and economic obligations to the community?

You must consider a wide range of matters in your environmental analysis. If you do your analysis right, the results can give you great expertise, which is of value to anyone seeking to develop organisational strategy and an assured competitive position.

Chapter 5

Looking to Leadership

· ·

· ·

Everything that an organisation does is the result of the actions and activities of people. And someone has to be in charge of those people and the organisation overall. In other words, you need a top person, such as a CEO, general, admiral, captain or head person. In other words, every organisation needs a leader.

An organisation's leader gives energy and direction, sets standards and ensures that the results are delivered. Leaders are also there to put things right when they go wrong and to see that the organisation's strategy and competitive position remain as strong as possible.

What is your contribution as a leader? How do your actions deliver the results that your organisation actually needs and wants? When you're told to do something that you feel is wrong, how do you respond? Your answers to these questions take you to the heart of leadership. Companies and organisations simply can't afford the bureaucracies, hierarchies and orderly processes that they've spent so many years building up.

On the one hand, delivering a blueprint for effective and successful strategic leadership isn't easy. Good leaders come from all walks of life and backgrounds. Some have military training. Some are graduates of the best business schools in the world. Others have no education at all.

In this chapter, I examine strategic leadership – what it is, where it's effective and how to make sure that when the time comes (if it hasn't already), you have all the expertise and characteristic to lead your team, department or entire organisation.

Looking at Leadership – Now and in the Future

Of all the things expected to change over the coming years, the need for greater leadership expertise is going to be very high on the list.

You're going to have to deliver results that are in the interests of many diverse groups and individuals – not just the shareholders or directors. While results are ultimately only delivered through the sales of products and services, you have to deliver the motivation, inspiration, vision and energy that are necessary to deliver sales. You can't sell in isolation! You're also going to have to ascribe to increasingly higher standards of ethics than have previously been the case. And the rewards of your leadership are also going to have to be shared amongst everyone – your staff, suppliers, customers and backers.

You can't lead from an office or a computer screen. Leading and directing companies and organisations must take place among people. After all, no one likes acting in the interests of people that you never see. So make up your mind to get out and about among your people – this is where your place is and ought to be.

If you're in a top position, you're going to be much more widely held to account over results. You have to face everyone for whom you're responsible, including staff, customers and shareholders, and be accountable for your actions. You're not going to be able to fall back on anodyne statements that your organisation's poor or declining performance is the result of difficult trading conditions, wars in the Middle East or credit crunches, without then going on to explain why and how these matters affect your organisation so badly. Although such explanations may have been acceptable to shareholders in the past, these fallback statements won't be enough in the future, particularly as resources become scarcer and demands ever greater.

To be effective now and in the future, you have to look harder at what the expertise of leadership actually is and how to use it to deliver company and organisation performance. (See the following section 'Leading Strategically' for a full definition.)

You must be able to deliver the expertise of leadership in a way that has meaning for today – not yesterday. Harking back to the good old days and saying 'Wouldn't it be good if Caesar were in charge?' can't suffice. (Besides, Caesar isn't in charge, he can't be, and even if he were, he'd be two thousand years out of date.)

What leadership is not

You have probably seen descriptions of leaders in the press and media that make you cringe! Perhaps Person X is appointed to a top job in a particular organisation, and he's described as being good at golf, or a socialite or a dynamic figure. The coverage rarely mentions whether Person X is good at his job or can deliver in the new set of circumstances.

Indeed, leadership isn't any – or all – of the following descriptions, which I took from 'the quality press':

✔ A safe pair of hands (whatever on earth that means)

✔ The right bearing (of course, 'the right bearing' is never quite defined)

✔ Good breeding (presumably from the middle classes, but never made completely explicit)

✔ The product of School X or Y (probably from the UK private sector, unless someone's making a virtue of the fact that he comes from humble beginnings)

✔ A member of a golf/sailing/cricket club

✔ 'One of us' or 'one of them' (for example, from the same club, school, class or location)

When you think about it, you can see why people prefer the preceding kinds of descriptions to precise statements of expertise. For a start, they're easier. You can fall back on clichés instead of doing the real hard work that's required when you're looking for people to lead and direct an organisation.

If you don't fall back on things like breeding and background, you're forced to start doing the job of hiring and promoting people properly! (Unfortunately, if you ask most hiring managers how to go about finding people for top jobs, they don't have any idea where to start.)

By avoiding assessing potential leaders properly you can also avoid exposing your own shortcomings!

Leading Strategically

Strategic leadership is a combination of expertise, personality, identity and confidence. To start with, strategic leaders must like and respect their companies and industries. They must know and understand everything that there is to know and understand about their companies, their products and services and how their companies conduct business.

Strategic leaders are essential at the head of any organisation because staff, customers, suppliers, investors and backers must:

✔ Know that leaders can do what they say they can do.

✔ Have confidence in a leader's character, integrity and expertise.

✔ Know that leaders act in the best interests of everyone, not just themselves or a small group of vested interests.

If you aspire to take on a top job in your organisation and do it exceptionally well, you need to know the expectations. Although every organisation has specific needs, top strategic leaders:

- ✔ Take and accept responsibility, authority and accountability for everything that goes on in the organisation and in the name of the organisation. If someone makes mistakes on your watch, you must accept responsibility in public at least. You can put things right with the individual in private afterwards.

- ✔ Devise and deliver a competitive strategy that delivers the results that the organisation needs for its backers.

- ✔ Create and deliver the products and services for customers' and clients' needs.

- ✔ Inspire the staff to work for the organisation through thick and thin.

- ✔ Inspire the confidence of the stock markets, media and everyone else who has a legitimate interest in the present and future of the organisation.

- ✔ Interact with people at all levels of the organisation, inspiring credibility and confidence in them at all times.

- ✔ Set an example of conduct, behaviour, commitment and performance for others to follow.

You have to be able to share and showcase all the preceding attributes – in forms, documents, meetings and presentations that people find understandable and acceptable. You must be able to understand what people need and want from you in such positions, and then deliver these expectations in ways acceptable to them, without compromising your own clear vision of the direction in which the organisation is going. (For a full understanding of how to communicate effectively with various people in business, see *Business NLP For Dummies* by Lynne Cooper.)

Strategic leadership is not a magic spell cast on some people but not others. You can acquire it by focusing on a few key elements – and being realistic about a few others – as I discuss in the following sections.

Envisioning your vision

Your vision – clear and direct – is the core of what you as a strategic leader must deliver. Your *vision* is what you see in your mind's eye about where your organisation is going and how it's going to look in the future. Your vision therefore gives life to your organisation's competitive position (see Chapter 2), strength to your direction and guidance to the ways in which the organisation conducts its affairs. Specifically, your vision:

✔ Sets standards of conduct and behaviour.

✔ Establishes your expectations for the company's products and services.

✔ Focuses everything and everyone on the positive and profitable – not just in money terms, but also in terms of reputation and standing in your industry and markets.

Your vision must be clear and positive, a call to action for others to follow. People need to know and understand what they're letting themselves in for, and *why* on earth they should follow you. You must tell and show them specifically what you're setting out to do, as well as *why* your vision is the best possible option for the company.

To share your vision effectively, you must have some distinctive characteristics and expertise, including:

✔ **Knowledge.** You must understand everything that your organisation does and how it does things. See the following section 'Becoming knowledgeable' for more.

✔ **Big and small picture:** You need to combine an overview of everything going on with full understanding of all the details that contribute to the success and effectiveness of activities.

✔ **Integrity:** People need honesty at the top of companies and organisations. Indeed, a leader's integrity is at the hub of everything a company does. When a leader's integrity is in doubt, people begin to question everything about the company, including the quality of conduct and performance, working practices – even the products and services.

✔ **Respect.** You need to value everyone else's contributions to the organisation, regardless of rank, status or occupation.

✔ **Enthusiasm.** Your passion for everything that your organisation does makes you its greatest advocate and cheerleader. See the following section 'Cheerleading and advocating' for more.

You can't expect others to have this kind of enthusiasm if you yourself don't. Every time people see you, you need to wax lyrical about your achievements, your brilliant staff and your excellent products and services.

Having said this, you also have to be honest! Your lyricism must be tempered with reality. You're extolling the (many great) virtues of your company, not just boasting or building up people's egos.

✔ **Speed of thought, word and deed.** You need to be able to master a brief very quickly on whatever subject may come your way and then deliver a credible, expert and accurate point of view on behalf of your organisation, whenever asked.

✔ **Decisiveness.** Your decisions must be accurate and timely. When nice and positive situations require decisions, accuracy and speed come easily. But when tough decisions need to be made, you have also to be able to take these, stand by them and explain to people the rationale behind your choices.

✔ **Transformation.** You need to lead your organisation into a radically changed market or industry, shedding the old ways of doing business. Some chief executives are unable to lead their firms through required transformations, and all stakeholders suffer as a result. Consider the global pharmaceuticals industry, which has been at the end of the 'blockbuster drug era' (one key consumer drug discovery that carries the whole firm) since the turn of the century. And yet, most leaders in this sector have been notoriously slow to change their companies' approach to R&D or to change their traditional vertical business and organisational structures. As a result of transformational leadership, the entire industry has been in slow decline for a decade!

Above all, you need to back your vision with courage and strength. You'll have times when your vision adversely affects other people (for example when you lay people off or when you withdraw product lines). As a responsible, strategic leader, you must face these people and be prepared to deliver your vision to their faces. Never release critical vision information – particularly if your vision contains difficult or potentially negative aspects – by email, text or, worse still, via the media.

Peter Nicholl, former Governor of the National Bank of Bosnia Herzegovina, provides a great example of vision combined with courage and strength as follows:

> *If you have this kind of vision, you must also have the character necessary to deliver and implement it. Difficult or tough decisions may not make you popular, but if a tough decision is necessary, you must make it – and you must also be able to explain honestly and openly why you made that decision.*

Colin Powell, former US general, Joint Chiefs of Staff and Secretary of State, reinforced the combined need for vision and courage by saying:

> *My job is to send people into battle knowing that some of them will die. I cannot avoid this. But what I can do and will always do is to explain to them why they are going into battle, the good that is to come out of it, and why they may be the ones who will be making the sacrifices.*

Powell was speaking of international warfare, of course. But the strength of his statement extends to business because it emphasises how leaders need to explain to people why they have to do things and why their efforts are so important. Powell's statement also implies that he communicates this information directly – face-to-face.

Cloudy vision

In one way, talking about a leader's vision is rather fanciful! The last thing that you need or want at the top of companies and organisations are individuals who deliver pieces of flighty guesswork, wasting organisation resources on ideas that have never been evaluated. For example:

✔ A Body Shop manager used her position as a key figure in the company to try and religiously indoctrinate her staff. The staff, she explained, worked at the shop because of a higher calling and customers were to be converted to her particular religious beliefs if possible. Essentially, her 'vision' was to save the world through converting people to her particular brand of religion. The whole thing evidently ran quickly into difficulties. Body Shop top management became involved, closing down the shop and removing the manager. When the shop reopened, it was under close supervision and scrutiny in an effort to restore its reputation and make sure that this kind of 'vision' never occurred again.

✔ A management consultant firm claimed to have seen the future of factory production, and it was 'world class manufacturing.' Persuaded by the firm's senior partners and top management, many manufacturing companies throughout the US north and northwest bought into this 'vision'. One of them, a major supplier to the motor car industry, quickly went from making a decent and acceptable return of 11 per cent profit, to the edge of bankruptcy, as the result of following the consultants' recipes. Soon other stories emerged of other companies experiencing similar problems after buying into the firm's 'world class manufacturing' vision. Finally the consultants were faced with having to justify their vision to the media, litigants and the world at large. Their answer was: 'World class covers a variety of meanings and so it is not possible to give a detailed definition.'

Not being able to define a vision says a lot about the sometimes spurious and phoney natures of corporate visions! Your vision must come down to you. You can't expect to take on anything substantial from some other 'visionary'; you must define your vision for yourself and your organisation. Whatever your vision, it must always stand up to scrutiny and critical evaluation. And it has to be capable of change and development to reflect changes in the world around and the competitive environment.

As economic resources tighten, organisations are going to be looking for expertise in organisational direction, rather than breeding or safe pairs of hands (see the sidebar 'What leadership is not'). Courageous, visionary, expert leadership is the type of leadership with which people can and do identify. This kind of leadership is certain increasingly to become much-prized expertise.

Doing the hard work

A myth still persists that leaders are born. It is true that some people exhibit 'leadership qualities and characteristics' that are evident from an earlier age than others. But even these people must go on to do the hard work of becoming leaders by developing their expertise, their communication skills and (in some cases) their honesty and integrity!

Think of sport and entertainment stars: talented people in these fields use their gifts as the beginnings of hard work, not as ends in themselves. And even if you're not a superstar, you can still make yourself into a decent player by working hard at particular techniques. You can surprise yourself by just how good you can become at something if you do work hard. Such is the case with leadership; you can surprise yourself by just how far you can progress if you choose to do so and if you put in the work.

Acquiring outstanding leadership skills starts by recognising that it's all hard work *now*. And you must do this hard work yourself – it doesn't do itself!

Many of the best and most successful leaders share an appreciation for the hard work of becoming great leaders:

- Richard Branson: 'I always took myself terribly seriously and worked hard.'
- Anita Roddick: 'I always worked hard at everything that I did.'
- John Harvey Jones: 'There is no point in doing anything half heartedly.'
- Philip Green: 'I love to see the results, and so I have to work for them.'

If you're going to succeed in reaching the highest levels of leadership, you must combine this kind of work ethic with strength of character, determination, ambition, commitment and drive. Only after you do all this can you develop the basis of your professionalism and expertise necessary for the top job that you're seeking.

Considering charisma

Sometimes people point to a controversial leader like Hitler and say, 'But he had charisma, and you can't manufacture that!' Remember this: Hitler, above all, was manufactured and not born. Before Hitler made any further progress, Hollywood film director Leni Riefenstahl, radio producer and propaganda expert Josef Goebbels and many other experts worked to present Hitler in such a way as to get the German military and civil service elites on his side.

Bullies in the workplace often behave badly because they've been put in a position of leadership or responsibility that they can't cope with. They've never worked on the skills that are now important to their leadership position, so don't know how to behave or conduct themselves. Indeed many bullying bosses only got to their current positions because they were good at their previous jobs, not because they had any aptitude for their current positions.

Charisma is about securing the confidence of others. In addition to being good at what you do, people must believe that you're good at what you do. So give thought as to how you want others to see you and then work these ideas into a *leadership persona* that gives everyone confidence in you and your expertise. See the following section 'Creating your identity' for more on this topic.

So work to develop your leadership skills. You need outstanding presentation skills and communication style because you want people to know who you are and what you stand for. Pay attention to how you behave and conduct yourself, the ways in which you engage others and the style (or styles) in which you present and exhibit yourself. And perhaps most importantly, be ready to modify or reinforce any of these behaviours based on the ways in which others receive you.

Keeping your feet on the ground

People who are exceptionally good at what they do – in sport, entertainment and yes, business – can easily start to believe their own publicity and begin to act as if they're the true saviours of the world. If you find yourself in such a position, beware! Other people can put up with vanity and over-confidence for a while, but eventually these behaviours lead to your removal – even if you're very good at your job. For example:

- Napoleon was a very successful general and victories on the battlefield led to his becoming emperor of France, a job he was also very good at – at first! But after conquering much of Europe, designing cities and roads and introducing a constitution and legal framework to the whole continent, he started to believe in his own greatness. And this belief led quickly to his downfall. Early in his career he worked hard and focused on what needed doing; later he guessed at things. As time went on, even his military campaigns began to end in defeat, not victory. The rest, as they say, is history.

- The only prime minister of Great Britain who has left office on the date of his or her own choosing is Tony Blair. Everyone else has been brought down by his or her own party or else forced out at an election – because each official held on too long. These leaders were vain enough to think that their parties and the country needed them. Indeed, the graveyards of the world are full of 'indispensable' people.

Nobody sets out to be like the preceding example, but many top leaders, after years of successes, end up losing touch with reality.

Make sure that you surround yourself with critical friends, not 'yes' people. Never reject criticism or disagreement because of your position alone; always argue your case, but if you got it wrong, admit it and then change your mind.

In 1940, after France fell to the German invasion, Britain was left to fight the war on its own. Neville Chamberlain, the country's prime minister, had been forced to resign. The minister for war, Lord Halifax, was also forced out of office. Winston Churchill took the positions of prime minister and minister for war and used his maiden speech in these positions to state, 'I can promise you nothing but blood, toil, sweat and many tears.' Amazingly, everyone – Parliament and the public alike – cheered him to the rafters! Not because of what he said, but because of the way he said it. They had faith in him and his ability to lead the country in response to the crisis facing it simply because he sounded as if he knew what he was going to do. And, of course, he subsequently proved it – by doing just that!

Creating your identity

Good leaders establish *identities* – combinations of recognition, awareness, expertise and credibility – both within their organisations and also amongst customers, clients, suppliers and backers. If you're in charge of people, they expect to be able to look up to you, and so you have to give them something to look up to. A key part of your leadership identity is confidence. People must believe you when you say that you'll do something and that you'll do it well.

Confidence comes from others knowing and believing everything you:

- ✔ Talk about
- ✔ Do for yourself
- ✔ Do on others' behalves

If you aspire to a position of leadership, you must build your confidence. Begin to do this by testing yourself against the preceding three factors. If you talk about something, be credible – and right! If you do things for yourself, they must serve wider interests also. And when you do things for others, make sure that you deliver what you set out to achieve. After you start along these lines, your confidence will soar!

Playing Key Roles

As a leader, you're going to have certain priorities that you must attend to and roles that you must fulfil. Put simply, other people demand these roles of you, and you have to be able to play these roles effectively if you're to do a top, senior job properly.

Being professional, being connected

Professionalism is a key ingredient to becoming a great leader. *Being professional* means that you have a personal as well as occupational commitment to everything that you do. You seek out new and better information all the time, drawing lessons from wherever you can find them. You're continually looking at ways of developing and improving everything about yourself and your organisation.

When you become the CEO or a top manager, make sure that you never lose sight of the operational and daily issues that make up such an important part of people's daily lives. You see how people deliver, not just their knowledge and expertise, but also how they deliver and impose their personalities on what they do. After all, you were in a lower position and probably grumbled like everyone else about your manager's remoteness or lack of understanding. So make the professional commitment never to hide in your brand new shiny office and car! Instead, get out and connect (or reconnect) with the people who really make your organisation function.

Make up your mind now to discover and understand everything that others demand of you as a leader. This sort of exhaustive research is the only sure foundation of success if you aspire to be a top or senior person.

Surveying a wide range of roles

When you research others' expectations of you, you're likely to find a large number of roles. Although you may feel overwhelmed, you need to have the lot – or something very close to it – including being:

- **The greatest enthusiast** for your company, organisation, products, services and activities. See the following section 'Cheerleading and advocating' for more information.

- **The biggest advocate** for everything that you and others do in the name of the company or organisation.

- **A consummate fix-it person** who puts everything right (or knows someone who can) whenever anything goes wrong.

- **A company loyalist** who is proud of staff and their capabilities.

- **A role and conduct model** who sets standards and enforces them, leading by example.

- ✔ **A promise-keeper** who always delivers – and never makes promises that you cannot or don't intend to keep.

- ✔ **An ethical authority** who acts at all times with the highest standards of probity and integrity.

- ✔ **A parent figure** who is fair and consistent in everything that you do.

- ✔ **A human being** who, after making a mistake, owns up to it. (And if one of your people makes a mistake, you own up to it in public at least – and then put things right as necessary behind closed doors.)

- ✔ **A cheerleader** who shares praise when the entire group achieves. (And if you all make a mistake or do something wrong, then you carry the can again – at least in public.)

The preceding may look like a wish list for the perfect superhuman, but that's not the case! The list simply reflects how much everyone expects of people in positions of power, influence and authority. Some roles may come more easily to you and fit your personality and skills more naturally, but you must know all that's expected of you and sign up for all of it when you take on any position of power, influence or seniority.

Fortunately, you can develop the skills needed to fulfil all the preceding roles. The following sections cover several essential roles and the skills required for each.

Becoming knowledgeable

Beyond the numerous leadership roles that I list in the preceding section 'Surveying a wide range of roles,' you need to become a bit of a know-it-all. In a good way, of course!

As a successful strategic leader, you must know and understand everything possible about your organisation and its workings because:

- ✔ You want to be a leader who interacts confidently with the media, answering questions clearly and accurately – and not getting collared by a reporter.

- ✔ You want to be prepared to say the right thing to anyone and everyone and not be caught off guard and say something inappropriate or crass.

- ✔ Your people (especially your staff) expect you to present your knowledge in ways that inspire complete confidence.

- ✔ You want to inspire faith and support from your backers and shareholders by being able to give a full and honest account of how and why you're using their resources.

Being this straightforward can be a real challenge. Many organisational cultures simply don't support honesty, directness and candour at all. Instead these companies have long histories of half-truth founded on years of mismanagement. All you can do as a leader in these circumstances is to push the barriers as far as you can – and make sure that if you can't tell the truth, at least you don't become one of the liars.

In order to know and understand everything about your organisation's competitive position, strategy, operations, direction and priorities, you need to get up to speed on your new job very quickly.

- ✔ If you're coming into a senior position from outside the organisation, you're going to have to quickly prove yourself. Otherwise, people soon start questioning your judgement, capability and expertise. In other words, they question *you* and why you were appointed in the first place.

- ✔ If you've been appointed from within (promoted from the ranks), people already know you – but through your old job, not your new one. These co-workers expect you to adopt your new role quickly. If you don't, they're likely to make dark mutterings about money, status or why you got the job at all – anything to chip away at your new-found position.

Managing by walking around

Authors Tom Peters and Robert Waterman coined the phrase *managing by walking around* many years ago in their book *In Search of Excellence* (Harper and Row, 1982).

Peters and Waterman consider managing by walking around to be a key behaviour of companies that consistently deliver excellent and sustained high-value performance. In every growing and developing company they profiled, the top person and people in the organisation walked the job, got to know everybody and listened to staff concerns. For example:

- ✔ When Michael Marks was chairman of Marks & Spencer, he visited each store every year. After a short meeting with the manager, he spent time with all the checkout staff.

- ✔ When Wal-Mart was growing into an international company, founder Sam Moores

Walton visited every store and made a point of turning up at midnight with trays of coffee and doughnuts for the staff who were working on deliveries, loading, unloading and shelf filling.

- ✔ Mark McCormick, founder of IMG which represents sports and entertainment stars around the world, rang all his managers at least once a week, unless he'd seen them during the week.

You do have such a difference to make as a leader through your sheer enthusiasm and interest in others. The professional bit and the expertise have to be there of course, but you have a real opportunity to add your own personal touch – through your energy and commitment. People respond to enthusiasm and commitment. So do it!

Within the first day or so of moving into any position of responsibility, walk the entire floor, office or workspace. Even if you've been with the organisation for years, get a sense of what the place is like from the point of view of your new post. Make face-to-face and verbal contact with everyone that you possibly can. Doing so does wonders for establishing a great beginning and can give you a bit of breathing space as you set about uncovering the intricacies of your new job.

If you work for a remote, virtual or global organisation (see Chapter 17), you can't easily get around to everyone in this way! But you can create an identity and credibility – and you must do it quickly! Utilise video links and conferencing, web casts, email, text – anything to get an impression of yourself out there among your people.

Cheerleading and advocating

One of the most important leadership roles that I list in the section 'Surveying a wide range of roles' is your ability to act as the greatest enthusiast, supporter and advocate of your organisation.

You are the main supporter and advocate for your staff, everything they do and everything that happens around them. You must sing their praises to anyone who'll listen – and especially to anyone who needs to know. Your staff expect this level of positive promotion from you. In the eyes of your staff, your performance as leader will take a downward turn if they don't see you actively and regularly supporting them.

Being the biggest supporter and advocate of everything that your organisation does means that you must have – and demonstrate – great faith in your products, services, direction, strategy and competitive position. After all, if you're in the very top job, most of the decisions related to these aspects come down to you.

Try to make your enthusiasm and sparkle infectious. You want to fire up people; you want them to follow you. So lead by example – a big part of your example is your positive demeanour while presenting yourself to staff and to the world at large.

You don't want to be one of those managers or leaders who says, 'If my staff don't hear from me, they know that they're doing a good job.' This approach is a mark of great disrespect. Get into the habit of praising everyone that you possibly can. And if you don't have time to praise your staff, make time! You are, after all, the boss – you can do what you want!

Leaders and non-leaders

Unfortunately, too many people in leadership positions are really non-leaders – a designation you want to avoid at all costs! Non-leaders are individuals who:

- Stay remote from everything, hiding away in offices and committees.
- Panic at the first sign of difficulty.
- Pull rank when faced with difficult lines of questioning and debate.
- Personalise professional issues.
- Surround themselves with 'yes' people and 'toadies', rather than people who can give genuine, expert and often unwelcome advice.

If you really want to be a leader and to hold a top job, you need to make up your mind *now* that you'll do none of these things. You must develop strength of character, which means you:

- Face people even when you know that the situation is going to be difficult or unpleasant.
- Panic inwardly when faced with difficulties but you then take time to work things out, pinpointing what needs to be done immediately and what needs to be done over the longer term to address the real issues.

- Argue things through if faced with difficult questions. And if you realise that you're wrong about something, change your mind, of course!
- Never personalise any workplace or professional issues. Discuss and debate with others, and then arrive at a conclusion that serves the best interests of the business.
- Never victimise others for having a point of view different to your own! Apart from being foolish, you're breaking employment law. You don't want to be one of the 15,000 or so cases a year in the UK that finishes up in front of a tribunal or the courts, having to explain why you picked on someone just because he or she had a different viewpoint to your own.
- Remind yourself – perhaps daily – that you need critics! Everyone does! Indeed for top leaders, critical friends who support, yet carefully consider everything that you propose to do, form a vital part of your ability to develop and sustain an effective and profitable business and career.

Make every effort to be a leader with character and courage. And make up your mind now never to be someone who hides behind rank, status or position.

Inspiring others

Never forget that as a leader, you're there to inspire! Your job is to generate excitement, action, commitment and achievement. (You can't do this if you're miserable, morose or a bully.)

Specifically, you must inspire:

- Everyone to work well and hard for you
- Customers and clients to keep using you and your services

✔ The public to have confidence in your company and its products and services

You can't inspire confidence in anyone or anything unless you know what you're doing and what you're talking about. You first order of business is to master the brief, find out what needs doing first and get acquainted with everything and everyone:

✔ **If you're given no specific brief or task to tackle,** you must create your own from your own knowledge and understanding that you must acquire very quickly!

✔ **If you're given a brief or specific tasks to tackle,** you still need to check if the brief is accurate and whether the tasks are the right tasks.

Immerse yourself in things as soon as you're appointed. You may only have a few hours or days, especially if you were parachuted in to sort out a crisis. Seek out everything and everyone that you possibly can about the organisation and all its works and workings. In addition, make yourself visible and known to everyone immediately.

Looking to the Future

As a strategic leader, you need to commit yourself to gaining new insights all the time. You can't predict where exactly an organisation – or sector, market or economy, for that matter – is going to go.

This element of uncertainty means you need to build the broadest possible base for your knowledge and understanding. Use every opportunity to visit others and see how they do things. Challenge your own preconceptions of things at every stage. If you do jump to conclusions about things, be honest enough to say so (to yourself at least!) and evaluate where things went amiss.

You don't want to be one of those leaders – who you've probably suffered under – who comes in with one good idea from a previous job. Every time something happens, his only response is, 'when I was at X Company, we always did this and so that is what I'm going to do here.' This response is no good. Companies and organisations need people who can deliver their expertise in the context of what is currently needed, not what used to be needed somewhere else.

Nothing ever stands still – especially not your expertise as a leader. Your expertise has to develop alongside your company or organisation and its competitive strategy.

Part III
Putting Strategic Management into Action

'This rambling club has certainly had a definite sense of direction since Sir Rupert took over.'

In this part . . .

1 show you how you can generate competitive action and how it works in practice. I look at finances and investment, as well as the nitty-gritty of products, services and markets. I examine how all these aspects behave, act, interact and react. I also point you towards the best opportunities currently available and give you hints on how to spot them for yourself.

Chapter 6

Assessing Your Competition

· ·

In This Chapter

▶ Becoming familiar with your industry and location

▶ Knowing your industry, competitors and alternatives

▶ Identifying competitive barriers

▶ Managing time, schedules, costs and reputation

· ·

Strategic leadership and management in action requires knowing and understanding exactly what you and your organisations are up against. No matter what plans and vision for the future you hold, you need to recognise the fact that other companies and organisations are successful, effective and profitable.

You must therefore examine where your competitors' strengths lie and also seek to locate their weaknesses. Knowing and understanding the value that they deliver to their customers and clients can help you shape the value that you choose to offer to yours.

Looking carefully at outside examples is key to strengthening your own strategic approach, operations and activities – all of which can ultimately sharpen your organisation's competitive edge. This chapter builds on and combines everything I look at in Parts I and II in an effort to show you how to fully assess your competitors so you stay ahead of them and respond effectively to their initiatives.

Assessing Industries and Sectors

Whatever your location, activities, strengths and weaknesses, you need to be constantly assessing and evaluating the state of the markets that you serve, and the industry or industries in which you work.

Of course, to begin to do this, you have to be as precise as you can about the industries and sectors in which you work, and the markets that you serve.

Things can, and do, change very quickly. Fashions and fads come and go. People's tastes and habits move on (see the sidebar 'Celebrity restaurants and nightclubs' for just a few examples).

You need to know and understand people's habits – and the effects that these behaviours and values have on your industry and your day-to-day business activities. You need to know what makes people change their habits and what the possible and most likely effects of these changes may be.

And above all, you need to understand that highly vague and yet hugely important quality of *confidence* – the perception or feeling of wellbeing that persuades people to go out and spend money in the first place. I tackle confidence in the following section because it serves as a starting point for everything else that I cover in the chapter.

Being aware of changes in confidence

Confidence affects everyone – consumers, suppliers, staff, investors and backers.

- **High levels of confidence** mean that you have to work less hard to generate business in the first place. People are disposed to spend their money on goods and services.

- **When confidence falls,** people look very closely and carefully at how they spend their money (if indeed they spend it at all).

You therefore need to pay particular attention to changes in confidence and the effects on people's willingness to spend. Often a fall in confidence reflects a decline in purchasing power. *Purchasing power* is a combination of the amount of money that people have available to them to make purchases, support an overall quality of life, pay essential bills and make discretionary purchases (the things that they want but don't need).

Consumer confidence and purchasing power are inter-related. Consumers need to have the confidence to spend money in your industry and on your products and services. They make their purchase decision based on knowing and understanding that you can deliver the value and benefits that they seek, at the prices and charges that you make.

- **If confidence is very high,** consumers have a high propensity or disposition to spend, and so you have the best possible chance of survival and profitability in your sector.

    Confidence rises when work and money abound, causing people to make all the purchases that they have long promised themselves.

✔ **If confidence is low or falling,** you must know and be aware of the effects on the sector overall. And even if you continue to do everything right, you may suffer nevertheless.

Any of the following can cause a loss of confidence:

- Credit squeezes

- Bad products and services put out by a competitor

- Introduction of a compelling alternative

- Negative media coverage

- Lack of reliability on supply and distribution sides

- Negative word of mouth

You have little or no control over any of the preceding. And you certainly have no control over how customers and clients may react to any of these situations. Whole industries can become completely destabilised as the result of a few actions by a few individuals or companies. For example:

✔ The house and commercial building industries changed almost literally overnight in mid 2008 when the credit squeeze caused the companies involved to stop work on the spot until they had greater confidence in the markets.

✔ The entire air travel industry has a reputation for adding fuel surcharges and high-price insurance policies, in spite of the fact that some companies do this and others do not.

The preceding example highlights why you need to know and understand where your money really comes from. If you depend on the sale of add-ons such as in the air travel section, your cash flow can be brittle.

You need to work on the basis that your customers and clients will only do business with you if they have full confidence in you, and if you can keep and maintain their confidence.

Knowing your industry and sector

If you want profit margins of 35 per cent per annum, you must go into industries and sectors that offer such returns. If you're a supermarket chain, publisher or mobile phone company (to name just a few examples), you must accept the returns on offer in these sectors, which are typically much lower.

So although you can influence your returns to some extent, you must be prepared to accept the returns that the sector typically delivers overall.

Celebrity restaurants and nightclubs

Restaurant and nightclubs frequented by celebrities – such as film stars, footballers and television personalities – are part of a very exclusive business sector – one that commands very high prices and profit margins. The presence of film, television, music and sports stars attracts other celebrities, as well as other customers; and as long as the celebrities turn up, the restaurant and club owners get massive publicity from PR features and photos in the news media and glamour magazines. As a result, the restaurant owners make high profits and gain great publicity for themselves, drawing in large numbers of people who want to 'eat with the stars.'

The problem is in keeping up these levels of hype. Celebrities, like everyone else, move on. When the 'next big thing' opens, the rich and famous move on – and so do the photographers and entertainment reporters. This faces the nightclub and restaurant owners with a major challenge: how do you continue to get the coverage that you once enjoyed? How do you sustain a business after the glitterati move on? Where now does a profitable future lie?

The answers aren't easy or pretty, and as a result, many businesses have to close. Or else they have to re-brand and re-position themselves as just ordinary restaurants or nightclubs.

Although hot restaurants and clubs may seem totally unrelated to your business or sector, you can still take several lessons from this roller-coaster popularity:

- Whatever your line of business, you're going to have good times and bad. Therefore, you need a core business that can sustain steady-state activities profitably.

- You need to be prepared to respond to a high-profile competitor who can pop up just like the latest celebrity restaurant – or else your business is very likely to die.

- Your organisation must be able to survive out of the limelight as well as in it. You must have something that is strong enough to survive without mass hype. You must be able to promote yourself on the basis that you need a particular volume of business to survive and not depend on a transient fashion.

- If your business does involve anything trendy or fashionable, you must plan for ways to deliver a profitable business long after the trend or the fashion moves on.

Assessing Locations

Location is another critical factor. Where you locate can have a huge influence on your enduring viability and prosperity. Different parts of the world, a country and any city or town are more prosperous than others. Often one side of the same street is more prosperous than the other. Companies fight each other to gain the best possible physical locations for their outlets and activities.

Location is also vital on the Internet. Companies try and get search engines such as Google to place them high on lists of search results.

Whether physical or virtual, your location has to be convenient for your customers and easily accessible for your staff and suppliers.

Factoring in prosperity

You need to assess all locations for overall prosperity, as well as the willingness of customers in the location to spend money on your products and services.

- **Areas of high prosperity** have customers with a greater capability to spend on *all* products and services, including yours.

  Even in a location with high prosperity you must consider whether customers spend on low-cost/good-value items. One of the trappings of prosperity is the ability to spend as you choose, not as you have to.

- **Areas of low prosperity** at first glance seem unappealing, but customers in these areas may have a high propensity to spend on your products and services if you're in the right line of business. For example:

  - The Thanet area of southern England, which has very high unemployment, has a large and very profitable low-cost/good-value used car market.

  - Many seaside resorts that have lost market to overseas package holidays have managed to gain prosperity as day-trip and short-break destinations.

  - Low-price supermarkets have set up profitable operations as alternatives to Tesco, Sainsbury's, Asda and Morrisons.

  - The fast food industry has a very strong niche in less prosperous areas, delivering a combination of convenience, choice and 'a treat' at a price and value that is acceptable to those in the area, even if it isn't necessarily cheap.

Examining specific locations

When you're considering going into a particular location and setting up business activities, what are you really looking for?

This question is well worth asking, and as with many such questions, you have to look at a combination of things to find your answer, including:

- **Hard business sense:** Can you conduct your affairs effectively in the particular place?

- **Strategic intent:** Does the location fit into the overall pattern and purpose of your activities?

- **Competitive scene:** Can you compete in a new location against everyone who already operates there?

> ✔ **Your personal and professional judgement:** Can you support and justify your choice of location on business grounds?

You have to be able to answer each of the preceding points in full. You don't just want to establish yourself somewhere because it's nice or because lots of others are going there. You must be able to generate enough business to be profitable after you set up there.

At its simplest, your assessment of a specific location boils down to a few basic answers:

✔ **Yes, you can compete – but do you and your entire organisation actually want to?** If the answer is yes, fair enough. But if the answer is no, you should pull out. You do yourself and your organisation no service by going anywhere where you do not want to be. Ultimately, you may need to walk away from a location that many may see as an opportunity.

✔ **No, you can't compete – but you want to!** In this case, you must put in place the means and resources necessary to compete, or you must walk away. For example:

• Many financial service companies that followed the crowd and set up call centres overseas have found that that they must buy and install their own technology – because the technology available in the new locations has been unsuitable for their purpose.

• Many manufacturing companies have been persuaded to set up in areas with no history of factory work. These companies have found that they must either train or import their workforces, delaying the opening of their businesses.

✔ **You can compete, you want to compete and you like the location – but the location doesn't like you!** If the location isn't currently open to you entering it (and you still want to), you have some options. You can go on a massive PR and community involvement drive to show that you're both good and serious about your interest in the opportunity. You can impose yourself on the location anyway. Or you can withdraw. Recent business news is filled with examples of each option:

• When the Channel Tunnel was commissioned, nobody in south east England wanted it. People feared it was going to hinder an area that was already declining by imposing construction and transport blight on 30 square miles of farmland and downland. Eurotunnel, the company in charge, responded with a major PR outreach to schools and colleges, highlighting the business opportunities that would be brought to the location. Eurotunnel also opened an exhibition centre and public library and archive. The result was that people very quickly became familiar with the fact of the tunnel's existence, and opposition faded.

- When Starbucks first tried to open a coffee shop in Primrose Hill in north London, it quickly ran into opposition from both local traders and residents. Local traders thought that if any major company came into the area, rents would rise and drive out all the independent coffee shops and other small businesses. Residents, led by celebrities, engaged in a campaign of media awareness, which led to Starbucks (in its own words) 'withdrawing gracefully.'

- When Nissan first opened its factory in north-eastern England, a powerful political and social lobby fought the company. These lobbies did not, at the time, want Nissan or anyone else coming into an area that had always had heavy traditional industries, such as shipbuilding and steel works. So Nissan worked the parts of the community that it considered important to successfully growing a business in the location. The company put up a small card in the Jobcentre window and within 24 hours received 20,000 applications for 6,000 jobs!

The companies involved in each of the preceding situations and responses are all quite big and powerful enough to go into particular locations anyway. But in each case, the company chose not to go forward without the active support of the community – and in Starbucks' case, the company chose to let go of an opportunity.

More generally, logistical considerations may make one location too expensive to serve. In theory, end-customers are appealing in terms of buying power and product and service preferences that coincide with the company's offer. But when roads are poor, distributors are few or local content requirements increase costs, the once-compelling location becomes less attractive.

Assessing Your Competitors and Alternatives

Having an enlightened view of your competitors, alternatives and rivals is essential because the companies providing them are good at their jobs too! (For a fuller discussion of competitors, alternatives and rivals, go to Chapter 3.) You have to recognise the things that they do well and the ways in which they're successful in delivering profitable products and services and enduring value to their markets.

You can – and need to – learn from your competition. Taking a blind, introverted or complacent view of everything that you do well (however well you may do it) is useless.

Gathering information from outside sources

You can discover insights anywhere and everywhere – trade press, professional journals, independent research reports and books (like this one!), and by networking. You can also visit other companies, organisations and conferences.

The important thing is that you take the examples back to your own place, evaluate them – and if they're truly any good, incorporate the good stuff into your own organisation (as appropriate and legal, of course). For example:

- ✔ One supermarket chain regularly sends out all its managers on visits, not just to other supermarkets but to companies from all sectors. Managers must come back with at least one example of something that the other company does better. A response from these visits along the lines of, 'We can learn nothing from them – they can't touch us' is unacceptable.

- ✔ The 80-year-old CEO of a £30 million building company still attends at least one professional or industrial gathering per week. He states, 'All I ever want out of each event is one good idea that I can take back with me.'

- ✔ The first purchasers of every new car model that comes to market are typically other car companies! These companies then take their competitor's new model, strip it down and see what it truly has to offer that they themselves don't.

Knowing your competitors and alternatives

Competition for the purchasing power of your customers comes from a wide range of places, products and services (see Chapter 3). So you have to take a broad view of where the competition for your customers' disposable income comes from. For example:

- ✔ The manager of a department store branch in a commuter town in the home counties recognised that his shop was opening too late to catch people on their way into work and closing too early to catch them on the way home. The shop was therefore losing sales of aspirins, sandwiches, soft drinks, tissues and vitamins – not to direct competitors, but to any business that chose to open earlier or later.

✔ The UK cross-Channel ferry companies took many years to realise that they were losing market share and sales to low-cost airlines and cheap package holidays. They recognised the Channel Tunnel as an alternative to their ferry services, but they took some time to understand that ferries were also in indirect competition with people flying with Ryanair, easyJet and others to remote destinations and then hiring a car.

REAL WORLD EXAMPLE

Lessons from the football industry

Over the past 20 years or so, the football industry has undergone major transformations, resulting in an ever-clearer divide between the haves and have-nots.

In particular, the haves include the big clubs that command brand and supporter loyalty. They've turned their position to ever-greater advantage through the sales of merchandise, television and film rights. The stars who play for these clubs at the top of the industry command their own premiums and high salaries because of their iconic status (sometimes alleged, sometimes real). To the clubs, player status carries a commercial value, apart from ability at the game.

The result of all this has been that the true nature of competition has been changed also. Clubs that don't form a part of the British and European elites now compete for what exactly? It's a fair question.

On the one hand, clearly non-elite clubs compete on a game-by-game basis against whichever clubs they happen to be playing, and this includes the elite clubs. Sometimes a smaller club even beats one of the big clubs. But in terms of trophies, landmarks (getting to cup finals, invitations to take part in prestigious tournaments) and other lasting achievements, the position of the British and European elites becomes stronger not weaker. These clubs have sought to secure this position even more firmly through forming their own 'club of clubs', the G14.

On the other hand, the non-elite clubs have had to concentrate on what they do have to offer (not what they don't). The best of these concentrate on their local communities, developing a much narrower focus and identity. This focus is driven by a recognition that if people from the local communities don't support them, nobody else will.

In all cases, this has resulted in changes in the customer bases and how they interact with the clubs. Customers (supporters) of the non-elite clubs have to have their loyalty actively maintained; and the product – the game at the weekend – has to be good enough to persuade them to keep coming back. The merchandise has also to be good enough to be capable of commercialisation on a local basis.

The main lesson is that, when an industry restructures in this kind of way, there are consequences for all the companies (in this case the clubs) involved. The big clubs have to continue to develop themselves as brands as well as performers; and this means being able to attract the best players in the world to come and work for them. Smaller clubs depend on local custom, as above, for their very survival.

And the game? The football? Some would say this is almost incidental! In many cases, it has shifted from genuine competition to the provision of entertainment. So not only has the industry structure changed, the core product has also.

Acknowledging Barriers to Entry

After you assess industries and sectors, locations, competitors and alternatives (see the preceding section), you need to look carefully at *industry barriers* – the things that you must have in order to even have presence in an industry. Barriers, of course, can include anything that prevent others from easily setting up in competition to you.

You need to analyse industry barriers for two reasons:

- ✔ In assessing an industry or location with the purpose of potentially going into it, you need to know and understand all the barriers and obstacles that are going to get in your way – all the things that you need to overcome.

- ✔ You need to know and understand just how much of a threat *other* potential entrants are to the industry or location – as well as threats to you and your organisation if another newcomer decides to enter the industry or location.

The main barriers that you need to assess are costs and reputation, which I cover in the following sections.

Contemplating costs

You need to assess the following costs:

- ✔ **Technology:** Including the costs of acquiring, maintaining and upgrading technology; the costs associated with the staff and expertise needed to run technology; the costs of replacing technology or writing it off when you have to; and the variable costs associated with operating technology (such as energy usage, Internet and database access charges and more).

- ✔ **Staff:** Including the number and expertise of workers you need; the wages, salaries and other contractual costs that you must pay; the accommodation, technology and equipment that you must provide.

- ✔ **Supply and delivery:** Including anything necessary – such as component volumes or transport fleets – to ensure that you have sufficient resources to sustain the nature, volumes and quality of activities that you're planning.

- ✔ **Marketing and advertising:** Including the ability to promote yourself as an employer, as well as promoting your products and services.

- ✔ **Additional financial charges:** Including the ability to underwrite all other costs; the ability, if necessary, to pay premiums to ensure that your own supplies and distribution networks sustain your activities.

 ✓ **Statutory costs and charges:** Including taxation; energy and infrastructure charges.

Think of all the preceding costs in competitive terms. For example, you may have to compete with other organisations on salaries in order to hold on to your staff. You may have to effectively overpay in order to ensure the continuity of your own supplies compared to those of your competitors (or if necessary, you may need to buy up the companies that provide key supplies of technology, components, raw materials and information). Additionally, if the market becomes more competitive, you may have to spend more on marketing, advertising and promotion.

All costs are potential barriers to entry and to conducting business activities effectively after you become part of the industry. Therefore, you must know and understand:

 ✓ What you have to spend currently

 ✓ What you may have to spend in the near and more distant future

 ✓ What you may conceivably have to spend if industry or location conditions change significantly

Guarding your reputation

Your organisation has a reputation to maintain, and maintaining that reputation is much more complicated today than ever before.

Reputation revelation: Body Shop and L'Oreal

When company owner Anita Roddick first founded the Body Shop and began trading, she stated: 'We are going to sell cosmetics with a strong ethical slant. The cosmetics industry presents unreal pictures of women which can never be achieved. We will not do this. We will not peddle false promises like L'Oreal and the other big cosmetics companies.'

However, when L'Oreal took over the Body Shop in 2004, L'Oreal actually had higher ethical standards – even though the Body Shop had a higher ethical reputation with consumers and within the industry. (L'Oreal's standards were, in practice, much higher in the areas of human resource management and practice, trading practices, fair payments to suppliers, product testing, ingredient quality and product labelling.) Still, this reality had not prevented the Body Shop from trading on its own unassailable ethical reputation for more than 30 years as an independent company.

Cost-cutting programmes

Many organisations believe that cost-cutting programmes are good strategic decisions that will solve problems (and save money in the process). However, a major reason why cost-cutting programmes don't work is the assumption that when costs are cut, nothing else changes; this is never the case.

✔ Financial services companies that cut costs by relocating call centres to India and elsewhere find that their reputations suffer. In addition to cutting costs, the customer base believes and perceives outsourced call centres to be a cut in service quality.

✔ Garment manufacturers that cut costs by having production carried out in Pakistan, Malaysia and Central America regularly have to deal with child labour and slave labour allegations. These situations have led, in some cases, to reduced sales in other parts of the world.

Conversely, one of the ways in which Tesco has managed its reputation – and enhanced its competitive position – is by allocating more resources to front-line staff. Consequently, the shelves are always full, and the checkout and service desks always open. This programme has caused some concerns among financial analysts, and an overwhelmingly positive response from everywhere else! And fortunately, the profits keep coming.

So the lesson is: look at the widest possible range of effects when allocating resources – especially when cutting resource allocations in some kind of short-term interest. It never works!

The traditional pattern of business was this. Companies had clearly defined markets, sectors and locations, and almost by silent consent they wouldn't tread outside these boundaries. The business situation today is much less clear. Companies and organisations cross national and regional boundaries, as well as industrial and commercial boundaries. Companies can and do become involved in sectors that they may never have dreamed of.

As a result, your reputation for delivering your products and services in your own ways is subject to very high levels of scrutiny and competitive threat. You need to know and understand where the threat to your reputation can come from – and how much damage these threats may exact on your organisation. For example:

✔ The big supermarkets today have a reputation for selling petrol cheaper than the specialist petrol retailers; and so 60 per cent of petrol sales now take place at supermarkets.

✔ The UK railways have a reputation for delays and cancellations, and so travellers who use these services expect delays and cancellations – even though passenger numbers keep rising (and statistically, the numbers of delays and cancellations are actually falling).

Part of what you must do when assessing the current state and potential threats to your reputation is ward off the competition and preserve your own position and status.

Losing a good reputation is a lot easier than gaining one. Indeed, you can even lose your reputation through the activities of your competitors delivering products and services better than you in terms of what the customers expect. Or you can lose your reputation as the result of one of your competitors, alternatives or rivals re-positioning themselves. For example:

✔ Sainsbury's reputation for 'good food costing less' has not changed, but the reputation of Tesco for variety and quality and Asda for lower prices has meant that Sainsbury's has lost reputation – and market share.

✔ The reputation of furniture companies such as Harveys and DFS hasn't changed; but the reputation of Ikea for delivering a full range of furniture at acceptable prices supported by a home delivery and after-sales service has meant that traditional furniture makers have lost reputation.

Responding to barriers: Resource allocation and management

Near the top of your list of commitments comes the need to manage your finances and your reputation – the two main barriers that others have to overcome if they're going to compete with you. Any business or organisation has some key areas into which you must put resources for this purpose.

Your decisions on how to allocate resources need to support your enduring best advantage (see Chapter 2). Additionally, resource allocation has to be completely integrated with how you:

✔ Make and deliver your products and services

✔ Present yourself as an employer

✔ Deliver your marketing and promotion campaigns

✔ Exhibit your attitudes and values to suppliers, customers, markets, backers and the wider community

You're committing resources to managing your reputation and your costs – in other words the two most significant barriers to entry. Therefore, be prepared to invest in everything that contributes to this overall purpose.

Knowing Critical Paths and Activities: All in the Timing

In order to be and remain competitive, you must operate in time. Customers will not wait forever for their goods and services. You need your supplies delivered to fit with particular production and delivery schedules. In general, the quicker you can do something, the more cost effective it is (provided that you also do things right, of course!).

So time is everything. In order to establish and maintain your competitive position, you must have an acceptable speed for production, output, delivery and response. In particular, you need to know:

- ✔ How quickly you can deliver products and services – and respond to requests.
- ✔ How quickly you can get new products and services to market.
- ✔ What the speeds of response are across the market – and whether you can match these.
- ✔ Whether you can gain any competitive advantage from speeding things up.

All this attention to time and speed helps you figure out whether your organisation and its processes can gain any advantage relative to everyone else in the sector. Time-related advantages can:

- ✔ Increase the value of your products or services to your customers and yourself.
- ✔ Increase the price that customers are willing to pay for your products or services.
- ✔ Give your organisation a distinctive and unique competitive advantage.

The effects of time-related changes may not be completely straightforward. For example, speeding things up may offer no commercial advantage. You may not be able to recover (fully or partially) the cost of additional resources and energy consumed in speeding things up. Indeed, some customers equate value with having to wait. Giving people an instant response can lead them to perceive a lack of careful consideration, quality or personalisation.

Assess all the time-related factors, but only concentrate on those that affect the value that you create or the costs that you incur.

The following sections cover many time-related considerations that you need to address when assessing your competition and establishing your competitive strategy.

The perils of fast decision-making

When you're faced with a strategic choice, your ability to maximise your advantage depends, in many cases, on the speed with which you can decide to proceed.

Of course, the speed of your activities and operations isn't an end in itself. Speed has to be tempered with accuracy, and accuracy is founded on expertise (see Chapter 5). If a potential opportunity presents itself, you must be able to figure out whether it is indeed an opportunity. You must assess and consider all necessary resources and then deploy them effectively.

Guessing at answers is useless, even if doing so yields a quick decision. Fast but inaccurate decisions invariably end up creating serious trouble:

✔ The London Olympic budget was originally calculated on the back of an envelope at £1.3 billion. The official estimate is now £14 billion; the final bill is likely to be much higher.

✔ The Millennium Dome was originally going to cost £20 million, all of which was to be recoverable from ticket sales. When the building was finally sold for £1 to a property company, it had cost over £750 million to construct.

✔ Sub-prime mortgage derivatives at the centre of the 2008 credit crunch are exceedingly time consuming to understand, which caused many risk management departments in many established banks in the UK and US to instead rely on credit bureau ratings and the actions of competitors – 'keeping up with the rivals.' But when these rivals disappeared along with the AAA ratings, the banks later regretted their haste and lack of care.

In all these cases, leaders made quick decisions without any serious regard to finance or logistics. And in each case, those responsible came to regret their haste in decision-making.

Paying attention to time: The shortest and longest

In general, you aim to do things in the shortest possible time, provided that you still satisfy the required standards and quality levels.

Doing things quickly can have some definite advantages:

✔ Matalan, the good-value clothing retailer, has scanned the clothes presented at fashion shows and translated this information into its product designs. Consequently, Matalan was able to cut lead times for getting new and top fashion designs to market from 30 to 40 weeks to 24 hours. This now sets the standards for getting new designs to market.

✔ One key area where Ryanair keeps its costs to a minimum is in using a single design of airliner, the Boeing 737-800 series. One airliner means that the company can streamline crew training, catering and product storage, loading and unloading and maintenance. Ryanair has also been able to implement just-in-time components and supply delivery methods, which keeps storage times (and costs) to a minimum.

Take advantage of speedy operations in the areas of data processing, finance, accounts and invoicing systems. By striving to have the shortest time possible in these areas, your cash flow improves and you can do more in the time allowed. You can similarly capitalise on developing communication and information systems that are fast, efficient and complete.

As important as knowing the shortest time for various activities is, you also need to know and understand the longest time that things can take without damaging your competitive edge, cost efficiency, market standing or reputation.

Rushing to market – even before products and services are ready – may be necessary in some sectors. For example, in the highly competitive computer games sector, Sega, Microsoft and Sony have all rushed out products to beat each other. And all these companies have done so knowing that their products had glitches. But if the drive to be 'on time' is overwhelming, you have to acknowledge that you're likely to stumble – and plan to address problems when they arise.

Be especially careful setting and managing expectations. If you promise results in six hours and deliver in four, everyone is happy. If you promise results for the same thing in two hours, and deliver in three, everyone is unhappy – even though you accomplished the activity in less than four hours.

Setting timetables

You don't want to spoil anything by jumping the gun and going into something under-prepared. You need to give yourself the best possible chance of success, and if this means taking just a little more time then so be it. See the sidebar 'The perils of fast decision-making' for more.

On the other hand, you need to recognise that if you give people lots of time, they typically don't complete whatever you're demanding until the last minute. And if you set really extensive or unconsidered deadlines, people very likely ignore them. See the sidebar 'A chocolate timetable.'

Pay attention to the damage that missed deadlines can cause. For example:

- The building and construction industries have enduringly bad reputations for missing deadlines and completing projects late.

- Everyone has waited in for deliveries of furniture, only for the supplying company not to turn up – often without explanation.

✔ Everyone has waited in for gas, electricity and water companies to turn up, again, only to wait in vain – often without explanation.

Formulate your attitude to timescales in the context of what is feasible, what the market needs and demands and how you secure maximum cost effectiveness. If you don't address each of these points, you weaken your competitive position.

After you recognise the time constraints under which you have to work, you still have flexibility to respond to the marketplace. For example:

✔ The bread and baking industries now recognise that they can't make assured and regular deliveries during normal working hours. They therefore make major deliveries between the hours of midnight and 6.00 a.m.

✔ easyJet has had so much trouble with passengers turning up at the last minute that it now includes the slogan 'If you're late, we won't wait' on all materials.

Never ever describe something as urgent or important. Instead always give a specific (and realistic) deadline. And if the assignment has a long overall timescale, then set interim deadlines and milestones for measuring progress along the way. Think about your own experiences: if someone gives you an important task to do this week, you'll probably do it. If a deadline is unrealistically short, you won't do it; and if it's too long, you'll leave it till the last minute – if not later!

A chocolate timetable

One of the world's top brand chocolate and confectionery manufacturers wanted to re-brand one of its product lines. The line, a range of flavoured chocolates with soft centres, had different names in different countries, and the company wanted a single name that transcended all national, cultural and social boundaries.

The company set up a product re-branding team that consisted of marketing, product development and wholesaling executives. The team met but came to no immediate conclusions; it arranged to meet again in three months' time. The next time the team met, there was again no progress, so they agreed to meet again three months later. And again. And again. And again.

After 18 months, the company Chief Executive asked about the status of the group's re-branding efforts. The group replied that they still weren't sure how to re-brand the chocolate, but they planned to meet again in three months. The Chief Executive said, essentially, 'No. You'll do the job today and finish.'

And they did! The chocolates were successfully re-branded and re-launched all over the world. The marketing campaign had a universal emphasis with the same main slogan, but presented in different languages.

The lesson? If you want an answer immediately, you get one. If you're prepared to let the answer wait, you wait.

British Airways and Terminal 5

On 20th March 2008, the Queen arrived as the guest of British Airways at the opening of Heathrow Airport's brand new Terminal 5. The largest enclosed space in the European Union, the terminal was built to make travelling with British Airways to and from London a pleasure. Incorporating the latest security, check-in and baggage-handling technology, the facility was supposed to provide everything that any traveller could possibly want while waiting for a flight.

Prior to the Queen's visit (around Christmas 2007), several serious concerns came to light, including technological glitches, a lack of staff training and insufficient capacity in the security and baggage-handling systems. If things were to go wrong therefore, they would go very badly wrong. But as the Queen walked through the terminal and met different groups of top managers and executives, she was assured that everything would work perfectly.

When Terminal 5 opened for business on the 27th of March, chaos quickly ensued. People were unable to get to their flights on time. Planes found themselves queuing for docking bays. The baggage system couldn't handle the peaks and troughs in baggage flow. The staff were unable to access their car parks – or indeed the terminal itself – because of problems with identity cards.

The result was extensive adverse publicity for British Airways, and a serious loss of overall confidence. Two top managers were forced to resign.

Why didn't the powers that be adjust the project's timeline? Certainly, you need to set timelines and then you do your best to stick to them; and if you have to change a timeline, then you can. (Of course, asking a small specialist contractor to delay is one thing – asking the Queen to alter her busy schedule is quite another!) Many in the airline industry, given what is known today, would go ahead and do everything exactly as it was done, trouble and all. Others would choose different paths.

Adjusting a timeline is a delicate matter. What you do in a particular situation must be the product of your own judgement. You have to recognise that you'll have trouble if you do go ahead, and trouble if you don't. The fallout of Terminal 5 does, however, reinforce the need for getting as much right as you possibly can in advance of opening for business.

Taking a strategic approach to time

People respond to different time-related issues differently, and as a savvy business leader you can and need to think strategically about what time means for you, your organisation, your customers and others.

For example, in 2007, the government announced 'a major review' of the A-Level school syllabus – a review scheduled to take place in 2012! No one took any notice of the announcement because a lot can happen in five years, including:

- ✔ The country will have a different government (regardless of whether it changes political party)
- ✔ Demands of the school-age population will change
- ✔ Available technology will change
- ✔ The availability of teachers and facilities will have to be addressed
- ✔ The content and objectives of projects will have to be established

Leaders of the project need to tackle all these points, but because the review is slated to happen in 2012, nobody has yet quite got started on them. And nobody is going to do so until the government produces a real agenda and structure and states specific objectives.

Long and indeterminate time-lines are problematic for everyone – not just public services. Corporations say things like:

> *We will introduce performance-related pay in three years' time.*
>
> *We will open a base in Cape Town/Brussels/Bombay in five years' time.*

The results of these statements are the same: nobody takes any notice until leaders publish a plan in detail. So you need to make sure that you have set dates (not just deadlines); and you need to have a reputation for making your set dates stick at all times.

Refining Your Competitive Position

Whatever your company size or industrial sector, you need to be constantly monitoring, evaluating and reviewing every aspect of your competitive position. You need to look back at everything that you do and assess whether you did everything that you set out to do. You also need to look at the reasons for success – as well as failure – so you can continually improve your performance. Above all, you need always to be looking for ways to improve each aspect of developing and securing your competitive position.

You therefore need to develop your own expertise in each of the areas I address in this chapter: assessing your competitors, managing your resources, working to time and maintaining your financial and reputational strength. You must know the details of everything as they apply to your company, your activities and your industry.

Although you're in charge, you don't have to do this alone. Encourage people around you to scan their activities and areas of responsibility for potential damage to your reputation, as well as for time and cost improvements. If people come to you with good ideas, listen, evaluate and take note of them – if the ideas are indeed good ideas, then implement them.

If you turn down someone's ideas, explain to that person, clearly and face to face, why you did so. Interacting this way is a mark of respect to your staff and improves communication all round. Honest feedback is good for collective and individual morale when staff know and understand that you're truly taking their commitment seriously.

The following sections cover ongoing competitive assessment activities in greater detail.

Steering and adjusting

Evaluate every piece of information – financial, sales data, competitors' performances – that comes your way. Use this information to further develop and improve everything you do.

For example, when you find costs leaking from your organisation, call other people's attention to the situation, find out what's causing it and improve things as quickly as you can. Similarly, if you find that your reputation is declining, find out why and take whatever steps necessary in order to restore it.

Your goal is to take a proactive rather than a responsive step towards making sure that your competitive position remains as strong as possible at all times.

Identifying and responding to significant problems

With effective monitoring and review processes, you can identify major problems and difficulties as they arise – and even predict where they may arise. You can also address the enduring matters that everyone has to face, such as delivery hold-ups and staff absences.

Good, you may be saying – that's exactly what I want. Well, not so fast.

Yes, some problems that come to light early – the effects of competitive action by others, a staffing concern or a technology issue – you can recognise and then tackle and manage. But the flipside is that if someone alerts you to a major problem, then you *must* tackle it immediately because now you know about it. Ignoring significant problems becomes negligence.

The situation reminds me of the famous scene in the movie *Titanic*, just after the ship hits the iceberg. The company Chairman, the ship's architect and the Captain all skirt around the problem until finally the Captain says, 'Will the ship sink?' The architect replies, 'Yes, she will sink.' Up until that point, the situation was in debate, but after stating the real problem, they had to tackle it.

Other examples of problems that have arisen and had to be tackled include:

- ✔ The vast amounts of data lost while in transit by UK public service bodies and retail banks.
- ✔ The damaging effects of battle fatigue in UK soldiers serving overseas.
- ✔ The postcode lottery for drugs and medical treatment in the NHS (which led one health authority to write to its clinicians ordering them to manage the media rather than attend to the postcode lottery itself).

Your own place of work is sure to have examples of these sorts of problems as well. Whatever they are, when they become apparent you must tackle them.

The earlier these types of problems become apparent, the less trouble all round. And if you're continually monitoring and assessing things, you get into the habit of seeing things directly as they arise and tackling them early.

Chapter 7

Appraising Investments

. . . .

In This Chapter

▶ Understanding the nature of investment

▶ Examining and anticipating returns

▶ Expressing your investment goals

▶ Making sound investment decisions

. . . .

*B*usiness leaders responsible for organisation strategy love to make – and talk about – investments. The prevailing attitude can be summed up as: 'If we put this amount of resources into something, we'll regain these returns on or by this date.' These individuals make complex calculations, present their plans and then proceed as if everything they predict is set in stone with the fact of a specific return absolutely assured.

And even when the world is not quite so certain, investment-focused business leaders can always hedge their bets and buy at an assured and low price in the future, protecting and assuring the return on investment. Or the organisation can take out formal contracts with another party to conduct the investments and deliver promised results (or face legal action). Or they can transfer or hedge against their risk of not achieving expected returns when expected.

All these approaches to investment are based on myths and legends. The truth about investment is very different – that's what this chapter is all about. I start by looking at what investment actually is and then walk you through the key phases and considerations that make up the investment appraisal process, finally considering the consequences of investment.

The current climate for investment is somewhat volatile – to say the least! Many companies, managers and individuals who thought they had investments on which returns were assured are finding themselves not only not getting the returns, but also losing their original investments. Therefore, before you invest in anything, you must know:

✔ What you're investing in and why

✔ The likelihood of receiving the anticipated returns

✔ What can possibly go wrong

You must actively manage investments if you really seek the returns; they will not and do not work by themselves.

Defining Investing

Investment is the process of putting resources into something, with the expectation of returns as the result. These returns may be defined or undefined.

In practice, however, all investments must have *defined returns* described in the most specific terms possible before you put in any resources (see the following section 'Getting Specific about Returns'). You can't simply state: 'If we put X resources into this, we'll get a return of Y per cent in a Z amount of time' unless you can state clearly:

- Why you defined the return and the time frame in the first place.
- Why the return is a good return.
- Why and how the return is feasible.
- What can possibly go wrong with your predictions and expectations.

You also need to look at what you may gain (and lose) from any investment you may be considering. For example:

- If you invest in opening a market for your products and services in Spain, your primary purpose is to secure a foothold in that country and to sell your products and services. However, you may also, as the result of making that decision, open up further opportunities in this location, which means you may then need to invest even more to produce and deliver your products and services.

- If you run a supermarket chain and decide to open a new store in a small town, you may face local opposition. To make locals happy, you may have to invest in opening, maintaining and developing things like community facilities, taking produce from local suppliers and providing community car parking.

- If you lead a retail bank, your reason for opening customer service call centres in India is probably based on taking advantage of technology, expertise and lower labour rates. However, you may find that the technology is not as cheap, and the expertise and the labour rates aren't as low as you once thought (because of the fact that everyone else is setting up centres in India also!), so you need to reconsider opportunities that your physical presence in the new location may deliver.

What a difference a year makes

If you're in any doubt about what investment is (and especially, what it's not), consider the following quotes. (They're both taken from the same publication, just over a year apart.)

✔ 'Economists may sometimes seem about as useful as a chocolate teapot but, as this year's Nobel Prize for economics shows, it isn't always so. On 14th October, the $1 million Nobel Prize for economics was awarded to two Americans, Robert Merton of Harvard University and Myron Scholes of Stamford University. Their prize-winning work involved precisely the sort of mind-boggling mathematical formulae that usually cause non-economists either to snooze or scream. That's too bad, for it ranks among the most useful work that economics has produced. Their work on how to price financial options turned risk management from a guessing game into a science.' (*The Economist*, 17th October 1997).

✔ 'Like the Titanic, Long-Term Capital Management was supposed to be unsinkable. The hedge funds' dramatic downfall and bail-out was the stuff of Hollywood disaster movies: fortunes laid waste, proud men (Nobel laureates no less) cut down to size, giant tidal waves threatening to drown some of Wall Street's snootiest institutions at the very least. Wall Street's finest were blinded by the reputation of Robert Merton and Myron Scholes who last year shared the Nobel Prize for economics for their contributions to the understanding of financial risk – and have now gone bankrupt in the process.' (*The Economist*, 3rd October 1998.)

Clearly, anyone who tries to make predictable the returns on investment is doomed to failure – even a venerable publication like *The Economist!* And anyone who tries to replace the need for hard and involved work with using a computer program is doomed to failure too!

You must look at what you're investing in and what returns are on offer – and then make sure that they come about! You cannot leave a computer program in charge of your investments. Do the hard work. Plain and simple!

In each of the preceding, investment is a process that leads to other opportunities and constraints – both of which require the decision to invest further, or not.

Investment isn't an isolated decision you make in a comfortable safe managerial office, moving resources around your organisation and the world and delivering assured results. Investment is a process by which you commit resources and receive returns. In order to know and understand what those returns are, and may be, you have to know and understand the full context in which you make your investments, as I discuss in the following section.

You can't make any part of investment appraisal predictable or assured. No computer program can do this for you, neither can any dominant market position – nor even this book. You have to take the broadest possible approach, which means building your own expertise so that you actually know what you're doing.

Getting Specific about Returns

Investment is complex, but you must make investments in order to produce the returns that you seek. *Investment appraisal* is the process of examining the relationship between an investment and its returns, and the extent to which the returns are acceptable (or not) to you.

The returns that you seek can be any, or all, of the following:

- ✔ **Financial:** Percentage returns on a capital sum stated over a period of time make up the most common type of returns. Financial returns are typically straightforward and simple to understand. In many cases, financial returns incorporate all that organisations and their managers calculate because they're more or less universally understood (or at least people *think* that they know and understand them).

- ✔ **Reputation:** Returns on your reputation may be positive or negative, just as with the financial returns. By investing in particular markets, products, services and ventures, you should be investing also in your reputation and expertise as a pioneering, progressive and profitable organisation. For example, every time Virgin Group goes into new ventures, part of the purpose is to enhance the reputation of the Virgin brand overall.

- ✔ **Time-based:** Pay attention to the speed of payback of the original investment. When funds are limited, speed of payback may become your most important consideration, even more important than financial return.

- ✔ **Maximising/optimising returns on existing capital technology and expertise:** Many organisations seek new outlets, ventures and markets because they have spare capacity in their existing production and service delivery facilities. What you're doing therefore is increasing the returns available from what you already have.

- ✔ **Market share:** If you decide a particular market share serves your interests, then you invest in ensuring that you achieve or maintain a specific market position. Your resulting position is, therefore, a type of return on your investment.

Each type of return feeds and reinforces the others. If your financial returns start to fall, your reputation is likely to suffer as well. If your reputation falls, so may your financial returns. So make sure that you make full provision for all aspects and types of returns on investment.

Whatever you do or don't do, you must invest in your core strategic position (see Chapter 2). If you seek cost advantage, for example, you must invest in maintaining this position. The same goes for seeking brand advantage; you must invest in marketing, advertising and developing and assuring consumers' perceptions of the quality of your products and services. And if you serve niches, or have a core position not based on cost or brand advantage, then you must invest in ensuring that you continue to know, understand, meet and deliver products and services with the promised quality, confidence and convenience.

Maximising returns

So how do you go about gaining returns – specifically maximising your chances of success and minimising your chances of failure? Start with some golden rules:

- If you want returns of 30 per cent per annum, you must invest in those sectors where 30 per cent per annum returns are possible.

- If you want to invest in a particular industry or market, you must be prepared to accept the returns that industry or market provides.

- The more players that invest in a particular market or venture, the lower the returns are likely to be. (This isn't always the case in practice, but it is the safest assumption to make.)

- Investing is more than a one-time decision or action. When you invest, you're investing in getting in, developing your position, maintaining your position, making upgrades and maximising other opportunities that come your way. You may also have to invest in getting out at some point.

Your returns on investment – not the other guy's

Whatever you choose to invest in, you must always be clear about what you expect to get out of it – and whether your expectations are feasible. Of course, you must take expert advice, but never assume that just because others are making a certain percentage return in a market sector or location, you're going to as well. For example:

- If you choose to go into budget airlines, you won't gain the returns made by Ryanair and easyJet; you're coming late to the party, and they've taken all the good bits.

- If you go into grocery retail, you won't make the profit volumes enjoyed by Tesco and Marks & Spencer; they already have their niches and markets.

Your investment decisions must be driven by what *you* can gain from a specific investment – not what existing players already gain. Pay attention to the aspects you're investing in: market entry, market positioning, attracting established customers from existing providers, delivering on promises and establishing steady streams of products and services that can (in time) give you an assured and profitable position.

Whatever you go into, always remember the statement made by the statutory financial services authorities in the UK: 'The value of your investments can go down as well as up.' This guideline applies to *all* investments. So when you assess returns, you need to ask yourself:

✔ What are the best possible returns for me and my organisation?

✔ What are the worst possible returns for me and my organisation?

✔ What level of return is acceptable for me and my organisation?

✔ What level of return is not acceptable for me and my organisation?

Your answers to these questions inform all your research, projections and forecasts. They inform any risk analysis that you carry out (see Chapter 14).

Considering the extremes

Ultimately, your assessment of any invest (see the preceding section) leads you to consider two vital questions:

✔ What if we succeed beyond our wildest dreams?

✔ What if we fail beyond our worst nightmares?

Both situations require specific consideration, as I cover in the following sections.

Beyond your wildest dreams

Succeeding beyond your wildest dreams sounds great! And it is – providing you can go on and satisfy the demand and the reputation that you've created!

All too often though, satisfying and maintaining extreme success is impossible. Your inability to fill the hole that you've so brilliantly created means that people may become frustrated with you and your products and services. It can also mean that competitors and new entrants may fill the demand that you've created but are unable to satisfy in full.

All too often, success that is beyond your wildest dreams is an illusion! You probably got these results by chance, because you didn't know what you were really getting into. So after you pat yourself and your colleagues on your backs, go back to the drawing board and make up your mind that you will do the groundwork properly in the first place in the future.

Beyond your worst nightmares

The problem of having everything go wrong is that more than your finances end up suffering!

For example, the companies and organisations that invested in financial products in the Icelandic banking sector simply assumed that the resources of a tiny economy and industry would deliver the results promised. These investors carried out no appraisal and no assessment of feasibility. The result? Everyone lost everything that they put in. (And if anyone gets anything back, it will be a bonus!)

Of course, if you do your job assessing returns properly, you already know the financial costs of failure. But total failure also affects your reputation and the confidence of customers and backers. It affects your ability to embark on any other new ventures that you may be considering. (This is especially true if you were trying to use a now-failed venture as a stepping stone into other things.)

More seriously, total failure may also affect the steady-state activities on which you've built your reputation over many years. If you lose money on a wild venture, you may have to curtail the things that you're good at because you no longer have the resources to support them fully.

Pressures on investments: Unrealistic returns

The questions and considerations I present in this chapter combine as a kind of *pressure on investment* to produce the desired rate of return. The work of economic, statistical and finance experts as part of your due diligence process is particularly valuable. (*Due diligence* is the legal and accounting process by which you satisfy yourself that everything you're considering is financially sound and above board.)

The data that your experts produce helps:

✔ Inform your decision-making process

✔ Bring down to earth those who see only a rich and glorious future

✔ Indicate where the hard work truly lies

✔ Indicate your true and likely rates of return

Even well-researched expert advice can't save you from some sets of circumstances. For example:

✔ Before he died, Robert Maxwell engaged Coopers & Lybrand to value the assets of his publishing empire in the USA. Coopers & Lybrand duly arrived at a figure of approximately $1 billion. Maxwell took one look at the figures, turned to the consultants and said, 'Double it' – and they did.

✔ Faced with financial losses on its original low-fare airline network, Laker re-valued upwards its ageing fleet of airliners in order to give the company a sound capital base (on paper at least). However, in this case, nobody was fooled, and at one point Laker's pilots had to carry cash to pay for refuelling their planes.

And of course, both companies went broke.

Whatever the pressures, returns on investment can only be achieved in the context in which you seek them, and the environment in which they have to be delivered. No amount of re-valuing, shouting or denial (see the section 'Denying problems' later in this chapter) can affect this fact.

A bridge to nowhere

In 1989, the Scottish Office (the UK government department responsible for Scotland) decided that the ferry service between the mainland and the Isle of Skye was no longer 'fit for purpose' (whatever that meant). So the office commissioned a bridge to be built and engaged Balfour Beatty as the contractor. Rather than receive a fee however, Balfour Beatty agreed to pay for the work itself and then recoup its costs by charging a toll to those who used the bridge.

So the bridge was built and duly opened – and then Balfour Beatty ran into immediate and insurmountable problems. Bridge users (the vast majority being islanders commuting to and from work on the mainland) simply refused to pay the tolls. A lot of trouble resulted, eventually leading to police action and court prosecutions. One Island resident who had refused to pay the toll 80 times, successfully argued that each of the 80 offences should be tried separately because the circumstances had been different in each case.

Eventually, Balfour Beatty threw in the towel. They went to the Scottish Office in 2000, made sure that they got back as much of their money as they could and then withdrew. Subsequently, Balfour Beatty has taken a much firmer line with payment assurances as a pre-condition of going into this kind of government work.

Noting important variables

In order to assess and then deliver returns, you have to take into account a huge range of variables and factors, including:

- ✔ **The rules by which your market plays and operates.** If you work in a highly volatile sector (such as football, films or pharmaceutical development) or engineering mega-projects (such as shipping), never expect orderly and predictable rates of return on a regular schedule. At the end of a project, initiative or venture, you may indeed achieve everything you sought, but along the way, you're certain to experience both surges and delays.

- ✔ **The assumptions that you make.** The most serious assumption that you always need to question is: 'We'll get our money back.' Unfortunately, this isn't always the case. See the sidebar 'A bridge to nowhere'.

If something sounds too good to be true, it always is. And if anyone other than a deposit account guarantees you particular rates of return, examine the small, very small and tiny print before you agree. Because catches always exist.

Clarifying Your Investment Objectives

Clearly one of your major goals or objectives with any investment is to produce a return on the resources, finance, expertise and technology that you commit. And in order to achieve your goal, you must be very clear about exactly what you want. This is where the hard work lies.

Whatever you go into is never as simple as it seems. Even if you invest all your savings in a bank deposit account for an assured rate of return, this 'assurance' depends on things like not having to make withdrawals in emergencies, being able to support yourself from income elsewhere, and not having others who may be looking to you to 'sub' them for any reason. (And even if you invest everything you have in a bank deposit account, you still must have some measure of confidence in the banking system overall.)

And all these possibilities exist for an investment in a simple form where your objective is clear! For the majority of business decisions, you need to take a much deeper view of what you expect from your investment, as I cover in the following sections.

Factoring in feasibility

Begin clarifying your investment objective by looking at *feasibility*, or the likelihood of getting the returns that you seek.

Your assessment of an investment's feasibility requires a very healthy dose of realism. For example, if you're investing in something that gives a predicted rate of return:

- ✔ Have you checked the conditions under which this rate of return is achievable?
- ✔ Do the conditions exist currently? If so, for how long?
- ✔ If not, how does this affect your targets and objectives?

What you are doing here of course is the hard work that all those who are sadder (and now hopefully wiser) did not do. See the sidebars 'What a difference a year makes' and 'A bridge to nowhere' for some particularly stunning examples.

Early on, you also need to look at the effects and consequences of an investment on your other activities. Consider the effects and consequences of things like:

- Delays and hold-ups
- Cost and price increases
- Sudden loss of major contractors and suppliers
- Fluctuations in sources of finance, capital, data, technology and expertise

Be aware that any projections you make assume a constant set of outside influences. For example, many mega-projects are financed on the basis of given and assured inflation and interest rates. These projects last for many years before their completion and delivery. You therefore need to take the widest possible view of fluctuations in currency and interest rates, inflation and energy costs.

The conventional wisdom that 'everything costs twice as much as you think, and everything takes twice as long as you think' is easy to follow when you're working on behalf of others. Somehow, though, when you're assessing things for yourself and your own interests, you forget! Rather than assuming that everything will work out exactly according to plan, be cautious and think about your own interests as you would think of others!

Researching rates of return

You must be able to give yourself a good idea of the rates of return that are available on investment opportunities. You need to look at each rate of return from the point of view of:

- Whether the rate is feasible, possible or achievable in the present and envisaged sets of circumstances. (See the section 'Factoring in feasibility' for more.)
- Who determined that a particular rate is right – and why other rates are wrong.
- How the rate was determined. (Often, rates are pure assumption, not based on calculations.)
- Why the rate was never questioned or debated; and if it was, why the other projections were rejected.
- The levels and nature of activities required in order to achieve the rate.
- The consequences of meeting, exceeding and under-shooting the desired rate at the end of the venture.

Playing a game of what if

What are the likely effects of the returns available on a project running very far behind schedule? Consider the A380 super-jumbo airliner project, which is running more than five years behind schedule. The original project plan stated that exactly 100 aircraft would be delivered by the end of 2008 – instead, the actual number delivered was 11.

In projects like this, you need to identify the things that you can and can't control.

✔ **For those things that you can control,** establish your own clear basis for delivering them, making sure that they work and contribute to the order, structure and execution of the venture.

For the A380 project, controllable aspects included ensuring that components were made and delivered on time. Unfortunately, these straightforward management issues were not dealt with effectively, and the deliveries didn't happen.

✔ **For those things that you can't control,** analyse and evaluate (see Chapter 14). Try taking a 'What if?' approach and ask yourself questions such as: What if the Euro halves or doubles in value? What if oil prices rise to $200 or $300 a barrel? What if my organisation loses a major contractor halfway through the venture?

For the A380 project, rises in the value of the Euro mean that the company is either going to have to take reduced prices, or else face the fact that potential buyers may withdraw and cancel orders.

Extreme 'What if?' questions help you create a good, clear and broadly accurate starting point for assessing the ways in which your rates of return are likely to change.

When assessing rates of return, make a habit of doing your own best, medium and worst projections on the basis of as much information as you can possibly gather. If things work out as planned and you've foreseen disaster, work out why you foresaw disaster. And the same with the reverse – if you'd foreseen success, with rates of return achieved, and it all turns out wrong, again, work out why.

Never forget that the sub-prime mortgage and finance market was based on an assumption that people with no money and a bad history of credit and repayment would pay off loans for which they were being overcharged relative to others. Looking back on it, the whole situation was extremely unlikely to happen as planned, and yet the entire 'sub-prime finance industry' was created and thrived (very briefly!). So question everything!

Rates of return can – and do – change, so you need to be as informed as possible about what can and does happen that cause rates of return to change – and the likelihood of these things happening.

Staying Competitive

A significant part of investment is about staying competitive and developing your strategic capability. For every investment you consider, ask yourself:

✔ How does this investment develop and enhance the organisation's competitiveness? Why?

✔ How may others respond to the proposal or venture?

✔ Where is the organisation going to add value as a result of the investment? Where is the organisation going to lose value?

✔ Where is the organisation going to enhance its cost effectiveness? Where is it going to lose cost effectiveness?

Your answers to these questions add to your clarity of knowledge and understanding. Above all, you don't want to go into something that's going to adversely affect your ability to compete. Pay particular attention to competitive concerns involving technology, anything new and peer pressure.

✔ **Technology.** Always ask yourself why you're investing in technology. Specifically:

• What are you going to gain that you don't already have?

• How are you going to measure and assess your returns on investment?

• How much disruption and retraining may the technology cause – what will this disruption and restructuring cost?

• Where is the technology going to add value and how much is it going to add?

• What can go wrong with the technology – and how much will repairs, upgrades and losses of production or service delivery cost?

Get to grips with these questions by going out and getting real quotes, estimates and prices for all the preceding. Then, just to be on the safe side, double the estimates you receive. That way, you can have no illusions about what you're letting yourself in for.

✔ **New markets, products, services and locations.** Whenever you venture into new stuff, you're moving away from what you know – and into things that you don't know. (Even if you're planning to take your established products and services into a new location, you need to be sure that this place is going to welcome you and place a value on what you do – be prepared to pay for it, which is a part of the cost of your investment.)

If you succeed in entering a new market, well and good. But will failing in the new market affect the esteem in which you're held by your present locations?

✔ **Peer pressure.** Be particularly cautious whenever you feel under pressure to invest in technology ventures, new markets and locations because everyone else in your industry is doing it or because dominant shareholders and backers want you to invest. You know the situation: a competitor is opening up activities in Poland or offering a low-cost product or introducing automatic production technology – and so you need to do the same.

Test all assumptions and be honest and realistic enough to examine why you're being driven down such routes. If your answer is peer pressure, be honest enough to say so to yourself and others from the outset. That way, you at least know how and why you're going into a particular situation, and you can better assess the problems and issues that you're likely to deal with.

Making Investment Decisions

After you gain a clearer understanding of what you're getting into and formulate a realistic assessment of the returns on offer, you come to the point of deciding whether to proceed with enterprises, ventures and initiatives. And if you're going forward, *how* are you going to proceed with those enterprises, ventures and initiatives?

Not proceeding with something is hard, particularly if you:

✔ Need to gain some return on your investment.

✔ Take personal involvement in the project and can't face the idea that you made a mistake.

✔ Find the proposal exciting and interesting in its own right (even though it is unworkable).

✔ Believe that the venture is pioneering (even though it may also be a red herring).

✔ Spent a lot of money hiring consultants to investigate things for you.

In these and similar circumstances, many organisations do attempt to make the unworkable workable, which simply leads to a subsequent loss of revenue, resources and reputation.

A German consortium put together a bid to take over Superdrug, the good-value pharmaceutical retail chain. The consortium did thorough research and spent many millions of euros in preparing to take over the company. In the process, the group found Superdrug and their own cultures simply didn't mesh well. (And Superdrug did not want to be taken over by the consortium.) The group eventually pulled out, despite its initial expenditure, because it didn't believe that it would gain the returns it was seeking.

Therefore, you must take the broadest possible view of investment when arriving at your decisions, as I discuss in the following sections.

Getting personal

You must know and understand not only the financial complexities of any investment but also the personalities involved, including personal preferences and the effects that behavioural and personal pressures can have on your supposedly rational and informed investment process. For example:

- ✔ You may choose to manufacture your own components in spite of the fact that the calculations state that buying them is cheaper. You decide to over-pay in order to retain control over volumes and quality assurance.

- ✔ You may choose to outsource some of your activities based on cost. By outsourcing, you forego in-house expertise and, instead, depend on a contractor.

Investment is always your choice, regardless of what any figures may tell you. Therefore, you must be aware of decisions that involve:

- ✔ Powerful or influential figures taking a decision and then using one set of figures to justify the choice. When others raise queries, the leaders have a set of figures that 'prove' that nothing can go wrong. When someone asks, 'But what if something *does* go wrong?' the response is: 'That can't possibly happen – the figures say so.'

- ✔ A powerful individual or group taking a decision and simply shouting down opposition and queries. When leaders respond this way to questions, the best thing that others can do is prepare themselves for trouble – or leave!

- ✔ A group taking a decision for reasons of excitement, adventure, prestige and triumph – but dressing up the endeavour as a sound business venture. This response happens in many organisations when they set out to become international players with overseas ventures. The reason for going overseas is (all too often) the excitement, although the stated reason is that a huge, untapped market exists and the organisation must go abroad and mop it up. (In spite of the fact that this amazing market has been coping quite adequately without the organisation until the present.)

Of course, people get carried away by the excitement of new opportunities from time to time. If you're a member of such a group, discipline yourself and seek to become the eternal questioner, the person who always says the wrong thing – the Jonah! And if you're not a member of the elite, you must find ways of lobbying against this kind of excitement. Hopefully, given recent financial crises, you can more easily gain a platform for expressing your concerns than previously.

Picking your path: The make/ lease/own/buy decision

The *make/lease/own/buy decision* is a critical decision. It arises from calculating whether any decision is cheaper, better value or more cost effective when you choose to:

✔ Make something rather than lease it or buy it in ready-made form.

✔ Lease something rather than buy it outright.

✔ Own something so that you have full control over its usage.

✔ Buy something rather than rent or lease it.

For example, should you:

✔ Make your own components (if you're a manufacturing company) – or buy them in from suppliers?

✔ Create your own databases (if you're a service company) – or outsource and subcontract to a specialist provider?

✔ Own and control your own supply side, suppliers, distributors, wholesale and retail networks and outlets – or use existing providers, transport fleets and others' wholesale and retail premises?

✔ Employ your own expertise – or buy it in on a contracted or consultancy basis when you need it?

To determine which path is most appropriate cost-wise for your organisation, you need to produce a set of calculations as the starting point for your considerations. This way, you at least know what is the most purely cost-effective option.

However, in the wider context of investing in remaining competitive, the answer, as always, is not so simple. You must also consider other factors, such as full control, effectiveness of usage and long-term advantage.

The key question in choosing whether to buy or lease is the question 'Why?' Why would you choose to do things one way or the other? In particular, you need to know and understand what you're foregoing for the sake of a cost advantage. For instance, if you're conceding large measures of control over critical activities largely because of a cost advantage, you need to consider whether this choice is really:

✔ Good business

✔ A cost advantage in the long run

✔ A cost advantage if something goes wrong

The pause that refreshes

White Water Soft Drinks (not its real name) is a very successful soft drinks production, bottling and distribution company in southern England. The company is highly profitable, producing excellent products. It has long held licensing agreements to produce soft drinks for Coca-Cola and the big UK supermarket chains.

White Water upgraded its production and bottling facilities and in the process ended up having spare production capacity. So, from its location in southern England, it looked to mainland Europe for potential new markets for its products. Market research stated that the soft drinks industry in northern France, Belgium, Holland and western Germany was worth £30 billion per annum. Calculations stated that if White Water gained just 1 per cent of this business, the company's return would be worth £300 million (even 0.1 per cent of this market would be worth £30 million). Excitement was all round! The company believed it would finally become a major international player.

Then one production manager quietly intervened, suggesting that he pick up some samples of the competition whilst visiting the continent for the weekend. Almost without looking up, the managing director of White Water agreed.

The production manager duly returned the following week with competitive samples – encompassing 39 different brands. (This figure counted Coca-Cola and all its works as one brand, as well as Pepsi-Cola, Schweppes and supermarket brands as one brand each.)

Moreover, the production manager had managed to have a word with one of the hypermarket general managers who stated that everything they did was dependent on central buying; even local providers were centrally sourced.

At this point, fortunately for White Water, a sharp dose of reality set in. The company thankfully forgot all the excitement that the initial market research generated and set out to research all its potential markets thoroughly before rushing in headlong.

If the answer is yes to all three aspects, then go with your decision. If, on the other hand, the answer is no to any of the three aspects, consider what changes would be necessary to shift the answers to yes. Or you need to arrive at the view that conceding large measures of control is not cost effective in the longer term.

Whatever your calculations state, realise that make/lease/own/buy decisions tend to be faddish and cyclical:

- ✔ In some circumstances, the ability to command the supply and distribution sides means that, not only are your own activities more or less assured, but you can limit the activities of competitors and alternatives, especially others seeking to buy in on the supply side or to use the same distribution channels and networks.

- ✔ In other circumstances, contracting out supply and distribution activities, as well as some specialisms, means that you can assure the costs of these activities.

Whatever the prevailing attitude, the same problems and issues endure: if you own these activities, you have to pay whatever the costs involved are. If you contract them out, you have to be able to assure yourself that they'll be available when required. So making your final decision takes knowledge and expertise – not just a set of calculations.

Denying problems

The other part of investment appraisal, decision-making and management that you must address is denial. If people want to do something, they can deny the existence of problems forever. And on the flipside, if people don't want to do something, they can deny the existence of opportunities.

Denial in investment decisions refers especially to people denying that:

- ✔ Anything can go wrong
- ✔ Any mistakes can possibly be made (or have been made)
- ✔ Markets are changing
- ✔ Products and services are inadequate

People often reinforce denial with counter-statements such as:

- ✔ We've invested heavily in this project.
- ✔ The consultants told us to do this, so it must be right.
- ✔ Everyone is really good at his or her job.
- ✔ Nothing can possibly go wrong.
- ✔ We're spending record levels on this project (particularly popular with government projects)

When denial occurs, you must confront it. You have to be prepared to acknowledge that things can and do go wrong, whatever your expertise or levels of expenditure. Be prepared and willing when necessary to put things down to experience, write things off and move on – and encourage others to act similarly. When things go wrong because of inadequate or incomplete investment appraisal processes, you have to be prepared to carry out a full inquest, identify your gaps in knowledge and understanding and then take steps to put things right.

Confronting mistakes and errors when everyone else is in denial isn't easy. Doing so requires courage and character, so prepare to be unpopular if you choose to confront such matters. However, confront them eventually you must if you're going to improve your decision-making processes – and improve the returns that you seek to gain on your investments.

Understanding how decisions are really made

Knowing how investment decisions come to be made is essential for many reasons, including:

- ✔ Developing an accurate, informed and expert decision-making process of your own.

- ✔ Gaining the habit of acquiring as much knowledge and understanding as you can in order to make accurate and effective decisions.

- ✔ Anticipating the effects of others' decisions.

- ✔ Realising that decisions driven by one overriding force typically affect everything else that you do.

So how are investment decisions really made? Of course, many are made rationally as the result of analysing and evaluating the opportunities on offer, allocating resources, calculating the returns and then implementing them. Others, however, result from:

- ✔ A single driving force, which is invariably short-term share or financial advantage.

- ✔ The need to get into a particular location, activity or industry, often on the basis of an opportunity becoming suddenly available or another company becoming available for takeover.

- ✔ A policy decision that requires guaranteeing your command of your supply or distribution networks by buying up a major company in these areas.

- ✔ The opportunity to gain (real and spurious; perceived and illusory) size and capacity advantage by merging with, or taking over, someone else in your sector.

- ✔ The opportunity to gain (real and spurious) 'synergies' and 'economies of scale' through merging with others.

When people uses phrases like 'synergies' or 'economies of scale' in discussions with you, make them define what they're actually talking about! These are jargon phrases, bandied about in newspapers, boardrooms and management meetings. They seldom get questioned, so *you* be the one who starts!

My use of the phrase 'real and spurious' in the preceding list is important because it reflects the attention to detail that people pay in advance of taking a decision. In general, the greater the detail, the greater the reality of the venture being considered. By contrast, the fewer the details (and the greater the generalities), the more likely it is that any figures produced – and also the whole premise for the venture – are indeed spurious.

Following focus groups

Focus groups and the use of (real and alleged) experts are very popular with many organisations and in a lot of different circumstances. The great strength of these research tools is that you can consult (ideally) with a wide group of interests and inform your progress. At their most positive, these forms of consultation refine and sharpen your thinking and where your priorities ought actually to lie – and where, therefore, you need to allocate and concentrate resources.

At its worst of course, this consultation is an abdication of responsibility. You probably know how the situation goes. Several people in a beverage focus group express interest in drinking stronger tea. So you go off and concentrate everything on producing stronger tea, only to find that stronger tea sells no better! But you have a watertight case – it was the focus group and opinion-former what done it! Not so, of course. It was you 'what done it' by slavishly following the focus groups and opinion-formers.

You must take what these tools come up with, analyse and evaluate the feedback and then make a decision that you're comfortable enough with to implement, resource and support.

Two other realities of the investment decision-making process to keep in mind are:

- ✔ **Organisations make decisions with short- and long-term results in mind.** Therefore, in practice you need to attend to both. However strong your line of reasoning, you still must at least indicate some early advantages in order to carry your backers and colleagues with you. This is the way of the world, and you have to be prepared to live with it.

- ✔ **Some decisions are made on the basis of the least harm, as well as the greatest good.** If you need to show 'some sort of progress' (and yes, an awful lot of investments boil down to this goal), consider allocating resources to a series of short steps or taking a minority interest in a joint venture, just to test the water or get started.

Anticipating the consequences of decisions

Anything in which you invest has consequences. Decision-making and investment appraisal are processes, not isolated events that lead to specific opportunities, prospects and chances. The investment decision-making process requires that you put on your evaluator's hat at regular stages along the way.

As part of this ongoing process, you must do your best to extrapolate where particular ventures and choices may lead, and prepare for both the direct and indirect consequences.

Direct consequences

Direct consequences are those that occur in response to what you do. For example, if you jump in the water, the direct consequence is that you get wet.

- ✔ The direct consequence of investing in Australia , for example, is that you must be prepared for any economic, social and political changes that may take place and compromise the returns. So you need to find out everything you possibly can about the economic, social and political background of Australia (or wherever it is).

- ✔ The direct consequence of investing in mega-projects (such as the A380 or power station developments) is that you have to invest in everything necessary to make them happen on the scale and time frame required. The Channel Tunnel project, for example, required assessing the enormous amount of equipment needed, as well as the volumes of concrete, cement, electricals, electronics, labour and expertise.

- ✔ The direct consequence of investing in information technology projects is the ability to generate capacity, security, connectivity, access and reliability for all those who need and want it.

Nobody can extricate you from the direct consequences of investment decisions. Investment appraisal is truly a process that leads to other things. So be prepared!

Indirect consequences

Indirect consequences are those that you can foresee in general, but not in reality until they actually come to pass.

If you do your homework properly, then you know and understand that generally, three years into a five-year venture, things like the price of oil or credit are likely to change. Of course, knowing generally doesn't mean facing a credit or oil change is any easier. Yes, on the one hand you knew something was going to come along, but on the other, now that you're faced with the reality, you actually have to do something. So what are you going to do – and *how* are you going to do it?

Indirect consequences are what contingency funding and contingency planning are all about (see Chapter 11). You need both strategies as part of your investment appraisal process if you're to maximise and optimise resource use and keep your competitive position as strong as possible.

You can gain an awful lot of clarity about indirect consequences at the outset of a project, if you take time to clarify your overall purpose and objectives (see Chapter 2). If you're clear about what you're letting yourself in for – as well as how and why – you can create a clear basis for dealing with everything else that's likely to come along.

REAL WORLD EXAMPLE

Big prestige, big demands

If a powerful or dominant backer states that you'll produce 30 per cent returns on investment, then you've no choice but to comply – or try to. Regardless of how much you know and understand that life is not like this, if the backer insists, then ultimately you must do your best to implement whatever the backer proposes, and to try and gain the returns demanded.

For example, the owners of Chelsea Football Club set out to buy the best squad of players and coaches in the world. The club was investing in success – trophies, a global brand and world renown. The only thing that went slightly wrong was the results, the bit that the club could not predict. Because winning was all that mattered, one coach, Avram Grant, was sacked for only achieving the runner-up spot in three of the four competitions that the club had entered.

And since then? Chelsea remains second in the UK Premiership – and in all of the other competitions which they have entered. So they've neither progressed nor regressed!

If you do invest in triumphs and prestige, then these have to turn a profit, or else you have to pay for them out of the proceeds of your ordinary steady-state activities. There's no other way. If you want to be, or to own, the biggest, the best, the brightest or the most glittering of anything, then it must pay its way – or you have to be able to afford to subsidise it from your activities elsewhere. For example, ThornEMI took on Robbie Williams on a £75 million contract so it could have Robbie Williams on its books; this contract must now be paid for out of everyday sales of CDs, DVDs and other goods.

You simply can't predict some indirect consequences. Of course, you can speculate along the lines of: 'If we invest in railways in Thailand, we may get the opportunity to move into the Thai tourist trade,' and you ought to have a good general idea about how this may happen. But what if the opportunity suddenly comes? Or what if the opportunity never arises at all? How are you going to respond – and what indeed are the consequences that arise (or don't) from the opportunity?

Power and influence – and consequences

When considering consequences, you need to be honest about your organisation's power and influence.

If you're a large international company, and suddenly need a presence somewhere new, you can simply go in and buy it. For lesser mortals (and companies and organisations), the process isn't so simple. You have to acquire the power and influence that you need relative to your own size, strengths, capabilities and sources of competitive advantage. For example:

- ✔ Amazon is able to drive down the wholesale prices that it pays because of the sheer volumes of books, music and other products that it buys from its suppliers.
- ✔ Although the Virgin brand is large, in no part of its huge range of activities does it have more than 10 per cent of the market.

These companies and others like them, know and understand their strengths and limitations, playing to their strengths and working within their limitations.

The problems – and negative consequences – come when a company gets an idea above its station, without the resources, capacity or reputation to back up the idea. For example:

- ✔ When Tarmac first tried to prospect for work in south-east Asia, it was genuinely surprised to learn that nobody knew its UK work, or indeed had heard of it at all.
- ✔ It took Microsoft a long time to get into the games console market on a viable basis, because it mistook genuine software expertise and an overall dominant reputation for the fact that people would therefore want to buy from it and not from the alternatives.
- ✔ Sony has regularly mistaken its dominant position for the illusion that people would therefore buy all things Sony – and this has led to failures in video, computer games, CD and cassette products over the years.

If you're a dominant player, you probably have the resources to accommodate these kinds of failures – and even force your will. But forcing your will is very likely to have significant consequences. People don't like being bullied or forced, and they typically do their best to find alternatives. If you really do impose on people, they'll most likely do everything they can to break away from you as soon as they possibly can. And then you gain no returns at all.

Chapter 8

Finessing Your Finances

I make *many* references to finance in this book. Indeed, you can't consider any business practice, let alone competitive strategy, without it. Finance is essential for you to compete – without it you simply don't have the resources to back anything you want to do.

In this chapter, I look at the wider aspects of what managing your organisation's finances is all about, including how to deal with finance, how to control it to the best of your abilities and make it work as hard as possible for you!

Even if you're not the Chief Financial Officer of your organisation, finance applies to you! You must look at company finances in exactly the same way that you look at all the other parts of your daily work. If you see that the finances don't seem to quite stack up, you must get on the case, find out why and, if necessary, raise your concerns as early as possible.

Balancing Obligations and Costs

Finance is the lifeblood of all organisations. Whatever you do (and wherever you do it) you need to have more money coming in than going out.

This financial philosophy seems so simple – and it *is* simple, providing that you know and understand how to meet your obligations and manage your costs.

Meeting your obligations

In order to meet your obligations, you must first know and understand what they are. At any time, you have numerous obligations and commitments for which you must pay, including:

- ✔ Wages and salaries, including employers' contributions
- ✔ Rent, rates, heating and lighting fees
- ✔ Fees and charges to consultants, contractors, subcontractors and suppliers
- ✔ Legal and accounting fees
- ✔ Taxes
- ✔ Contracted obligations to suppliers, distributors and transport contractors
- ✔ Insurance for staff, your premises and activities

You can also be more or less certain that from time to time you'll need to pay:

- ✔ Maintenance, replacement and upgrade charges
- ✔ Marketing and advertising fees
- ✔ Pay rises
- ✔ Increases in energy costs
- ✔ Changes in interest and exchange rates
- ✔ Gas, electricity, energy and transport costs
- ✔ Waste disposal charges and obligations
- ✔ Fees to specialist subcontractors and experts, when required

You also have to pay to service the finance in the form of interest and overdraft charges from time to time (see the sidebar 'Considering the costs of finance' for more). So you have a long list of obligations that you need to be able and willing to meet.

Unfortunately, organisations frequently find that they can no longer meet their financial commitments without incurring serious difficulties. For this reason if no other, finance must be a priority for all. If you're faced with this kind of crisis, make sure that you alert individuals in charge early of financial problems. The earlier you alert the appropriate people, the easier they can work to put things right. And if you can't put them right, at least you're not throwing good money after bad!

Considering the costs of finance

The particular sector in which you work affects your *costs of finance* – the interest, overdraft charges and other fees you must pay to service any money you finance. You need to know and understand sectoral economics, particularly typical cost, price, charge and payment structures. For example:

✔ Working in retail or catering means a steady cash flow and regularity of income, but if you work in these and similar sectors, you need to have capital, overdraft and flexible finance facilities to underwrite your ability to buy in the stocks that you need.

✔ Working in civil engineering or computer project work means that you're likely to be paid large amounts of money at irregular intervals. Thus, you're likely to incur financial charges while managing your regular bills, including wages and energy charges. For some projects you may also have to underwrite the costs involved in acquiring and beginning work before you're paid at all.

The key to understanding how much you're going to have to pay for your finance is knowing and understanding what actually goes on in your business and other competing businesses in your sector or industry – rather than what you'd like to happen. Several things shape your cost of finance including:

✔ General credit availability

✔ Underlying zero-risk financing costs (in the UK, this is the Bank of England Rate)

✔ The borrowing company's risks and operating prospects, as perceived by the lender

✔ The proportion in the capital mix between debt (cheap) and equity (much more expensive)

Managing your costs

In meeting your obligations (which I discuss in the preceding section), you incur *costs* – charges that you must pay when demanded or required. You must know and understand what these costs are and the consequences of incurring them.

Costs you have to be aware of include:

✔ **Fixed costs:** You incur *fixed costs* as a condition of setting up in business and maintaining your business. Fixed costs include premises, energy charges, wages and salaries and any other elements that you can't easily change.

Treat your staff as a fixed cost. Doing so ensures that you engage only the staff that you want and need. Although you can vary staff costs based on how you pay (or don't pay) overtime, you can't easily vary the cost of your core staff. Yes, you can use agency staff, but the charges for these services are more or less predictable.

If you make lay-offs, the immediate effect is to vary your costs *upwards*, not downwards. Think about it. You're paying people to leave you and not to work for you! Lay-offs can take many years to achieve the cost savings that you're hoping to achieve immediately.

✔ **Variable costs:** You incur *variable costs* as the result of the volume of business that you actually conduct. Variable costs include some heating and lighting, raw materials, distribution, telephone, overtime and other things that change according to your business volume.

✔ **Consequential costs:** You incur *consequential costs* as the direct consequence of the ways you organise your activities. For example, if you spend large amounts of money on research and development, significant R&D costs are a consequence of the ways you do business. If you're sloppy and slapdash and incur fines, these costs are also consequences of the ways you conduct business.

✔ **Sunk costs:** When you've no reasonable prospect of recovering the amount you pay, a cost is considered a *sunk cost*.

Increasingly, production and technology costs (especially software) are categorised as sunk costs. You must buy quality technology while realising that with the pace of technological change, you're likely to have to scrap equipment at fairly short notice (even if your current technology works fine) and purchase newer technology, in order to remain competitive.

✔ **Switching costs:** You incur switching costs as the result of changing from one set of activities to another. For example, if you change from a manually operated system to something that's electronic, you incur some sort of switching cost.

✔ **Opportunity costs:** These refer to your next best option for an expenditure or investment. Whenever you choose something, you have to give up some other opportunity.

✔ **Marginal costs:** You incur *marginal costs* as the result of conducting one further activity, such as producing one additional item or unit of service.

Calculating marginal costs is essential so that you know and understand when you're up to full, or near full, capacity. You calculate marginal costs by assessing the costs each time you introduce extra activities. When you reach full capacity, your marginal costs – the cost of the extra activity – include capital investment in new equipment and technology, overtime and hiring new staff.

Hedging on the future

To an extent, you can manage your costs by buying commodities (such as crops and minerals), raw materials, database access, energy and utilities supplies at assured future prices. Basically, you contract to buy whatever it is that you need at an assured price, thus guaranteeing a price for the duration of the contract. By doing this, you' re hedging your bets – effectively betting that the fuel, commodity or supply won't go down in price relative to what you've contracted to pay.

From a strategic management point of view, you must know the detail of the particular cost for the duration of the contract for each of the above factors; so it becomes another key aspect of defining the basis on which you're going to compete.

From a strategic management point of view, identifying, arranging and classifying your costs in the categories I list in the preceding bullets ensures that you concentrate on what is important to your business. Classifying your costs also helps to ensure that you approach each cost based on its consequences to your business, rather than as a mere expenditure. With this strategy, you can focus on:

- The value that you're going to get from technology or staff.
- The benefits of more efficient and effective forms of cash and capital management.
- The increased suitability of your organisation's premises and facilities.

Choosing Your Financial Structure

Strategically speaking, you have several sources of finance on which to build your business, including:

- **Deficit finance.** You take out money in the form of a loan that's normally guaranteed by you against the future of your business.
- **Partnership finance.** One or more partners with financial assets, business angels or venture capitalists put money into your organisation, typically in return for a contracted share of the business.

- ✔ **Share capital.** You sell shares privately to family and friends – or publicly on a recognised stock market, such as Wall Street or the London Stock Exchange.

- ✔ **Personal wealth.** You invest your savings in the organisation with the hope, expectation or promise of future returns.

- ✔ **Bank loans, gilts, bonds and overdrafts.** You enter into an agreement with your bank to use its money to support your business – and to eventually repay the borrowed money. Loans and overdrafts normally act as working financial instruments, to get you through a particular short-term matter, and so these tools are normally integrated into other financial structures.

You may be able to choose amongst these various finance structures, or some outside forces may choose for you.

- ✔ If you're a new venture and business start-up, you may have a clear view about what structure you prefer.

- ✔ If you're an established organisation, existing backers or board members are likely to steer and pressure you in particular directions.

Whatever your situation, you need to know and understand what you're letting yourself in for – and the likely opportunities and consequences for your competitiveness associated with any finance source. (Even if you have little or no control over your business's finance sources, you can at least recognise and assess where the problems and issues are likely to arise.)

If you do have any control over your financial structure, your first decision is whether you can work with the structure proposed. If you can't, you must do whatever you can to change things – or you must withdraw from the venture.

Assuming you can work with your proposed finances, you need to be aware of the following aspects of any financial agreement:

- ✔ **The balance of control:** Your financiers want some kind of influence over what you do with their money. In many cases, they may want the final say in what you do, as a condition of agreeing to back you.

- ✔ **The nature of business activities:** Although your organisation may be fairly clear about what it does or intends to do, backers often significantly influence *how* your business goes about developing and operating.

- ✔ **Staffing:** Backers may insist that you hire specific executives or experts as a condition of their backing. If the financing is significant, the staffing requirement is often a financial manager because the lender is keen to ensure that you keep your books in a proper manner. (This expectation most commonly results in large corporate shareholders making appointments of directors to public limited companies.)

✔ **Returns:** Securing backers for some ventures and initiatives may require you to give preference or assign a pecking order for future returns. For example, in order to remain viable, Eurotunnel, the Channel Tunnel operator, had to engage upwards of 200 banks to put money into the venture. As a condition of their support, the banks insisted that they gain priority in the distribution of any future profits. As a result, shareholders slipped down the pecking order, and share values collapsed – even though the venture gained a sound financial structure with its bank-based finance.

✔ **Bank loans:** With any form of bank loan, you must be aware of the conditions in which the bank may withdraw the facility. In particular, banks get very jittery if you try to extend the period of the loan without giving full details as to how you intend to use the additional time and why the extension is necessary.

Every form of finance carries its own consequences, including loss of control, demands on returns and loss of ownership or direction of the venture. Even if you secure 100 per cent shareholder capital, you have to meet your obligations to shareholders in the form of dividends. So seek to understand fully the particular financial demands associated with any structure you're considering.

Assessing Financial Performance

The starting point for determining, measuring and ultimately assessing financial performance is: how much money do you need to make in order to cover costs, meet obligations, deliver the returns demanded by your financial structure – and make a profit or surplus?

To assess financial performance, you must know and understand in detail your strategy for dividing your income among reinvestment in the business, share dividends and profit-related pay for staff. You also need to be clear where your priorities lie – such as meeting your obligations, making returns or reinvesting in future activities. If you know that you have commitments which you're going to have to pay for in the near future, you must make sure you hold back some resources for this purpose.

Setting expectations

To assess financial performance, you must have a clear view of what your expectations were, and whether these expectations were reasonable and feasible in the circumstances. (Go to Chapter 7 for more on establishing financial expectations.)

Figuring out what went right

Great financial successes are often not fully evaluated. Organisations and their managers tend to put great successes down to their own brilliance and excellence – and then move on in the assurance that their genius will see them through all future decisions!

After an excellent return, you must assess the reasons behind *why* you did so well. You need to know and understand the conditions that were in place that helped deliver your excellent return, including the following indicators:

✔ You met your deadlines

✔ You delivered (or exceeded) the quality and volume that your customers expected

✔ Your levels of pricing and charging are accurate

✔ You're better at specific issues of value to your customers than your competitors are

All the preceding can point to future success. Whatever you do in the future, you need to ensure that you never compromise these aspects.

As your business progresses and develops, you need to pay attention to the extent to which you meet or don't meet your expectations (if you expected to make 30 per cent annual profits, but in fact are only making 20 per cent, for example), as well as the reasons for meeting or not meeting expectations. Assessing your financial performance in this manner helps inform your forecasting processes, increase your understanding of your market sector and develop greater product and service knowledge.

Establishing best, medium and worst outcomes

As with all aspects of organisational performance, you must know the amount of financial outlay you can support. You also need to know the returns that you need – and want – to make.

To set these guidelines and goals:

1. **Examine what is feasible in your current economic circumstances and sector.**

2. **Establish your baseline as to how much you need to make in order to meet your immediate obligations.**

3. **Working from your baseline, make financial projections and forecasts that combine various trading conditions, environmental pressures and sales volumes.**

   This way, you begin to consider what you're doing in the full context of everything that's happening in your markets and the environment (see Chapter 6).

Defining Your Assets and Liabilities

You may think that defining your assets and liabilities is easy. After all, your accountant does all the work for you, right?

From the point of view of delivering annual accounts, yes, your accountant is indeed responsible for defining assets and liabilities! But from the point of view of developing your strategy and improving your competitiveness, you need to take a much more detailed and informed look at everything that you do, how you do it and how you pay for it.

- ✔ **An asset** is anything that is working for you productively and positively
- ✔ **A liability** is anything that you no longer need, or which needs replacing.

In the following sections, I consider in detail how to look at assets and liabilities from the point of view of what they deliver for you as you go about your daily work.

Noting your assets

Assets include anything that delivers value, revenue, profit and income to your company or organisation. Assets also support and enhance your reputation and underpin customer and client confidence and expectations.

Cataloguing your assets is a complex exercise. When you do so, you may find that some products or services are unprofitable – but also you have to keep them going so that customers and clients remain familiar with what you do or so that they have a choice. If you remove the unprofitable products or services, you remove any perception of choice. So you have to decide whether the unprofitable products and services are assets or liabilities (see the following section).

If you sell product or service clusters, you may find that part of the cluster is sold at a loss. You have to choose whether to keep the loss in order to keep the other elements going. For example:

- Ryanair sells many plane tickets at a loss, but it relies on the ancillaries – baggage charges, in-flight food and drink, car hire deals and targeted media offers – to raise its income (or revenue) to £60–£100 per passenger, per flight.

- Department stores sell razorblades at a loss and rely on selling 'the shave' – including shaving foam, brushes and after-shave – to generate a surplus from sales of the full package of products.

In the preceding cases, the loss-making items – the tickets and the razorblades – remain assets and have to be treated as such.

Looking at your liabilities

From a strategic management point of view, *liabilities* are anything that harms your profitability, revenues, reputation or the value of your products and services.

In considering where your liabilities lie, you look at each loss-making product and service (as I discuss in the section 'Noting your assets') and decide which are:

- **Liabilities under any circumstance,** in which case you stop producing and delivering them.

- **Liabilities in their present form but changeable,** in which case you can adjust your approach to them. (For example, you may choose to buy in a product or service for an assured price and charge, rather than making or producing it yourself.)

- **An asset,** in which case you work with the product or service as I discuss in the preceding 'Noting your assets' section.

Anything that damages your reputation is a liability. For example, if you use contractors who produce sloppy work, or retail outlets that take a cavalier attitude to your products and services, then your reputation suffers and these contractors or outlets are liabilities. You need to persuade the contractors or outlets to change their approaches to your products and services, or you need to change your contractors and outlets.

Consider everything to be assets until you prove them to be liabilities. And when you find that something is a liability, you must divest yourself of it or discontinue it.

Selling assets

Many company annual reports mention sales of assets. *Sales of assets* occur when you sell off a part of your organisation or business, including property or capital equipment (old computer hardware, old production lines) that doesn't form a core part of your trading activities.

In an ideal world, you only sell off your liabilities! Of course, in practice things don't always work out this way. You're likely to find yourself selling (and often having to sell) things that you still hold in high value. You may, for example, do this in order to bolster other parts of your business, to raise ready cash at short notice, to fund changes in your activities or to support entry into a new market.

In practice, sales of assets rarely realise their true value because individuals buying your assets typically know that you're being forced to sell. The main exception is when you sell off something of value to two or more potential buyers who are prepared to outbid each other in order to acquire the particular item.

Shifting between asset and liability

Asset values can and do change, rising and falling over time. Furthermore, assets can and do turn into liabilities, especially in the case of technology, premises and capital goods.

When an asset turns into a liability, or when an asset's apparent value declines significantly, you can choose to:

- ✔ Try and sell it off.
- ✔ Write it off as a loss altogether.
- ✔ Keep it going for some good and sound business reason. (For example, keeping old but well-loved product lines going because you have a reputation based on their historic worth.)

Whatever your choice, you must look at what contribution the item, product or service makes to your business. Balance your need for cash and the amount that you're likely to receive for the item to determine whether a sale is worthwhile.

REAL WORLD EXAMPLE

Positive versus negative assets in the football industry

All industries and commercial sectors use complex ways of assessing whether something is an asset or liability, including the football industry.

For many years, the football industry has bought, sold and traded players as commodities (like crops in the coffee industry). The clubs buy and sell players between them on the basis of players' asset values. Asset value for a football player is based on whether he:

✔ Can be commercialised by the club he is joining

✔ Has a brand value all his own (like David Beckham, for example)

✔ Can secure sponsorships and endorsements

✔ Helps sell tickets for matches

✔ Helps sell television and broadcasting rights

✔ Helps attract other good players to the club

✔ Opens up possible branding and merchandising activities in a particular part of the world

✔ Plays well (which is, ironically, almost an after-thought)

If a good player with a high asset value joins a particular club on a five-year contract and plays well (or well enough) for the duration of his contract, the club gets the best of all worlds for the period. After five years, the club can sell the player as a demonstrable and realisable asset.

But if the player suffers a serious injury after two years, does his injury make him a liability? Maybe – or maybe not. The player's asset value depends on what else he continues to deliver. If the player is no longer on the field of play but continues to sell merchandise or help attract other players to the club, he is nevertheless an asset.

On the other hand, if a player delivers everything and remains injury free, he can, nevertheless, become a liability because of a bad attitude or unwillingness to play to the best of his capabilities. He is therefore sold on as soon as possible, ostensibly as an asset, but actually as a liability.

Monitoring Costs and Revenues

The other key area to be aware of is the relationship between costs and revenues. For the purposes of this section, *costs* include all charges you incur in your particular business, and *revenues* include all the money that your company generates in practice.

As with all aspects of organisation management, you have to have a fully informed and expert view of what is feasible for costs and revenues within your business and your sector or industry.

The following sections explore situations involving costs and revenues.

Falling costs and rising revenues

Diminishing costs and increasing revenues. Sounds like your dream scenario! But even if you're fortunate enough to experience this combination, you need to know and understand why it's happening, how long it's likely to be sustainable for and what can possibly go wrong.

If costs are falling and revenues are rising throughout your sector, be aware that others are going to be desperate to get in! If you're truly in this position, guard it well – and keep on doing all the things that you're clearly doing right! For example, Ryanair cut its costs back when it first went into low-fare mass air transport by streamlining everything from its airliner fleet to maintenance schedules and ticketing procedures.

Rising costs and rising revenues

When your costs and revenues are both rising, you need to work out whether the costs incurred are supporting the rise in revenues. As your revenues have been rising, you may have become sloppy about costs. Or maybe you can point to a real connection between cause and effect:

- ✔ Increased spending on advertising is resulting in more customers coming to you now – or in existing customers spending more.
- ✔ You're generating short-term sales advantages through product and service discounts.
- ✔ You're generating additional business through contracting out arrangements (for which you have to pay, hence the rise in costs).
- ✔ You introduced an after-sales package (the rising cost) but doing so has brought in more customers because they now like your fuller service and are prepared to pay for it.

The fact that revenues are rising does not mean that you can become complacent about costs. You always need to know what is going on – and why!

Rising costs and steady or falling revenues

Increasing costs and stable or diminishing revenues is a fairly common position in which an organisation finds itself. From a strategic standpoint, you need to look at what you're going to do to restore your competitive position.

Rising costs fall into two categories:

- ✔ Those that you can do nothing about
- ✔ Those that you can influence

Some costs that you can do nothing about include energy, transport, taxes, electricity, water and fuel. In practice, you should also look at wages and salaries as being largely outside your control, at least in the short term. (Though you can of course tackle wage and salary costs in the longer term through tying pay to performance, recruitment freezes, organisation streamlining or, if all else fails, redundancies and lay-offs.)

When faced with rising costs and steady or falling revenues, concentrate your efforts on ensuring the maximum possible usage for the energy, transport and fuel you consume. Work to make your premises as productive as possible, for as long as possible. Send out transport fleets as full as possible, as often as possible. Tie staff performance, wages and salaries to organisational objectives and priorities.

Costs that you can tackle, even in adverse trading conditions, include:

- ✔ Wastage rates
- ✔ Staff absenteeism
- ✔ Machinery, technology and equipment usage
- ✔ Advertising and marketing operations
- ✔ New product and service development

Concentrate your efforts on ensuring that everything you can control operates as efficiently and effectively as possible. In particular, work to change people's attitudes about wasting energy, transport, fuel and water resources. Address staff absenteeism (whereby you're effectively paying people to be away from work) by asking them why, and so getting at the core of why people are taking time off; address your staff's real concerns and remove all the reasons why people don't come to work. (For more, pick up a copy of *Managing For Dummies* by Bob Nelson, Peter Economy and yours truly.)

Making Strategic Financial Management Decisions

Base your organisation's financial management on the resources that you have available and the nature of your income. Sounds simple doesn't it? And yet you'd be surprised by the numbers of managers, companies and organisations that partially or totally miss this concept.

The core problem in many cases lies in the assumptions you make. These problematic assumptions can occur at all stages of the development of your competitive strategy (see Chapter 12). For example:

- ✔ **Planning stage:** During this stage, you may share projections of a certain possible income – and this figure eventually becomes a reality in the minds of everyone involved.

- ✔ **Delivery stage:** During this stage, you assume that a product or service is going to fly off the shelves, and as a result you start spending the money before you even put products on the shelves.

- ✔ **Implementation stage:** You assume a specific income, and when it comes in at less, you cannot support the development of what you have implemented. Or your assumptions focus on gross rather than net income; as a result you now have to account for things like transport costs and taxation – the things that you conveniently missed earlier!

So you have to look at financial management in terms of the relationships between your costs, income and expenditure.

Connecting costs, income and expenditure

Of course, you employ financial specialists to ensure that the financial structure and management of your business is as strong as possible and delivers this strength in the context of how you conduct your affairs.

You must distinguish between:

- ✔ **Costs,** which are charges you incur. See the preceding section 'Monitoring Costs and Revenues.'

- ✔ **Income,** which you generate as the result of the costs that you incur.

- ✔ **Expenditure,** which you have to make on a daily basis to pay for resources and support all your activities.

Many may say that the distinctions are fine and semantic! But a bit of discipline and attention to detail ensures that you gain a close understanding of what is truly going on as you conduct your business.

Seek to know and understand where your financial management strength lies. For example:

- ✔ If your company is a project-based organisation and receives large amounts of money at irregular intervals, such as in civil engineering, then you must pay for the costs that you incur on a daily basis from somewhere – from what money you manage to retain from the irregular payments or else from overdraft or contingency/emergency facilities.

- ✔ If your company is in fast-moving consumer goods or services, such as food retail, you need to use a portion of your steady and (hopefully) assured cash flow to service the business itself. Some money needs to go to making sure that your products and services are on the shelves and available for sale in the appropriate volumes required to maintain cash flow, customer confidence and inventories.

Budgets and various reports – which I cover in the following sections – help you support your decisions regarding costs, income and expenditure.

Getting more from budgets

Organisations need *budgets* – agreed volumes of finance and resources to enable them to support and energise their businesses. But beware! Budgets can be minefields. (See the sidebar 'Out-of-control budgeting' for some particularly bad examples of what you need to avoid.)

You have two basic approaches to budgeting:

- ✔ **The zero-based budget:** You calculate from scratch at the start of the year or period the cost of everything that you're going to need, and then submit your figure for approval.

- ✔ **The present situation base:** You take this year's budget as an accurate assessment of cost and add a bit for things like fuel, energy and transport costs.

Another school of budgeting suggests that budgets should only include variable costs and that fixed costs should be taken out of them and remain the domain of the organisation as a whole. (See the earlier section 'Managing your costs' for more about fixed and variable costs.) Certainly, following this path means you aren't drawn into staffing, technology and capital expenditure issues as part of your budgeting process. And in turn, you know and understand your fixed-cost base and can therefore concentrate on the operating costs only.

Never-ending financial management decisions

Financial management is a continuous process, not a simple set of actions. One financial decision leads to others as you seek to balance your costs, income and expenditure.

For example, one UK car manufacturer experienced a large reduction in production for ten days, which cost the company many hundreds of thousands of pounds. The problem lay with some key, special components for the chassis of one of its models. The components were brought in on a just-in-time basis, up to three times a day from a particular supplier. For many years, the relationship had worked fully and effectively, and then suddenly the deliveries didn't turn up.

Working together, the company and its supplier traced the problems to major road works on one of the motorways and upgrades of one of the supplier's production facilities.

After much discussion, the car manufacturer and component supplier generated the following solution:

✔ The car manufacturer would pay a 10 per cent premium to guarantee supplies.

✔ Failure to deliver at any point on the part of the supplier would result in the particular delivery being free for the car manufacturer.

The car company now had to recoup the 10 per cent premium from within its own facilities. Of course, it could simply have passed on the cost to its dealers and eventually its customers. However, it instead chose to speed up the production process. Rather than producing 55 cars per year per staff member, it now produced 62 cars per year per staff member – an increase which more than recouped the supply-side cost increases.

Although this solution sounded very rosy, it created a new problem: would the car manufacturer be able to sell its increased output? As things turned out, the company was able to sell the additional cars, but only if it opened up new markets in new locations (especially central and eastern Europe) where there was no particular history or familiarity with the company's particular makes and models. And so on. And so on.

Knowing and understanding where your finances are going and how they're being used is the main outcome that you're seeking in the budgeting process. Of course, you also need to know and understand where the fluctuations between projections, forecasts and realities occur. As long as your budgeting process and structures deliver these two broad outcomes, then they're doing their job.

Reporting activities to stakeholders

In the interests of financial probity, your own integrity and assurance and the law, you have to report a 'true and fair' reflection of your trading over the past period to your key stakeholders, including shareholders, backers, staff, customers and suppliers, as I cover in the following sections.

Out-of-control budgeting

Incredibly, some organisations still make managers and section heads fight each other, and the organisation, for resources – rather than allocating what is needed on an expert and informed basis.

In circumstances like these, managers typically overstate their resource demands, knowing and understanding that someone will cut their demands. So these managers go down the path of adding 25 per cent to budgets, the powers that be cut things by 25 per cent and it's all a nice little game, right? Well, not always.

One manager at a defence contractor returned from the annual budget-round doing his best to look glum. He had, after all, just had his budget halved. He had however, not over-stated his budget by 25 per cent – but by 300 per cent.

When money is involved, what you can procure is often limited only by what you have the cheek to ask for. After the over-statement of budgets starts spiralling upwards, the cosy little game is over.

External shareholders

Externally, you must report your activities at least once a year (and many organisations now also produce half-yearly summaries). You have to provide an independently audited statement of:

- ✔ Income and expenditure (your Profit and Loss account)
- ✔ Capital and financial structure (your Balance Sheet)

You must also deliver this information to the appropriate financial, taxation and company authorities.

Internally, plan to provide and make available *at all times* statements of progress, successes and failures. The financial implications of all statements of progress and what now happens in the company as a consequence are, after all, of vital importance to the staff. And they are of interest to everyone: customers need to know that you're viable, suppliers need to know that you're going to be around for the long term and backers want their money back!

Staff

The staff are also legitimate stakeholders. Where once staff only took interest at the time of annual bonuses or pay rises, now they're much better informed because:

- ✔ The law requires provision of financial information to staff and consultation on business strategy and practices in matters such as joint consultative committees and works' councils.

- If you don't tell staff about what is going on, they assume that you're being somehow dishonest with them – or worse.

- People are much better informed than ever before. As a result, staff are more prone to question everything around them.

- As a result of a long history of employment volatility, staff take a more active interest in where their next pay packet is coming from (or not).

So the best practice that you can adopt is to keep people fully informed. And if this isn't possible because of the culture and habits of your organisation, then at least:

- Tell no lies

- Put out what information you can

- Assume that staff will find out anyway

One of the reasons that people come to work (however much they may truly love you) is to earn a living. In days of rising prices and economic volatility and uncertainty, staff quite legitimately need to know where they stand. They also want to know about their next pay rise or bonus, why they're only getting a certain percentage increase and why this is the right amount. If you can't explain these points, prepare to watch the best of your staff start shuffling their feet and looking at what's available elsewhere.

Customers and suppliers

Reporting financial management information to customers and suppliers is about:

- Managing the information that goes out into the public domain.

- Managing any financial crises that you may have.

Customers and suppliers read the information that gets out into the public domain, the same as everyone else. So they form their own view of just how good and sound you are financially. If your customers and suppliers have any questions over your financial soundness, they're very likely to begin shuffling their feet, like staff.

Your suppliers have their own interests to guard, exactly the same as everyone else. They don't want to become one of the creditors appearing at a bankruptcy court. All responsible suppliers keep checks on their customers; they typically run credit checks on you at the outset of your relationship with them – and they take this as the start of a process, not an end in itself.

Shareholders

Shareholders have put their money into the company. They're therefore entitled to know that you're using their money to the best advantage on their behalf as well as your own. In addition to seeing annual reports and projections, your shareholders are also likely to read the papers, watch the news and financial media and log on to your website.

Your shareholders have a large range of information at their disposal, so whatever you say to them had better tie in with what they're reading.

(And if it doesn't, then you need a really good and clear explanation of the differences, and why the media has got you so wrong).

Everything happens much more quickly now than in the past. Shareholders who'd glance at share values and truly wake up only when their dividends arrived, now take a much more active and enlightened view of how much their investments are worth. And if they lose confidence in you, they'll withdraw their money like a shot!

Your customers want products and services from you in which they have full confidence. Whether it's supermarket goods, a new car or a package holiday, they expect to be able to come back to you for replacements, upgrades, after-sales, the next package – anything that they value. They therefore need to know and understand that you'll be in existence! And once they get the idea that you may not be, they'll look elsewhere.

If you think that some sector is immune to customers' information demands, recall that in recent times the public has raised questions over Arthur Andersen (accounting), Lehmann Brothers (capital finance), Northern Rock and Bradford & Bingley (retail banking). Loss of confidence can happen anywhere. So, in your case, manage it!

Assessing Returns

Part of the financial base that you need to expand, grow, consolidate and remain competitive comes from your *retained profits*, the money you keep after you meet all the obligations and commitments that I cover in all the preceding sections of this chapter.

Are the profits and surpluses that you generate sufficient to fund what you need now – or want to do in the future? To answer this question, you need a clear and informed view about the rates of return that you're generating. If these are excellent, satisfactory or adequate, then continue to do the things that generate these returns. If they're not satisfactory, then your strategy needs attention so that the finances return to a more assured base.

Chapter 9

Matching Products and Services with Your Customers and Clients

*Y*our products and services are at the centre of everything that you do. They're the main reason (some may say the *only* reason) that your organisation exists.

So you must know and understand in full detail how your products and services work in terms of:

- ✔ The value and benefits that they deliver to your customers.
- ✔ The income that they bring in for you.
- ✔ How they contribute to your company as individual products and services.
- ✔ How they contribute to your company as a whole or as a package.

In addition to knowing your products and services inside and out, you must also be extremely well versed in the behaviours and wants of your clients and customers. You're operating in a competitive world!

This chapter gets down to the nitty-gritty of choosing the products and services you offer – as well as figuring out who exactly purchases and uses your products and services.

Observing Product and Service Lifecycles

With the exception of the wheel, all products and services have finite lives. Some products and services have long lifespans; others are very short.

You never quite know what your product or service lifespan is! So always pay attention to how well individual products and services are doing.

You need to know and understand:

✔ How long the lifespans of your products or services are – or can be.

✔ Whether you can influence or extend the useful lifespans of your products and services by re-branding, re-designing or re-packaging.

✔ When you need to let go of products and services as they near the end of their lifespans – as well as when you need to kill them off.

Because products and services have different lifespans, most companies choose to provide a mix of products and services. A mix of products and services allows some ideas to come and go quickly, balanced by longer life products and services. Furthermore, a mix of products and services allows things that don't necessarily stand alone or deliver a profit on their own to contribute to the overall profitability of your business. For more on product and service mixes, see the section 'Mixing It Up: Product and Service Mixes' later in the chapter.

Products and services typically follow a series of major events, from creation to extinction. Figure 9-1 shows the product and service lifecycle.

You may be able to reinvigorate individual products and services, as well as product and *service clusters* (things that you sell together, like cars and after-sales packages), through re-design, re-packaging, re-presentation, marketing activities and promotional campaigns.

Be aware that modifications that have no value to present or potential customers may only increase your costs. For example, the manufacturer of a chocolate bar who changes its product's image with a shinier wrapper and larger, more colourful lettering may imagine that he has 're-branded' or 'repositioned' his product successfully. But sometimes sales don't change at all – because the consumer only cares about the chocolate within.

The lifecycles of products and services differ depending on whether you're looking at a generic, company-specific or specific product or service. For example:

> ✔ The car is a generic product.
>
> ✔ Nissan, Ford and Renault comprise company-specific products.
>
> ✔ The Nissan Micra, Ford Zetec and Renault Megane are individual or specific products.

Each of the preceding types of products has a different lifecycle. The lifecycle of the car is much longer than that of the companies, or their individual products.

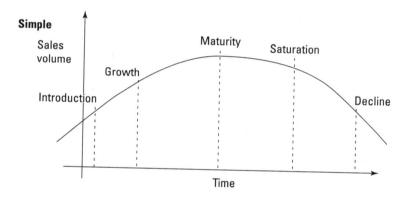

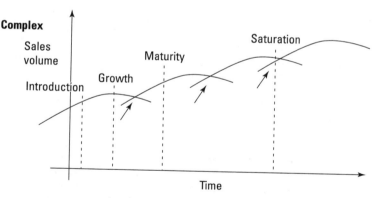

↗ Marketing efforts, strategies, campaigns

Figure 9-1: The product and service lifecycle. The model indicates the conception, growth, regeneration, renewal and extension of the effective and profitable life of particular products and services. The figure also indicates relationships with successful and effective marketing activities.

On the other hand, when car companies introduce new models, they also constantly review, upgrade and extend their product ranges. New models widen customer choice – or at least the perception of customer choice. Regenerating and rejuvenating the existing range takes place through any, or all, of the following changes:

✔ New colours or colour schemes.

✔ Extra and add-on features, such as air conditioning, satellite navigation or sunroofs.

✔ Changes to technology, such as more fuel-efficient engines or more reliable starter motors.

✔ Changes to the service package, such as assured finance plans, extended warranties or subsidised and assured upgrades to new models after a certain length of time.

Mixing It Up: Product and Service Mixes

You and your organisation are likely to offer a combination of products and services – old and new ideas, blended with creative packaging, presentation and positioning (see also Chapter 10).

In practice, most organisations serve multiple customer or client *niches* (precisely defined market sectors and segments) with specific products in their mixes. And in practice, most organisations also tweak their product and service mixes to serve each specific niche (for example, by making specific features available to different niches according to what is of value to them).

With product and service mixes, you have some important choices to make. For example:

✔ Do you offer everything under the same name, as the Virgin Group does? Or do you have different distinctive and overtly unrelated names for different products and services, as Sony does with brand names such as Aiwa, Vaio and of course Sony. (For Sony, each brand denotes different prices and perceptions of quality to target different markets.)

✔ Do you provide a full range of accessories or add-ons, as Nissan does with many of its lines? Or do you make your core products and services compatible with those of other organisations, as anyone who makes and sells DVDs does?

✔ Do you keep the full range of activities necessary to create the product or service in-house, like the traditional Japanese companies do? Or do you rely on subcontractors and outsourcing to deliver some of the products and services on which your reputation stands or falls, like the retail banking sector does?

Mastering the mix: The 80/20 rule

As applied to product and service mix strategies, the *80/20 rule* states that 80 per cent of your profits, turnover and income come from 20 per cent of your products and services. The remaining 80 per cent of your products and services exist to support the dominant 20 per cent and ensure that customers have choice. If you remove the unprofitable or not-as-profitable products and services without considering the whole, you remove the reality and perception of choice – and your customers are likely to look elsewhere, seeking out more choice.

The choice is yours! The main thing to know and understand is *why* you do things in the ways that you choose and *how* your choices can influence your business and future.

Researchers have devised several ways to describe the products and services that go into a mix. I cover two particularly useful ways in the following sections.

The Boston Matrix

The Boston Matrix is a way of classifying your products and services based on the criteria of growth and market share (see Figure 9-2). The matrix is widely attributed to Brice Henderson, at the time from Boston Consulting Group (BCG). The matrix is sometimes referred to as the Market Attractiveness or Market Strength matrix.

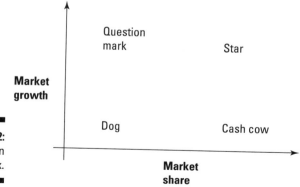

Figure 9-2: The Boston Matrix.

The Boston Matrix divides products and services into four classifications:

- ✔ **Dogs** (low share of low-growth markets): These products and services are likely to be unprofitable, ageing and 'old fashioned.' You might only keep them if they have some distinctive positive feature (for example, something on which you've built a traditional or enduring reputation without which your present reputation may be diluted).

- ✔ **Question marks** (low share of high-growth markets): The cases for these products and services, potentially tomorrow's breadwinners, are questionable or not yet proven. Not all will succeed.

- ✔ **Cash cows** (high share of low-growth markets). These products and services are your main, steady and present sources of income.

- ✔ **Stars** (high share of high-growth markets). You expect to make high profit volumes on these products and services for as long as both the high market volumes and high levels of growth persist. In other words, stars are today's and tomorrow's breadwinners from which future cash cows will emerge. Stars normally need high investment and support to maintain their position.

The Boston Matrix helps you clarify where your income and growth is coming from – and where it is *not* coming from.

After you identify where your products and services fall within the Boston Matrix, ask yourself the following key questions:

- ✔ Do you kill off dog products and services – or do these give you the reputation on which all your other products and services are so successful?

- ✔ How do you decide whether to develop your question marks?

- ✔ How long will your cash cows remain so? And how can you replace their income when they come to the end of their lives as cash cows?

- ✔ What do you do with your star products? Why are they stars – and how long will this last?

By asking these questions, you're starting a debate about everything that you do. The reason you're calling into question everything you do is because no matter how good things may be at present, your particular state of affairs can only continue if you keep paying attention to *why* you're so successful – and keep doing the things that deliver this success.

Keep accurate and current data about all your products and services – and continually ask questions about *why* they perform as they do. Also, make sure that you get full assessments of the reasons for any changes in their performance (upwards as well as downwards).

As I state several times in this book, you must evaluate fully your successes – and here I go again! Saying, 'Oh, such-and-such product or service is doing well, so no need to worry about it' is foolish. You need to know *why* something is doing so well, so that you can keep doing whatever is accounting for the success. Also, you can apply the lessons you discover to other products and services in your portfolio which may need a bit of TLC.

You must ask yourself these difficult questions, honestly and often. Numerous outside forces threaten your downfall, so you must be prepared to respond appropriately and quickly to difficult circumstances. For example, a credit squeeze, clever competitors or the emergence of a new alternative can kill off your stars and cash cows. So pay attention at all times to possible threats to your own present prosperity. See Chapter 3 for more on various competitive forces that can threaten your business.

The Ford Model

Planners at the Ford Motor Company devised the Ford Model of product classification in order to identify in detail where the company was making and losing money. The approach classifies products and services into four categories:

- ✔ Those that attract
- ✔ Those that sell
- ✔ Those that make money
- ✔ Those that lose money

Products and services can, and do, fall into more than one category. For example, Ford itself:

- ✔ Uses its sports and luxury cars to display in the showrooms and so attract buyers, but these products lose money in the showrooms because they do not sell in sufficient volumes.
- ✔ Makes mass sales of its Ka, Mondeo, Zetec and Fiesta models.
- ✔ Makes money from finance plans, service agreements and replacements and upgrades.

You can apply the Ford Model to other companies, organisations and industries. For example:

- ✔ **Ryanair** uses its low fares to attract, but it loses money on ticket sales. The company's mass sales are low fares (and not-so-low fares). It makes money on add-ons and ancillaries such as baggage charges, car hire agreements and in-flight food and drink sales; Ryanair depends on high-volume sales in each of these areas to generate overall profit volumes. Ryanair also makes money from credit card sales, late bookings and priority boarding.

✔ **Supermarket sales** aim at delivering an average *spend per checkout visit*, which requires stores to have a range of products and services available to meet these spends. The product and service mix on supermarket shelves is based on the belief that although many products indeed remain unsold, the choice that's generated results in the target spend per checkout visit. So, for example, many supermarkets lose money on newspaper and magazine sales, yet not to stock these items reduces the choice, and therefore the attractiveness, of visiting the store.

Look at your products and services in this way: classify them according to how much money they bring in (or don't); categorise your various products and services and begin to assess your business's strengths from this point of view. Be sure to pay attention to connections between products and services. For example, if Ford doesn't sell enough of its mass market cars, it also doesn't sell enough of its finance plans either, thus taking a double hit.

Considering service

When establishing the products and services you're going to provide, you also need to determine the *level of service* (the support you give to your products and services after you sell them) that you're going to offer. Pay particular attention to how much your desired level of service is going to cost in terms of money and also people, as well as how you're going to deliver this service.

Of course, you want to deliver the best possible and continuing level of service so that your customers and clients know and understand you to be a truly excellent organisation. But you also need to be realistic about:

✔ The amount of direct access to your staff and yourself that you can provide to your customers.

✔ The ways you use telephone, email, Internet and other communications options to interact with customers.

✔ Whether you contract out some – or all – of your service functions, including customer service and financial services. (Many retailers today hire outside organisations to operate shipping, returns and financing.)

✔ How you support product and service replacements.

✔ Whether you exclude any services and for what reasons.

When considering your service polices, you're really addressing customer confidence that you can:

✔ Deliver what you say you'll deliver

✔ Put right any mistakes that you make

So put yourself in the position of your customer. Decide what you would want if you were a customer, and make up your mind that this is what you're going to deliver at all times.

The Ford Model is simply another way of seeing how the mix of your products and services stacks up. What you're concentrating on with this model is where you make and lose sales, and where you make and lose money.

Pondering Quality and Value

Considering the quality and value of your products and services is part of determining your business's mix. While clients and customers expect certain qualities and values from your products and services, these terms are nevertheless very hard to define! They're almost notions in the realms of 'I don't know what quality and value are exactly, but I know them when I see them.'

Some business experts describe quality and value as different aspects of the mix of expectations that customers hold about products and services, including the prices they pay, the usefulness they gain, the presentation and packaging and the ways in which you support the products and services after you sell them.

Quality and value are reflections of the confidence that clients and customers have in your organisation's strengths and your product's usefulness (or *utility*), combined with their feelings about the prices and charges that you ask them to pay.

Within this hugely vague definition though, there are some universal expectations, as follows:

- The durability of your product or service
- The speed of access to you and your staff when things go wrong
- The contribution that your product or service makes to your customers' overall feelings of wellbeing
- The prices that you charge

In particular, the prices that you charge give a clear reflection of the quality and value that you aim to deliver. For example:

- A management consultant who charges £200 per day is known – or more importantly perceived and believed – to be not as good as one who charges £2,000 per day. And perception is likely to remain true forever, even though some consultants new to the market may charge less just in order to gain a foothold.

- Perfumes and fragrances carry high prices because their core market consists of people buying these items as gifts for loved ones. The high price tags reflect the value and esteem in which the person receiving the gift is held.

Flying short-haul club-class at British Airways

A number of branded and flag-carrying airlines provide what many consumers know, believe and perceive as high-quality, club-class service (in contrast to basic, economy service).

On its short-haul routes, British Airways offers a small number of club-class tickets. BA sells these tickets at up to ten times the price of economy tickets. (In many cases, club-class airline tickets are bought for business travellers by their companies and organisations as part of the airline's reward package.) In return for buying a club-class ticket, you receive the following benefits and values:

- Lounge facilities while you wait for the plane

- A large, extensive buffet from which you can eat as much as you like

- Hot and cold drinks (including alcoholic drinks)

- Free computer usage and Internet access

- A large range of newspapers and magazines

- A children's play area

- Seclusion from the rest of the airport

- Comfortable chairs for sitting and relaxing

After you're on the plane, club-class flyers are secluded from the rest of the passengers at the front of the plane. You receive priority boarding, a wider choice of drinks and a three-course meal. A single steward is dedicated to serving the club-class passengers only.

Interestingly, customers can fly short-haul club-class with British Airways in two ways:

- Buy a club-class ticket, which usually costs more than £500 per ticket, one way.

- Buy an economy ticket (for approximately £50) and then buy an upgrade, which usually costs about £59.

In essence, British Airways offers two very different value propositions for the same service. British Airways' strategy shows that you can offer the same quality and value for different prices, but you have to be certain that in doing so you don't dilute the value gained by one part of the operation. British Airways protects itself because businesses purchase many of the full-price club-class tickets, making this type of ticket much less of a consumer product than an economy ticket plus an upgrade.

More generally, British Airways' club-class ticket situation highlights the need to pin down the marks of differentiation that define different levels and perceptions of 'quality' and 'value' as closely as possible.

In the preceding cases, you're not only looking at value – you're also looking to deliver a value proposition. A *value proposition* is the reflection of what you deliver and how you deliver it, in the eyes of the customers as they make up their minds whether your products and services, *and the ways in which you present them*, are worth what you charge for them.

Clearly, *subjectivity* – other people's points of view, which may or may not be well informed – affects the perceived quality and value of your products and services. If you can, try to look at your products and services from the point of view of your customers and clients. Ask yourself again: 'Is my company truly delivering the kind of quality and value that I'd expect if I were a customer or client of my organisation?'

Developing New Products and Services

In order to continue to deliver high quality and good value (see the earlier section, 'Pondering Quality and Value'), you need a steady flow of new products and services. New products are essential for all companies and organisations – even ones that offer a single product or service. Bottom line is: you always need to be looking at ways of improving.

Your understanding of the market and your customers' needs and expectations is critical in developing and introducing new products. However, you must balance your new product efforts with your established business and avoid diluting your core strengths. Unfortunately, companies don't always balance these competing interests well. For example:

- ✔ The financial services and insurance industries currently have a reputation for introducing new products at rates that are more advantageous to new customers than existing customers. For example, new customers receive introductory discounts on policies and finance plans that aren't available to existing customers who renew their policies.

- ✔ Car companies introduce innovations such as sunroofs and wide windscreens which look attractive but increase the temperature inside your car when driving in sunny, hot weather.

- ✔ Confectionery companies use nuts to create new, richer chocolate mixes – but nuts cause allergic reactions in some customers.

- ✔ Publishing companies spend a lot of time, energy and money developing magazines and web publications, even though their history of success is in book publishing.

Proceeding through a process

Develop a process by which you scrutinise and evaluate every new idea, product, service and innovation *before* you go any further in its development. Consider every new enterprise from multiple points of view, including:

✔ How much the new endeavour will cost.

✔ How much you think that you can charge for the product or service.

✔ How much resource it will consume.

✔ How (if at all) it will affect your present range of activities.

After you conduct a pre-evaluation of a new service or product, you need a process that covers each of the stages of development in full detail, as Figure 9-3 shows.

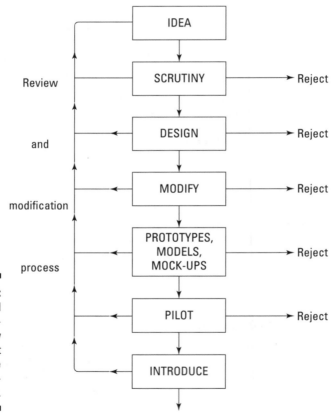

Figure 9-3:
Essential stages during new product and service development.

Regardless of the way you go about developing your new products and services, your process must be clear and specific. As Figure 9-3 shows, every stage of the process must be resourced and supported.

Stages aren't isolated events. You must tackle problems whenever they arise, and this can mean that some things may suddenly become urgent. You must have the resources and the flexibility to get involved at each stage as the need arises.

Looking for results

As Figure 9-3 shows, at each stage in the process you have to look at the results of what you've achieved so far. For example:

✔ If your product or service doesn't look quite right at the design, prototype or mock-up stages, go back to the drawing board. Keep your options open and try reworking your ideas. Eventually you must cancel the idea, decide to go with it or put it on ice. (And if you choose to let an idea sit for a while, you can always turn it over to another individual or team for further refining.)

✔ If your product or service doesn't seem ready during the market testing and piloting stage, ask yourself if you have tested it with the right set of customers. Perhaps in your eyes your prototype idea seems great but for some reason just doesn't work. Consider turning over the idea for a more detailed evaluation by your staff or (if you don't have staff) experts in the field. That way, when you choose to go ahead (or cancel or postpone), you can work from a fully informed position.

Changing your mind

Be open to changing your mind at all stages of the product or service development process. You may have to alter your views on:

✔ Whether your idea is good – or not.

✔ The costs, resources and time required to get your idea to market.

✔ Your idea's design and appearance.

✔ Where you add (or lose) some quality and value.

✔ How much time and money to spend getting a prototype fully up and running.

✔ Supply, distribution and logistics problems.

Yes, you really need to consider all the preceding – and more when developing a new product or service. Pay attention to the details of everything that can go right – as well as everything that can go wrong. You don't want to be one of the many companies and organisations that launches a new product or service with great fanfare and then lives to regret the decision.

The chances of any innovation reaching market are very slim. New ideas and proposals always flow thick and fast. So tackle everything with a large dose of realism.

Never ever commit more than you can afford to any new venture. Regardless of the thoroughness of your research and evaluation, you never quite know what's going to happen until your idea is up and running. So before you do start:

- ✔ Have a clear idea of how much you're going to lose if your idea doesn't work out.

- ✔ Estimate how much you're prepared to lose in the pursuit of trying to make your idea work.

- ✔ Refine and expand your expectations so that you look at the entire situation from both pessimistic and optimistic points of view.

You're not being the Jonah (honestly!). You're simply making sure that you cover all bases.

Getting emotional: Vance Packard

Working in the consumer boom of the 1950s, US journalist and author Vance Packard developed a rigorous and far-reaching study of new product and service development that focuses on maximising the chances of successful introductions and minimising the chances of failure. The core of Packard's work, which he explored in *The Hidden Persuaders* (Penguin, 1975), still holds good even after all these years.

According to Packard, effective products and services have to target at least one of the following human emotions:

- ✔ **Vanity and ego:** Buying things because they make you look or feel good.

- ✔ **Immortality:** Buying things because they, and by extension you, will last forever.

- ✔ **Recognition:** Buying or owning something as a way of looking good.

- ✔ **Status and exclusivity:** Buying something because you're one of the chosen few who can own it.

- **Achievement:** Buying something because what you can then do with it represents an achievement in and of itself.
- **Esteem:** Buying or owning something that makes others look up to you.

If your products or services do not press one or more of these triggers, they stand little chance of reaching the market.

Be honest with yourself! Look at the products and services that you make and sell. How many press at least one of the Packard buttons? How many of your products and services that haven't done so well also failed to press any of the Packard buttons?

Packard's work highlights the fact that organisations need to give people an active (rather than passive) reason to come to them for their products and services. See the sidebar 'Packing a Packard-style punch' for more key insights from Packard's work. So when you're planning new products and services, target your customers' humanity, their emotions and their human side – rather than their rational responses.

Packing a Packard-style punch

Examples of Vance Packard's insights into consumers' emotional responses still resonate throughout the marketplace.

For example, one of Packard's earliest and most critical findings was with cake mixes. Unilever wanted to know why its cake mix packages weren't selling. The mixes were complete; all customers had to do was add water. Packard found that customers didn't feel as if they were baking their own cakes – but rather those of Unilever! So he suggested re-designing the cake mixes so customers had to add their own eggs and thereby believe that they (and not the company) were baking the cakes.

And it worked! Unilever cake mix sales doubled in six months. Furthermore, a mix requiring eggs has become the industry standard – as well as a successful and profitable product category for more than 50 years.

Packard identified many other powerful tactics that target people's emotional rather than rational responses:

- New electronic devices such as telecommunications gadgets and computer game consoles sell out within hours of coming on to the market. Although rationally, you really should wait six months before buying these items so that glitches, teething troubles and operational quirks can be identified and ironed out, many people get into a frenzy to purchase the newest items so they can show off their purchases and claim to be one of the first to own the items.

- 'Buy two, get one free' offers give the impression of getting something for nothing, but this is hardly the case. Rarely do you consider the costs spread over the three items or consider whether you actually want three of the items.

- Slogans such as 'See how much you can save' during a retail promotion target people's influence over their finances, but what the slogan actually means is more like 'See how much you can spend'.

Whatever your line of business, never underestimate the value of being able to connect with people's emotions. After all, if everyone behaved rationally, they'd simply go for the cheapest option. And they don't! People go for what they want and then find reasons why they didn't go for the cheapest (refer to the preceding list of Packard reasons).

Getting to Know Your Customers and Clients

Being effective and competitive in delivering your products and services is knowing and understanding your customers and clients.

Even in today's information-rich world, many companies and organisations lack insight into who actually buys and consumes their products and services. Identifying and understanding your customers and clients must be a top priority. Specifically, you need to know and understand:

- ✔ Your customers' and clients' habits, needs and (especially) wants; see the following section.
- ✔ What makes them satisfied, happy, sad, angry, frustrated or contented, and thus reinforces their present habits or else causes them to change their habits.

Knowing and understanding these customer insights shapes the products and services you offer. The following sections explore various ways of getting personal with your customers and clients.

Identifying customer demands, needs and wants

You must be able to clearly pinpoint where your customers' demands, needs and wants truly lie. They may not know themselves – but you at least need to try!

Take an overall approach and try to identify the following for your customers and clients:

- ✔ **Demands:** Your customers' desire for products and services that do what they expect and more. Your customer has to have confidence in the product or service so he can say. 'I bought this from company X, and I am absolutely delighted.'

Think of the Ronseal strapline: 'It does exactly what it says on the tin.' Your customers need, want and expect that you will deliver exactly what you promise.

✔ **Needs:** Like everyone on the planet, your customers and clients only really need food, water, shelter, heating and clothing – everything else is choice. While customers' choices are limited in many cases, most make use of you only until they find an alternative for these essential items.

✔ **Wants:** This category is the nub of the whole question, so focus on your customers' wants. But what do they want? Well, they want:

- Full confidence in you and your products and services
- To know that they're getting value for money
- Good service
- An instant point of contact for redress when things go wrong

Your customers' wants are subjective. Because no crisp definition exists, you need to make your own. For example, your definition of 'good service' requires you to manage people's expectations of and confidence in you.

In order to do this, of course, you have to know your customers and what they expect from you. And how do you find out this information? You go and ask them! Then, having asked them, you put what they want together with what you think is right – and you deliver. Always!

If you don't define what you mean by good service and other customer wants, your customers don't quite know what you stand for and how you work. Eventually, they'll gravitate towards those people and organisations that do.

Characterising your customers and clients

You need to know and understand how your customers behave and what they respond to. One useful way of looking at your customers and clients is based on various types – including mercenaries, loyalists and others – as the following sections outline.

Mercenaries

Mercenaries are customers who buy purely based on price and value (see the preceding section 'Pondering Quality and Value'). Mercenaries are prepared to go from shop to shop, looking for what they consider to be the best value. To mercenaries, 'best value' is nearly always based on price or product and service certainty – or both.

Make sure that your mercenaries stay with you. Although most people aren't pure mercenaries, everyone nowadays is bombarded with messages of quality and value. You must remind your true mercenaries at all times that your prices and value are indeed excellent and exceptional – and that they'll remain exceptional. Otherwise, the mercenaries seek satisfaction elsewhere, especially from others who press the price and value buttons.

Loyalists

Loyalists are customers who choose your products and services because they have full confidence in everything you do and produce. You can further divide loyalists into:

- **Active loyalists:** People who think that your products and services are excellent, so they buy from you continually. Active loyalists include people who always buy their newspaper from the same place or go to the same bar or pub or restaurant.

- **Passive loyalists**. People who think that your products and services are excellent but rarely buy from you. (Marks & Spencer has a large passive loyalist customer base; people know and believe that M & S quality is very high, but in practice, most customers rarely use the company.)

Make sure that your loyalists are active and not passive. Active loyalists are who your livelihood depends on – not customers who think you're great but never actually use you!

Apostles

Apostles are super-loyal. They have utter faith in you and everything that you do. Having come to you either on a mercenary or loyalist basis, apostles now take everything that you do as a company as a matter of personal trust and commitment.

They also expect you to treat them as family. They expect personal responses to all requests and demands. When your business with apostles is successful, these customers are your greatest asset. They market you and sing your praises to the skies.

You'll generate this kind of loyalty in some people. But you'll also make mistakes along the way. Unfortunately, if you let down apostles, they can become terrorists (see the following section).

Guard your apostles to prevent them from becoming terrorists (see the following section). Make sure that you always treat apostles with respect and always quickly deal with apostles' complaints when they arise.

Terrorists

Terrorists are often apostles whose faith has been broken. Terrorists turn on you with all the strength they can muster. To gain revenge for their broken faith, they may:

- ✔ Complain to the papers and media
- ✔ Start 'anti-you' blogs and websites
- ✔ Go on consumer programmes such as *Watchdog*

If you find yourself faced with terrorist customers, you need to do whatever is necessary to put things right, including:

- ✔ Recognising when terrorists are indeed right and dealing with matters in full.
- ✔ Recompensing them quickly and thoroughly whenever complaints arise (apart from anything else, doing so may nip any possible serious problems in the bud).
- ✔ Addressing the media openly and completely when you have to.
- ✔ Countering any bad publicity that you experience with your own positive PR.

Passing trade

Passing trade includes customers who deal with you on the occasion during which they happen to be passing by your premises and locations. These customers thought they'd 'just call in' and see what you did and how good you were. Some organisations, such as country pubs and restaurants, some bookshops and souvenir shops, actually depend on passing trade for their livelihoods.

Passing trade now also applies to Internet browsers and surfers – customers who may just happen upon you by chance. When these individuals do just happen upon your products or services, you want them to be pleasantly surprised. See the sidebar 'Passing trade on the information superhighway' for more.

Treat passing trade as a bonus, rather than as your core customer base. Of course, doing this is not as simple as it seems.

Make sure that your presentation is first class so that when trade does pass, these customers are drawn to what you have to offer. And when people do try out your product or service, ensure that they get full satisfaction, excellent attention and a pleasant all-round experience that they remember. And finally, you must note the enduringly precarious position if you depend on passing trade for your livelihood.

Passing trade on the information superhighway

The Internet is a burgeoning source of passing trade. People who visit your website need to be instantly attracted so that they click through your various pages in order to see what you truly have to offer. People who are searching for particular products and services online (just as in real-world settings) need to be drawn in so they come back as often as possible and grow into being a substantial and regular part of your customer base.

Keep an eye on just how much business your website generates; evaluate it for hits, of course, and even more crucially, evaluate it for contacts that then lead to sales. Over time, you can come to know and understand whether your website is a generator of business, a high-tech PR tool or a part of the furniture.

In some cases, you can also translate passing trade into your loyalist or mercenary customer bases, provided you accept the limitations of the passing trade. Make sure that you do provide the products and services that your passing trade buys when it comes to you and then start to build a wider reputation for having these things at all times – so you can begin to develop a base for those who need and want them.

Competing for Customers and Clients

After you analyse your customers and clients and begin drawing accurate conclusions as to how they behave and what they value, you still have to make sure that your products and services deliver what's demanded at all times. In the process, you're going to have to compete for customers and clients.

Working with a strength – or not

To compete successfully, effectively and profitably for customers with existing rivals, competitors, substitutes and alternatives (see Chapter 3), you must have one (or more) of the following going for you:

- ✔ **Size and strength** supported by lots of capital so you can generate a substantial physical presence.

- ✔ **Brand and promotional strength** so whenever you introduce a new product or service, people quickly understand your new item and take notice.

✔ **Customer and client confidence** that your existing activities are competitive within your marketplace.

✔ **A specific value or quality proposition** that's of value to the customer base and which the other providers don't deliver.

✔ **A specific cost advantage** that allows you to offer the same product or service as your competitors – but at a greatly reduced price.

✔ **A specific quality advantage** that allows you to deliver much higher value at the same price – or much higher value for an increased price.

If you don't have any of the preceding advantages, then very likely you need to serve specific niches where you can generate a core position based on confidence, reputation, local standing or specialisation. (See Chapter 2 for more on niches.)

In many markets, many of the players have neither cost domination nor brand advantage. In these (often) large and diverse markets, you're likely to take some customers from some competitors some of the time. But your position is never as assured as when you can take a distinctive and clearly understood cost, financial, value, quality or brand strength with you into battle.

Growing your own customer base

If you're to grow your own customer base, you must have one or more of the following.

✔ A new product or service that nobody has ever thought of before.

✔ A new take on an existing product or service that delivers value to a customer base that hasn't previously used these products or services, but which may do so now.

✔ A new location for an existing product or service.

✔ Re-design, re-presentation or re-packaging of existing products and services so that they don't look like the existing products and services.

After you establish one or more of these positions, you must carry out the hard work of customer and client analyses and decide if you need to build a mercenary or a loyalist customer base. (See the earlier section 'Getting to Know Your Customers and Clients'.)

You must be as certain as you can of everything before you make an investment or commitment to grow your own customer base. For instance, you must determine whether your new customer base (which has never existed before) is truly going to be big enough and last long enough to support profitable activities in the future.

You also need to be satisfied that *you* are the right company or organisation to serve this newly identified customer base. Many companies identify new markets, only to realise that they can't exploit them. For example:

- ✔ The big UK supermarket chains have many value lines, but they have had to leave the low-cost end of the market to niche providers such as Aldi and Lidl.

- ✔ British Airways initially refused to accept the Ryanair/easyJet proposition that low-cost air travel was feasible. When British Airways eventually decided to start its own low-price airline, Go, the enterprise failed.

Even if you do generate a whole new customer base, realise that:

- ✔ Others will try to get into your new market.

- ✔ Others will take your product and service as their starting point – and try to add their own distinctive mark or value.

- ✔ Companies with their own strong cost or brand advantages will use these strengths to try and drive you out of your new market.

Chapter 10

Putting Your Competition in Context

In This Chapter

▶ Seeing and assessing opportunities

▶ Minimising constraints to maximise your chances of success

▶ Knowing your competitive environment

▶ Staying competitive

This chapter brings together many of the elements I discuss in Parts II and III, in order to show how to increase your chances of successful and enduringly profitable activities.

So you need to be clear as to where your organisational and operational strengths and weaknesses lie (see Chapters 2 and 3), where your strategic and competitive preferences lie (Chapter 4) and why you've decided to go ahead with your project or investment. This clarity gives you collective and individual confidence – confidence that you're going into business and presuming success and profitability.

Unfortunately, too many business decisions aren't clear or rational. Many companies, organisations and managers do things for reasons that have only a passing relationship with what anyone is actually good at – or what they ought to be doing in the name of producing and delivering excellent products and services.

Whatever you set out to achieve, you must be clear about some key factors, the *context*, of your decisions:

✔ The opportunities that are certain to come your way

✔ The constraints within which you'll have to work and operate

✔ The nature of your competitive environment

✔ The nature of competition in your sector

As long as you have these clear in your mind, you can proceed with assurance and certainty because I explore each of these key factors in the following sections.

Spotting Opportunities

Opportunities are only opportunities if you think that they're opportunities! Markets always have gaps, such as a lack of a luxury brand or a lack of a good-value alternative. These gaps suggest that something can fill them, and whatever you fill them with is an opportunity.

Yet so many gaps remain untackled, left to others to fill because identifying and taking advantage of opportunities is largely subjective. After all, gaps exist only if you think they do and can then produce a line of reasoning to support your supposition. Two companies may look at the same scenario; one sees the opportunity and the possibilities, while the other sees only the risks and the pitfalls. And both can be right!

Companies and those responsible for strategy and direction must identify gaps as opportunities and then be willing and prepared to put in the hard work to turn the opportunities to their commercial and competitive advantage – topics I examine in the following sections.

Distinguishing between opportunities and non-opportunities

Knowing whether something is an opportunity when it presents itself is a talent that's born of hard work, expertise, enthusiasm and collective and individual commitment to an organisation, its products and services. Identifying opportunities is about:

- ✔ Seeing and assessing the potential for delivering something you're already good at to other markets and locations, or in different ways.

- ✔ Seeing and assessing prospects for new inventions and ventures – then going successfully into the unknown.

If you do go into the unknown, your first duty is to find out as much as you can. Duncan Bannatyne (founder of a fitness club chain, provider of residential facilities for the disabled and a major figure on the BBC's 'Dragons' Den') says that he's always staggered by the number of people who come to him and ask him to invest in them – with ideas that they know nothing about and often haven't even bothered to research! So when encountering something that you think is a good idea, research, research and research it again – before committing the organisation, or its backers, to anything more.

Seeing

Seeing opportunities comes as a result of a pioneering leader's expertise. Your expertise comes from your ability to master a brief quickly and comprehensively (see Chapter 4). You need to gather enough knowledge and understanding of the operating environment overall so that you can spot opportunities at the earliest possible stage, without necessarily having full or perfect knowledge of a given situation, product or service.

Assessing

Whatever the opportunity, you must find out as much as you possibly can. You have to look hard at what you now know and then realistically assess whether you're looking at an opportunity or not. See the sidebar 'The Seattle Coffee Company' for a closer look at this process.

The Seattle Coffee Company

Two American expatriates, Don and Ann Ryder, founded the Seattle Coffee Company in London. They started their company because they saw what they perceived to be a gap in the London market. Unlike the Ryders' experiences in the US, Londoners had nowhere to buy good quality coffee and other refreshments that could be taken away or enjoyed in a comfortable, inviting environment. In fact, matters came to a head when Ann tried to buy coffee on her way to her job in London and had to persuade the shop owner to provide her with a polystyrene cup so she could take her drink with her.

The Ryders researched what they perceived to be an opportunity and concluded that a gap did indeed exist in the market. However, they had to make further assessments to determine whether this gap needed filling or could be filled on a commercial basis. The Ryders gathered evidence from fast food chains, railway catering facilities, small independent operators and department store restaurants, as well as trying out the idea on opinion groups. Evidence from

their research demonstrated that the identified gap could be commercially filled, and the Ryders decided to go ahead with their business idea.

They opened their first shop in London in 1993; and in Don's words, 'It worked in five minutes.' Londoners indeed found that this type of coffee-drinking experience was of value to them – an experience for which they were prepared to pay. The Ryders subsequently opened a further fourteen shops in London and elsewhere in England; and they sold out to Starbucks in 2001 for £30 million.

Here's the main lesson from the Ryders' success: always be prepared to do the work to back your judgement. The Ryders were prepared to see more than just the gap, which may have been no more than the inability to buy a coffee on the way to work. They were willing to put in the hard work to prove or strongly indicate that the gap existed and it could be profitably filled.

You're likely to commit a lot of time and energy to the process of identifying opportunities. You may have fired up everyone for the opportunity. The pressure to go along with things can be overwhelming, but you still need to know in detail what you are or may be letting yourself in for.

Taking a critical eye to an opportunity can be challenging – especially when an expensive, 'expert' consultant identifies the opportunity. Regardless of a consultant's bill for services, *you* still must be capable and expert enough to do your own evaluation of the opportunity. You don't want to be led into expensive and damaging ventures just because the groundwork carried a high charge.

Taking advantage of opportunities

Taking advantage of opportunities that present themselves requires hard and expert work. Nothing else does the job. Nothing is going to come to fruition unless you're prepared to do whatever's necessary to give it life and make it happen.

Your hard and expert work includes thoroughly understanding:

- ✔ The products or services you're proposing
- ✔ The locations and markets you're considering
- ✔ The financing required
- ✔ The customers and clients you're targeting
- ✔ The history of similar ventures elsewhere and by others

You must be capable and willing to do this hard work. Failure to know each of these aspects of opportunity means that you're guessing at the potential and the likely range of outcomes.

In his best-selling book *In Search of Excellence,* Tom Peters (see Chapter 18) highlights the challenges facing new ventures. 'If you were a rational thinker, you would never start', Peters says. 'The chances of a new product or service making it to market are zilch. This is made worse by the fact that the best ideas come from the wrong people in the wrong place at the wrong time in the wrong jobs in the wrong locations.' Clearly, you're up against major hurdles when identifying, assessing and taking on new opportunities. You must be prepared to tackle all these challenges if you want to market new ideas successfully.

Knowing your position

Another important aspect of identifying and assessing opportunities is determining what _position_ you're in to enter into a location or market.

The following sections cover the advantages and disadvantages of various positions – being first, second and later to take advantage of an opportunity.

First mover

The advantage of being first mover is that you're the first! The field, location or category is open to you. Providing that you do all the groundwork that you can, you have a major opportunity to corner the market before others wake up to what you're doing. So recognise the following:

- ✔ If you're successful, you're going to earn the recognition and standing that you quite rightly deserve! You put in the hard work, and now you're to gain the rewards.

- ✔ If you make mistakes or have not got things quite right, others who follow your lead are likely to see and right your errors, enabling them to steal a march on you.

Even if you do most things right most of the time, others' speedy response may mean that you have the field to yourself only for a limited time. You must make things count as quickly as you can.

Second mover

You can gain second-mover advantage if you're prepared to hold your actions, while at the same time closely observing the progress of the pioneer.

Evaluate everything that the pioneer has done and is doing, recognising and respecting the pioneer's successes and strengths – but at the same time assessing everything in terms of mistakes the pioneer's made and improvements you can make.

Late mover

If you choose to enter things late, you have the great opportunity of coming in having learned from the mistakes of everyone who jumped the gun or who followed the paths of the pioneers.

You can, for example, see the effectiveness of technology, the realities of profits, the shortcomings of how others are doing things. You can use everyone else's previous experiences to your advantage. See the sidebar 'Lots of java in London' for some examples.

Lots of java in London

When Starbucks opened its first coffee bars in London in 1998, it developed a trend started by the Seattle Coffee Company (see the sidebar 'The Seattle Coffee Company') – and an extremely profitable industry! Many others were attracted to come into the sector, including small independents and chains such as Caffe Nero, Coffee Republic and Costa Coffee.

All these companies started to compete for shop space, street presence and customers. It quickly became apparent to all the companies that in terms of the market size, volume and profitability, there was one chain too many. And so they all worked very hard to make sure theirs was one of the chains left standing!

The wisdom was, and remains, that Starbucks (the first mover) would survive, along with two others. One of the later movers – Caffe Nero, Coffee Republic and Costa Coffee – was going to be driven out. Thus the later movers were competing with each other for survival, not just customers.

And there the story rests – for the moment at least! But the core problem of who is going to survive and who isn't has not gone away!

On the other hand you may be too late! You need to have a fully informed view of whether you can satisfy your demands in the market and further (and profitably) develop the market.

If you don't jump into a market, you can still be an interested onlooker. From your sideline position, you can always choose to become involved if you see an opportunity as the market develops. Yes, you may come late to the party and miss out on first- and second-mover advantages (see the preceding sections), but you may be able to buy up one of the existing, struggling players at a good price, potentially gaining profitable business without having had to do any groundwork. Morrisons, the UK northern regional supermarket chain, was such a company. It bought up Safeway and found itself suddenly a national player with 10 per cent of the UK grocery market!

Considering Constraints

Whatever you go into or decide to do, you encounter constraints. *Constraints* are limiting factors that can pop up in various areas of business including your physical, economic and competitive environments.

✔ **Specific constraints in your physical environment** include questions of accessibility and convenience for your suppliers, customers and clients; traffic bottlenecks; speed of turnaround and processing times for products, services, data and information; supply of components and raw materials; energy supplies and assurance of supplies; the ability to attract and retain staff; staff access to the work premises (especially if your staff commute).

✔ **Specific constraints in your economic environment** include cash flow; support for organisation finances; profitability of products and services, individually as well as by groupings, clusters (such as bread, butter and jam) and overall. As we discuss in Chapters 6 and 9, organisations need to know which products bring in the highest and lowest levels of value.

✔ **Specific constraints in your competitive environment** include the nature of your competitors' and rivals' operations; the things that your competitors do better than you (your rivals always do something better than you, so be honest!); the things that you do better than your rivals; the strength and priority of price wars and marketing campaigns.

Simply recognising constraints is probably the most important thing about them. When you're assessing specific ideas, ventures and proposals, take the time to look for all constraints that are bound to be present. Refer to the preceding bullets to see that you've considered all the areas of possible restraint. I provide full details on environmental scanning and evaluation in Chapter 6.

Moving before others do: When to cut and run

The pace of change seems forever to be accelerating. Even the best-laid plans may disappoint because too many others have recognised the same (or a similar) opportunity at around the same time as you.

The consequences of such crowd behaviour were severe during the 1996–2000 Internet bubble, and may be re-occurring with some Net-based social networks currently. With so many companies crowding into the market niche at the same time, no one (or almost no one) survives. At the very least, market share projections become rubbish, as five or ten times

the number of expected competitors are in the market!

The answer? Move out first, even if doing so means leaving some money on the table. In Dallas, Texas, Mark Cuban sold his Internet company, Broadcast.com, a couple of years before the bubble burst and is still a billionaire. By contrast, the company that sticks with terrestrial stores in fields that are rapidly becoming 'all-Net' (DVD and music sales, travel) only has itself to blame when it finds that it has held on to an obsolete business model for too long.

Avoiding constraints

You can only avoid a constraint after you acknowledge that it exists and identify the influence that the constraint has on your activities and those of your rivals and competitors. If you don't fully understand a constraint or aren't prepared to acknowledge its influence on your business, you're going to lose at least a part of your competitive edge.

For example, if you need to take on extra staff in order to meet your obligations, you must either accept the cost of the new people or else change your obligations. Nothing else will do – no third way exists! And yet, people still try to find a third way, and in the process get mired in projections and technology-driven alternatives – anything but concentrating on the core matter.

Turning constraints to your advantage

After you acknowledge your constraints you can, in many cases, turn them to your advantage. For example:

- ✔ **If, because of your location, you have a struggle to recruit people to come and work for you,** turn this situation to your advantage by offering flexible hours of work and times that may suit a wider section of the population.

- ✔ **If your customers complain about delivery delays for your products or services,** turn this to your advantage by offering heavy discounts on repeat orders after you've sorted out the complaint. You can then include the heavy discounts in your pricing for this repeat business.

- ✔ **If your suppliers have problems getting supplies to you because of traffic bottlenecks,** arrange with them to deliver at quiet times (late evening or even overnight). They may not want to make deliveries at these times, so you must offer incentives that include a cash advantage (which you can sustain because you now have better assurance of supply) or some sort of longer-term contract.

Being able to operate within constraints is a fact of organisational life. Being able to turn constraints to your advantage is a fundamental part of strategic management and is likely to add to your competitive edge.

Of course, as with everything to do with competitive corporate strategy, your edge may not last very long. As soon as your competitors and rivals see what you're doing, they'll follow your lead and do their best to do what you're doing – or do it even better than you. But this process is what being competitive and remaining competitive is all about. Think of dealing with constraints as part of a process and not an end in itself.

Getting Comfortable with Your Competitive Environment

Being able to identify and evaluate opportunities effectively comes from knowing and understanding your environment (see Chapter 4) and the companies and organisations you compete against (check out Chapter 6 for more on this).

Having a thorough knowledge of your environment and competitors helps you typically to see and anticipate competitive decisions that you and your competitors are likely to make.

Being comfortable with your competitive environment means knowing and understanding how it works, and the likely, possible and potential actions available to your competitors and which they may take. When you know your competitive environment, you can answer the following questions (and many, many more):

- If you or your competitor starts a price war, how are your customers likely to react? What is the likelihood of them going to whichever business offers the lowest price?

- By how much must you lower your prices to make a significant impact on customer behaviour?

- Do people really change their habits for the sake of a small saving? (And if the answer is yes, will they continue with you if the prices go back up again?)

 Have responses available and ready for the preceding competitive situations. That way, when another organisation takes competitive actions against you, you have actions of your own to implement. For example, if a competitor brings down its prices, you can be ready with things like your own 3-for-2 offers, after-sales packages or warranties when required.

Succeeding, Failing and the Bits in Between: The Nature of Competition

Your stakeholders – everyone who has an interest or a stake in what you do and what you set out to achieve for them, regardless of whether you deliver – measure and evaluate your success and failure. Specifically:

✔ Your backers expect the returns that you promise them.

✔ Your customers and clients expect the products and services that you make available.

✔ Your staff expect good wages and salaries, a good quality of working life and opportunities to progress within the organisation.

✔ You personally may expect to achieve recognition, a good reputation and positive press coverage and publicity.

You can only realise all these expectations if the conditions in your market or operating environment and your organisation itself are capable of delivering, and willing to deliver, on your expectations. Otherwise, you have to answer to your own colleagues, directors and senior managers.

The following sections explore your possible outcomes: success, failure and something in between.

Dealing with success

Even if you're clear about what you set out to achieve – and you achieve it – you can still run into trouble.

There's a Chinese proverb which states, 'Beware of what you wish for; your wishes may be granted.' Many people create and implement competitive strategies very successfully from the point of view that their organisations achieve what they set out to achieve. Successfully meeting a competitive strategy may create problems for yourself and for others:

✔ **You may be holding up a mirror to the past failings and shortcomings of others.** The fact that you made something work may cause resentment among others who tried to do something similar and failed.

✔ **You may attempt to prove someone wrong.** You know the sort of thing: 'Let her run with it, she'll fail and then we can get rid of her.' Only she succeeds – and then what do you do?

✔ **You may be defying the norms of the industry, location or sector.** If you're in a sector that has established time and cost bases, you can't wish these away.

You cannot make a baby in one month by working nine times as hard!

✔ **You may have set standards that you now need to live up to.**

You can only measure success against what you set out to achieve. Success is ultimately both subjective and a value judgement. Additionally, measures of success and failure change as circumstances change.

Learning from setbacks and improving

And what about failure? It does, after all, happen to everyone, and you have to be prepared for it.

The most important thing with all failures is that you learn from them. You need to evaluate where and why things went wrong, and then make known the findings so that:

- Everyone knows and understands where and why things didn't work out.
- You do your best not to make the same mistakes again.

You may have to face the fact that failures occurred because you didn't understand what you were committing yourself and the organisation to or the extent of resources required for the venture. If this is the case, you need to learn these lessons collectively and individually.

You may also have to face the fact that some failures are caused by collective and individual negligence, incompetence, complacency and vanity. If any of these problems caused your failure, you need a collective and individual will to change these attitudes so that you remove them. No organisation can continue to sustain failures due to these factors. You must get to the heart of *why* you implemented a poorly thought-through strategy or vanity project. You can only begin to do this after everyone agrees why the previous failure came about.

When dealing with individuals responsible for these types of failure, you must firmly and unambiguously reassign vain, complacent and negligent individuals to other duties. (The same goes for the incompetent unless they learn very quickly.)

In practice, many organisations aren't willing or able to assign responsibility for failed vanity projects to specific groups or individuals. Instead, many prefer (and certainly feel more comfortable) to put down such failures to:

- Adverse market conditions
- Difficult trading conditions
- An uncertain environment
- The war in Iraq
- Bad English weather
- The strength/weakness of the Euro
- Cheap Chinese labour

Placing significant blame on any of the preceding factors ought to be unacceptable. After all, everyone's already heard of each of the above and any top organisational leader already knows that each of the preceding does or can exist. Any leader worth her salt should have been ready to implement strategies and responses to these potential threats.

If your company or organisation blames its misfortunes on any of the preceding, challenge the findings (in public if you can, in private you must). Go through what went wrong yourself. Establish where mistakes were made. Identify assumptions that were wrong or not tested. With this type of analysis, you can significantly diminish the amount of unjustified blame.

Although everyone does make mistakes, you need to try and do everything as right as possible, as often as possible. If you're effectively creating competitive strategy, you can expect to make fewer and fewer mistakes the more you use and develop your expertise.

Dwelling between success and failure

Between success and failure lies a multitude of sins, errors and omissions! Arriving and remaining somewhere between success and failure is the actual aspiration of many organisations and their managers, reflecting the comfort zone of many managers (and indeed many organisations).

It reflects also what many managers gain their greatest (or at least most assured) rewards for achieving – steady and satisfactory performance, getting most things right most of the time. Many corporate cultures don't, in practice, reward excellent performance, so satisfactory performance becomes a great strength and an aspiration in itself.

In many organisations, a quest for mediocrity becomes the primary strategic drive, supported by corporate cultural notions such as:

✔ Even if you haven't fully succeeded, at least you haven't failed. So you can't be called to account for failure or be blamed for something that hasn't happened.

✔ As long as the organisation is making more money than it spends (a profit), you can concentrate on doing those things that you're good at and being rewarded for them.

- What gets measured gets done – which tends to be reflected in a simple rather than complex set of performance measures and aspirations. (Often the focus is on satisfying shareholder interests rather than all stakeholders.)

- The organisation claims to have a 'good year' when it describes most performances as 'not too bad' or 'no worse than anyone else's.'

If you want to change a situation where these collectively mediocre attitudes about performance, strategy and competitiveness exist, you have to be prepared to engage with all aspects of the organisation. Your journey is going to be long, and you're certain to encounter resistance along the way. In many cases, you'll be asked to leave. In order to succeed, you must have clear thinking, strategic and competitive expertise and organisational and market knowledge and understanding. (Thankfully, all topics I cover in this book!)

Whatever your level of performance, you have to change and develop all the time. Things that are pioneering today become tomorrow's mainstream and then passé and obsolete shortly afterwards. For this reason, you can only sustain something that's adequate or satisfactory in the very short term. For all organisations and their leaders, the message is clear: change or die.

When satisfactory is your best

US psychologist Herbert Simon coined the word 'satisficing' in an effort to describe the performance that organisations most often achieve in practice. Simon contended that at one extreme was excellent performance, which very few people achieve, and at the other extreme was unsatisfactory or unacceptable performance, which organisations can't sustain if they want to survive.

In between these extremes, Simon saw a performance level that was at least satisfactory; and this he called *satisficing*, or 'the practice of delivering enduring satisfactory performance.'

The drive for satisfactory performance is neither necessarily wrong nor unacceptable. Indeed, satisfactory performance may be the only thing that an organisation is capable of, and it may be the only thing that the present management or collective culture is capable of delivering.

Sometimes, encouraging people to think more deeply about how to develop the organisation is both traumatic and also unproductive. At such a point, you need to take a more pragmatic view of your drive for performance improvement. After consideration, the best that you can achieve from people, at least for the present, may be something that's merely satisfactory – and this is in many cases the main lesson to take away from Simon's work.

Part IV
Enhancing Your Competitive Strategy

In this part . . .

Progress is great, but making and sustaining it within your organisation is even better. I investigate changing needs and wants and how your organisation needs to and can develop and evolve in order to be competitive. I also explore important ongoing efforts, including effectively managing risk and setting and maintaining standards of work and behaviour.

Chapter 11

Pulling Together a Comprehensive Strategic Plan

*N*othing I cover in Parts I, II and III is of any use or value if you can't put the various strategies and suggestions together into a practical plan.

So that's exactly the purpose of this chapter: to make sure that you can translate the ideas in the book into something that's valuable, worthwhile, achievable and ultimately profitable.

I first show you how to combine your understanding of activities, values and barriers into a comprehensive strategic plan. Then I offer advice on how to really live your plan – allocating resources, evaluating outcomes and reviewing progress.

Assessing Activities

The first step in pulling together your strategic plan is to assess all the activities that you propose to undertake in the pursuit of what you've chosen to do in pursuit of your strategic goals. Assessing activities means you look at:

- ✔ **Primary activities,** those involved in making and delivering your products and services.

- ✔ **Support activities,** especially administration, financial and human resource management.

- ✔ **Consequent activities,** especially marketing and advertising; and also maintenance of equipment.

- ✔ **Legal activities,** including financial, industrial and operational compliance.

Your assessments form the basis for everything that your organisation or company does now and in the future, including:

- ✔ The size, strength and status of the organisation itself.

- ✔ The primary purposes that your organisation serves.

- ✔ The ways in which you organise the work that your organisation carries out.

- ✔ The ways in which you divide up the work of various departments, divisions and functions, as well as the priorities and procedures you establish.

- ✔ How you're going to create and deliver rewarding and interesting jobs and work for your staff.

- ✔ The kinds of people that you're going to find and hire to work for you.

- ✔ The range of technology and equipment you're going to need.

- ✔ The premises, buildings and locations in which you're going to work.

- ✔ How you're going to meet and deliver your legal obligations such as reporting accounts and keeping track of sales, pay roll, purchase orders, profits, losses, income and expenditure.

- ✔ How you're going to pay for all this! Regardless of whether you're starting up a new business or continuing an existing one, you're going to have to spend some money.

- ✔ How you'll deliver and assess your future results.

Base your assessment of activities on knowing and understanding what your organisation is capable of and is willing to do. You do this by establishing which customer bases your company serves when it delivers products and services (see Chapters 2 and 3). You then use your knowledge of customers, products and services to create the sort of organisation required to do so effectively and profitably.

This capability and willingness must be disciplined and harnessed to ensure that you:

- ✔ Optimise cost effectiveness and cost efficiencies.
- ✔ Allocate resources that best address your priorities.
- ✔ Provide everyone with the facilities, tools and technology they need.
- ✔ Promote good working relationships through effective communication.

Monitoring Value

In order to remain competitive, you need to look at your strategic planning constantly in terms of where you and your organisation are gaining and losing value (see also Chapter 9).

Identifying value gains and losses is sometimes very clear. For example, paying attention to cost efficiency and inefficiency points you towards areas where you're gaining or losing value. Then concentrate on activities that add value to what you do and remove or minimise those activities that are losing value.

Beyond cost efficiency, you have several things to consider in terms of adding and losing value, which I now cover in the following sections.

Adding value

Value does not always refer to financial matters only. (Although one test of whether an action is valuable is whether it increases the company's financial value.) Broadly, you add value when any activities bring benefits to your customers and clients. Specific aspects of your business to look at for adding value include:

- ✔ **The quality that you produce and deliver.** Quality is a reflection of design and appearance. Quality products and services deliver benefits to your customers and clients – benefits for which they're prepared to pay the prices that you charge.

- ✔ **The volumes that you produce and deliver.** Are you producing enough products and services to satisfy demand? Answering this question isn't as simple as it may seem. If you make too high a volume available, you lose exclusivity. If you make too little available, people may turn away from you altogether.

✔ **The convenience of access of your products and services.** As with volume, you have to strike a balance. Make things too easily accessible, and they become a mass commodity; make things too exclusive, and people look elsewhere.

✔ **The expectations of clients and customers.** You must meet people's habits and expectations, so you have to know in detail what these are. In general, meeting expectations means:

- Having both an online and physical presence.

- Offering multiple points of contact where customers and clients can buy your products and services.

- Providing ways for people to contact you for maintenance, upgrades, repeat purchases and (though you hope not) complaints and problems.

✔ **The amount of time that people are prepared to wait for your products and services.** In general, people want your products and services instantly, or they want to be given a specific date on which they can have them. Whichever time frame you establish, your customers and clients expect you to deliver on the date you've promised. See the sidebar 'Toying with time' for more ideas on important aspects of value assessment.

Losing value

Where and how you add value is fairly straightforward – you just need to identify where you're adding value and see that you continue to do so or improve on the value you're already adding.

If you don't attend to identifying and promoting opportunities where you're adding value, you lose value – which means eventually that you lose customers and clients. And when you lose customers and clients, you lose money.

You lose value – and customers and money – when any or all the following happen regularly:

✔ You keep people hanging on the phone or waiting at checkouts for too long.

✔ You can't connect people to the right person on the phone or the customer can't find the right contact through the Internet.

✔ You have constant hold-ups on the supply and distribution sides, with your goods and services arriving late for your customers as the result.

✔ Your technology – including production and service delivery technology, as well as administrative and information systems – is unreliable.

Everyone hates complicated electronic telephone systems (at the end of which you have to hang on for ages before speaking to an actual human). The same goes for staff who blame the computer for failure to deliver goods and services. So be very careful if either of these are commonplace in your organisation. Customers and clients only put up with these inconveniences if some benefit outweighs them (or if you have a captive market). Rest assured that people will turn away from you and towards those who provide a known and perceived better service.

You also lose value (and therefore customers and clients) if your staff:

- ✔ Are poorly trained
- ✔ Don't know or understand the products and services that you deliver
- ✔ Exhibit bad, slapdash or 'don't care' attitudes

Make sure that your staff know and understand the standards to which they're required to perform – and make sure that you enforce these standards through HR and staff management policies.

Toying with time

People need to know where they stand. Customers and clients can be quite happy to fit in with your time frames providing that you do what you say you'll do.

Look at the successes of companies that keep their word and meet expectations:

- ✔ **Tesco.com:** The Internet grocery service provided by Tesco gives a time frame of one hour in which your groceries will be delivered. If Tesco fails to meet this, it notifies you in advance, or it pays a refund. This policy assures customers that they'll have their groceries when they need and want them, as well as the fact that Tesco doesn't completely disrupt its customers' lives in order to deliver purchases.

- ✔ **Ikea:** Ikea normally gives a time frame of three hours in which it delivers purchased furniture. Ikea offers no refund if it fails to meet this delivery promise, but the company does undertake to notify you of any

delays or changes in delivery schedules. Additionally, as furniture is a *considered* (or at least semi-considered) purchase – one that you think about a bit before actually buying – Ikea can easily and legitimately manage customers' perceptions so they accept deliveries within a wider time frame.

By contrast, consider the reputations of those organisations that don't effectively manage their time-related expectations. Everyone has stories of having to wait in for gas, electricity and water companies to turn up and deliver services. These companies give a time frame of 4–6 hours, or they expect people to wait in all day for them. And frequently, the company doesn't turn up. You've ended up taking off the day from work – and everyone is frustrated and very angry. No organisation wants a reputation like that, so make sure that you never keep people waiting like this!

Noting (and Overcoming) Barriers and Blockages

In addition to assessing activities and value as part of your overall competitive strategy, you must also look at the hurdles – the barriers and blockages – that you must tackle and overcome in order to be as effective as you possibly can be.

Busting the barriers to entry

Barriers to entry or to beginning certain activities exist, and you have to overcome them whenever you consider new ventures. See the sidebar 'Barrier busters!' for some notable examples of organisations and individuals who surmounted major entry barriers.

Look for entry barriers in all the following areas:

- ✔ **Cost:** These include start-up costs, the costs of sustaining and developing your activities and any required maintenance activities. You're also certain to need contingency funds available to meet surprise expenses that you genuinely couldn't have foreseen.

- ✔ **Reputation:** In addition to your own reputation, you must consider the reputations of those already in the sector you're targeting. If the established organisations have good and high reputations, you need to spend time and resources persuading satisfied customers and clients to switch to you.

- ✔ **Capital:** If you're going into activities that require high levels of capital outlay, you need to have a clear view of how long it'll take to recover your money, how much you need to pay to underwrite your activities and the effects of anything that may go wrong along the way.

- ✔ **Distribution channels:** Do you have access to distribution channels – or do you need to create your own? And if channels do already exist, can you make use of the same opportunities as existing players – or do you have to pay for access anyway?

Distribution can be a major barrier. You must follow a detailed line of investigation to find out who really controls distribution. Established influential players are likely to see you coming from a very early stage; and they may do everything in their power to prevent you gaining access to these channels.

Barrier busters!

If you're facing high barriers to entry and commencement, you must have a strategic approach to overcoming them. And even then, you may need a large measure of luck if you're to be successful. For example:

↙ **The Beatles:** The Beatles were turned down by 23 record companies before being signed up to Parlophone, a division of EMI, in 1961. The reason that they were turned down by so many was due to the huge proliferation of 'beat groups' (which the Beatles were not, but their name confused matters). Consequently, one of the group's particular barriers was that nobody was able to listen to them properly. In particular, one record company told them that 'the era of beat groups was coming to an end.'

↙ **Harry Potter:** The Harry Potter stories of J.K. Rowling were turned down by 14 publishers before being accepted by Bloomsbury.

The reason – the barrier – was that publishers receive so many unsolicited manuscripts that most of them aren't properly scrutinised.

↙ **Roots Sauces:** For many years, Henry Wood produced Roots Sauces (savoury sauces for adding to meat dishes) in his mother's kitchen. He had tried to commercialise them but had failed because he could not assure the volumes of production required by large supermarket chains; and small volumes of production simply meant that his products would be yet another marginal product in the already saturated food sauces market. Henry Wood was able to overcome this barrier by gaining television coverage on 'The Dragons' Den' (the BBC entrepreneurial ideas show), and by securing backing from the Peter Jones organisation, a major business 'angel' organisation.

By considering barriers, you take a pragmatic and informed view of what a specific market or sector requires of you in order to get in and develop a presence. If the barriers to entry are high (getting into the sector is both difficult and expensive), you may still choose to go ahead – but you must do so with your eyes open.

Breaking through blockages

Blockages occur in all organisations. Blockages are the points where work piles up, delays occur and you fail to deliver products and services at the speed required and demanded. Whenever blockages occur, they always reduce your effectiveness, and consequently your competitiveness. You must therefore look at where and why these hold-ups and delays occur – and what you can do about them.

Exit barriers

Getting into some activities and gaining a presence in some markets can be expensive – and so can getting out of certain activities. Whatever your business, industry or sector, make sure that you don't enter into something without knowing and understanding the consequences of things going wrong.

Exit barriers that you need especially to be aware of include:

✔ **Write-offs:** If you made a mistake and need to get out of something, you must have an informed view about what to do with the capital and resource you outlaid. Can you re-deploy them elsewhere? Or do you have to write them off completely? You may have to consider any move into new sectors as sunk costs rather than capital with an expected return.

✔ **Reputation:** If you have to come out of a sector, activity or location, you must consider the effects on your reputation. Is leaving one area going to harm your activities elsewhere? Will people start to question the whole of your activities just because you made a single mistake? Can you sustain your overall reputation, even if some activities go wrong?

Your answers in both of the preceding areas are matters of your individual expertise and informed judgement related to your unique circumstances. However, you don't want to destroy an enduringly profitable and successful business simply because you fouled up in one area. Just remember that all companies and organisations need to make progress – and many have made, and continue to make, mistakes along the way.

Before you bust up blockages, however, you need to make up your mind that you're going to take a fully informed view – indeed a strategic view! You don't simply want to move problems in one area by resolving one issue in isolation from the rest of your activities, only to introduce new blockages elsewhere.

Managing your competitive strategy and edge involves looking at the operational factors that deliver your products, services, administration and support, seeing where things are going wrong, and considering what can and needs to be done to put them right. In order to do this, you need to know and understand everything that goes on in your organisation and your domain.

What happens in individual organisations clearly varies, but areas that are particularly prone to blockages include:

✔ **Supply side:** These blockages include delays in the supply of components for manufacturing processes. Particularly when you have *just-in-time deliveries* (small volumes of components delivered on a regular basis) you must ensure that the vagaries of transport and distribution networks don't negatively affect your ability to operate.

Supply side blockages also include hold-ups in data processing caused by delays in access to databases or other technologies (which is often part of a capacity problem). Furthermore, you don't want to be held up by crashes and shutdowns in any of your data sources.

✔ **Distribution:** Delays occur, and you lose both sales and reputation if your distribution channels are inadequate and you can't deliver your products and services to customers and clients quickly enough. Distribution blockages include physical outlets and also your Internet and technological presence and capacity. (You especially don't want to become one of the all-too-many organisations whose website crashes as the direct result of people wanting to use it and buy from it!)

✔ **Maintenance:** You don't want to lose customers, clients, production and reputation as the result of having to take time out to maintain and upgrade your facilities.

✔ **Support functions:** If you have hold-ups in processing your invoices, you're losing cash flow and finances, and therefore affecting your overall competitiveness. You need to gather what you're owed as quickly as you can – not to do so effectively means that you're subsidising your customers.

One school of thought states that while indeed you should get your payments in as soon as possible, you should nevertheless pay out as slowly as you can. This is good practice, but you must never default on, or delay payments out for reasons of expediency. Nor should you breach contracts on the supply side. To do so simply means you gain a reputation (and so lose competitive edge) for being a bad payer. And although organisations have indeed got away with these types of behaviours in the past, after the story circulates that you're a bad payer, people are only going to do business with you if they have to.

Putting It All Together

Combining your insights into your activities, value, barriers and blockages requires balance. You must look at each aspect in relation to other aspects and try to consider everything that you do in an overall context. So begin by looking at your product and service portfolios in terms of:

✔ Products and services that attract

✔ Products and services that sell

✔ Products and services that make money – and lose money

Thinking in terms of your overall context is a lot easier when you're thinking about your products and services than, for example, administrative support and other functions, but you must take the same kind of approach to your support functions. You must know and understand where everything adds and loses money, so you must consider:

- ✔ Speed and accuracy of data processing.
- ✔ Regularity and frequency of data errors.
- ✔ Capacity of production, administrative, support and information technology.
- ✔ How much technology you have, and how often the technology is actually in use, and for what purposes.
- ✔ Premises costs.
- ✔ Patterns and locations of work.

To fit each of the preceding aspects into your overall context, you need to look primarily at whether you can sustain the costs incurred, and whether these costs are an acceptable proportion of your total costs.

Making this type of determination is a value judgement rather than a rational calculation. You need to know the basis on which you're calculating any value that you ascribe to an activity. Keep the following tips in mind:

- ✔ With any support function, you can often find opportunities for one-off savings. For example, you can often combine roles with existing staff when someone leaves you, rather than replacing them. But make sure that you don't disrupt everything for the sake of a single small saving.
- ✔ If you want to radically alter the cost base on which you carry out support functions, make sure that you ask the staff for their input early on. They know where inefficiencies and blockages are occurring.
- ✔ Never lose sight of the fact that although you, of course, want to keep support activities as simple, efficient and cost effective as possible, support functions are essential – which means you have to pay for them.

Managing the Whole Endeavour

Congratulations to you! You have a clear view of what you're setting out to do and to achieve. You've established a basis for conducting your business effectively and profitably with effective systems and structures in place. You know your activities, values, barriers and blockages – you put everything in the full context of the products and services that you set out to deliver. As a result, you can see everything that you do in detail as well as in the totality of your organisation and all its processes.

Now what?

Well, now it's time to go about executing, managing and maintaining your business based on your strategic plan – all of which I address in the following sections.

Allocating resources

All the challenging work you do to set up your strategic plan provides you with a rationale for how you prioritise activities and allocate and manage the resources at your disposal. As long as you allocate resources in the name of retaining and developing your overall effectiveness and competitiveness, where you place your resources is a matter of your choice.

Every time you propose to allocate resources to a particular department, division, venture or initiative, you must be able to answer the question 'Why?' Seek to answer this question in clear and unambiguous terms by stating clearly what you expect the allocation to achieve and why you chose to allocate the resources as you did. See the sidebar 'But why?' for more ideas on how to justify resource allocations.

But why?

Answering the question 'why?' – as in 'Why did you allocate half of next year's budget to this new project?' – may seem straightforward to you. However, you need to be aware that people take decisions to allocate resources for many reasons other than maintaining and developing competitiveness. For example:

✔ Decisions to update computer and IT systems are often taken in response to demands for the latest, rather than the most effective, technology.

✔ Decisions to allocate personal assistants may be taken for reasons of status and prestige rather than operational effectiveness.

✔ Decisions to outsource some functions are taken in response to shareholder and peer/industry pressures rather than the best use of resources.

At least one £100 billion merger has fallen through because the two Chief Executives of the companies being merged were unable to agree on the placement of their offices in their new premises.

So if you do allocate resources for any reason other than operational effectiveness, make sure that you know and understand all the consequences and can answer fully any and all questions on why you're proposing something.

All we ask: Meet your deadlines

Semco is a Brazilian manufacturing and Internet venture company (see Chapter 19 for more on this organisation). Since its restructuring many years ago, the company has invested in fully flexible hours and work goals. The company allows everyone to set his own daily production quotas and targets, and to come and go as he pleases. Employees are subject only to meeting absolute deadlines, timescales and delivery schedules.

The company has invested in removing the barriers as to why people do not, or will not, come to work; and do not, or will not, do anything after they get there. The company is effectively saying: we'll resource everything that you need,

want and ask for; now you've no reason not to deliver what we need, want and ask for.

The result is that the company has survived all the economic turbulence of the South American continent of the past generation. It has weathered the storms of hyper-inflation, lack of accessibility and a chaotic transport, supply and distribution network. By concentrating on a clear allocation of resources to the staffing side, and targeting absolute deadlines only, Semco has removed all the administration, progress chasing, quality assurance and production scheduling that other organisations have to pay for.

Being guided by priorities

Your organisation's true priorities must guide all your resource allocation decisions. (See the sidebar 'All we ask: Meet your deadlines' for one company's unique take on resource allocations.)

Being led by your true priorities is complex, so you need to understand the full complexities involved. I can offer one bit of advice: return often to your core purposes, products and services, and promises to give the best possible customer satisfaction (see Chapter 2). Yes, you must also attend to your staff's comfort, resourcing and expectations as well as your backers' demands on returns. But if you always return to your core, your true priorities emerge.

Working with limited resources

If you can undertake everything you want by using your existing resources, good for you. Everything is going to be just fine in your organisation!

But if you have more proposals than you can resource, you do have choices to make, as Figure 11-1 shows. You basically need to decide whether you're going to attempt everything – in which case some things will be under-resourced – or whether you're going to do only those things that you know you can resource. Making that choice isn't always easy, especially when you have powerful figures on your case wanting everything done – whether or not you have the resources to do them!

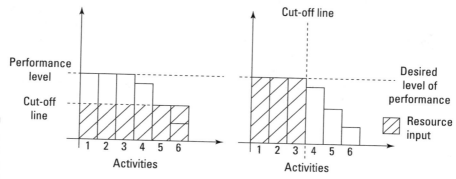

Figure 11-1: Two scenarios of working with limited resources.

a) Everything is attempted, but is unsatisfactory

b) Only those ventures that can be properly resources are attempted

Monitoring, reviewing and evaluating

The final key part of staying competitive is to ensure that you monitor, review and evaluate all the activities that are part of your plan on an ongoing basis. Nothing is constant or assured; everything is ultimately capable of being changed, developed and upgraded.

You must continue to scrutinise the details of everything that goes on in your organisation. The following is a concise, though comprehensive, list of critical factors that have to be at the core of any strategic approach to monitoring, review and evaluation. Check frequently on:

✓ Performance of systems, technology, departments, groups and individuals.

✓ Strategic clarity and focus.

✓ Customer and client focus, confidence and reputation.

✓ Speed and accuracy of technology support and IT systems.

✓ Attention to your cost base; as well as responding to cost increases and changes.

✓ Staff expertise, capability and commitment; as well as staff development and improvement.

✓ The currency of your technology, processes and systems.

Although the preceding list may be short, every item must be scrutinised constantly and in full detail if you're going to maintain your organisation's clarity, focus and direction.

This list should also form the core of all your reviews of organisational progress. Use it as a key element in staff meetings, performance appraisals, committees, consultation processes and organisational reporting. This type of simple, straightforward list helps to keep everyone focused on the core priorities and purposes of your organisation. If you don't use this list (or a similar one), you need to remind people in other ways about what their core purposes are; and if you don't remind them, people have a way of serving their own core purposes.

Chapter 12

Defining and Establishing Organisation Structure and Culture

*I*n order to compete effectively, you must have an organisation that's capable and willing to do so. Yes, this sounds silly and obvious! Yet in many cases, organisations created for one purpose or set of circumstances, fail to develop and evolve when their original purposes, products, services and markets move on.

As a result, these organisations continue to sell dated products and services in order to support businesses that are no longer fully efficient and effective – which inevitably leads to these organisations making less, at greater cost, with more malfunctions.

So in order to remain competitive, an organisation has to evolve in terms of its capabilities, attitudes, values and beliefs – just as it does with its performance. This chapter addresses how your organisation can remain successful by creating a structure and culture that fits your competitive strategy.

Establishing an Organisation Culture

Organisation culture is the combination of attitudes, values, beliefs, performance and relationships that make up the daily and (ultimately) enduring ways in which an organisation and its people work, act, react and behave.

Surveying common culture types

Before you can make adjustments to your organisation's culture you need to be able to describe your current culture. Business experts often describe organisation cultures based on some archetypes or stereotypes:

- **Power cultures:** Everyone determines success based on her position or relationship with the individual (or sometimes group) who holds the most power and influence in the organisation. See the later section 'Seeking out sources of power and influence' for more.

- **Role cultures:** Everyone works to adhere to clearly defined roles, job tasks and functions.

- **Task cultures:** Everyone works to deliver exactly what she has been told to do, normally in terms of sales and output.

- **People cultures:** The organisation exists for the primary purpose of supporting those individuals who created it and who work in it.

- **Pioneering cultures:** The organisation celebrates – and even requires – entrepreneurial and adventurous spirit.

- **Paternalistic cultures:** Everyone works to the direction of the person in charge – often the founder of the organisation, or the founding family.

- **Conformist cultures:** Everyone is required to do things in the precise ways demanded by the organisation; these demands are often very comfortable for individuals who can accept the conformity, but not for those who can't.

You may look at the preceding definitions of culture and conclude that task cultures are right or good, whereas perhaps role cultures are wrong or bad. This isn't necessarily the case, at least not in isolation. You can find many very effective and enduring role cultures, such as GlaxoSmithKline. And many task-oriented organisations lack focus or direction because staff pursue maximum output without considering the context, such as double glazing and other building products merchants. Don't let the sound or appearance of words drive your judgements. You need to assess each case, each organisation, on its own merits.

In practice, most organisations combine characteristics of the cultures in the preceding list. In fact, finding pure forms of various organisation cultures is quite rare. You're more likely to see a dominant culture type in the organisation – or a lack of any distinct culture types. Organisations that don't seem to have a distinct culture type are typically fragmented, divided, and dominated by powerful individuals, experiencing constant in-fighting among staff groups and special interest factions.

REAL WORLD EXAMPLE

Strength, cohesion, unity of purpose – and caution

Creating a strong and cohesive organisation brings its own responsibilities and challenges. For example:

✔ **The Nazi SS** had a very strong and cohesive culture for members. It was deliberately created as the elite of the Nazi regime and empires, which in turn reinforced its strength and solidarity. SS leaders tapped into this extreme strength and cohesion when they ordered members to carry out exterminations and mass murders; and the strength and cohesion made these acts very easy and straightforward for the members to do.

✔ **Boo.com** was a short-lived retail online footwear company. Established in Sweden in 1998, the company lasted less than three years. During its lifetime, the company was a wonderful organisation to work for. The culture was fully inclusive, integrated and pioneering – it was going to change the face of footwear retailing across the globe forever! Everyone was given a high salary, state-of-the-art workstation and top quality premises. Staff considered Boo.com an excellent place to turn up to for its own sake. When footwear sales didn't materialise, members of the company took refuge in their own mutual admiration and comfort in their culture, rather than attending to pressing business decisions.

Clearly, creating a strong and cohesive organisation isn't an end in itself. You also have the responsibility of making the organisation work ethically and profitably.

And if you do ever need to change people's beliefs in any way, be prepared for a major challenge. The strength, cohesion and unity of purpose that you built in the first place can be very difficult to alter.

Figuring out what really counts in organisation culture

REMEMBER

Whatever your organisation culture (see the preceding section), it needs all the following characteristics to be fully effective:

✔ **Strength:** The organisation must be based on a positive set of values to which everyone can ascribe. See the sidebar 'Strength, cohesion, unity of purpose – and caution' and Chapter 5 for more on organisation values.

✔ **Unity of purpose:** People need to know why they're doing what they're doing – overall, as well as within departments, divisions, functions and groups.

✔ **Cohesion:** Everyone respects the capabilities of colleagues.

✔ **Commitment:** Staff want the organisation to succeed in its overall purpose and specific departments, divisions and functions to meet their purposes.

✔ **Progression:** People embrace necessary change and advancement.

✔ **Pride, team spirit and esprit de corps:** Everyone needs to be fundamentally comfortable with belonging to the organisation.

In order to achieve all the preceding characters, an organisation must value each of the jobs and tasks within the organisation. A fundamental equality and humanity of treatment of everyone must exist – especially if you want to maximise your chances of creating a competitive organisation.

Exploring attitudes, values and behaviour

Instilling and developing the required attitudes, values and behaviour comes from the top of the organisation. As I state in Chapter 10, encouraging these areas throughout an organisation constitutes the cornerstone of strategic human resource management.

Whether you allow these attitudes, values and behaviour to emerge over time or set specific standards yourself, your people need to behave and interact – collectively and individually – in a consistent manner throughout the organisation.

In order to have a consistency of attitudes, values and behaviours in your organisation, everyone must:

✔ Have a positive attitude to the organisation and the work that it does.

✔ Respect each other and the work that everyone else does.

✔ Treat everyone as fundamental equals, regardless of position, rank, status or occupation.

✔ Believe that staff management processes and procedures are transparent, fundamentally cooperative and inclusive.

The preceding list of desirable attitudes forms the basis for what you can then ask of your staff with a clear conscience! If you create the conditions where everything is positive, open and transparent, and if you reward people well, you're then entitled to expect staff to:

✔ Commit to the company, its products and services

✔ Act in the best interests of the organisation at all times

 ✔ Identify problems earlier

 ✔ Treat all customers, clients and suppliers with respect

To instil positive attitudes, think about the reverse. Identify reasons why people do *not* want to come to work – and then do everything you can to remove these reasons. Indeed, if you can remove all the things that people say – boredom, bad relations, lack of interest in the work and so on – you're well on the way to victory!

If you can instil positive attitudes and values – and reinforce them with your daily actions – you can transcend any glamour or excitement that may not be immediately apparent in your organisation.

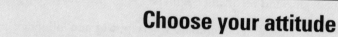

Choose your attitude

As the leader of an organisation, you need to create and instil positive attitudes and values for everyone in it. Consider the following:

Negative attitudes and values in situations where you may expect positive attitudes and values:

 ✔ The film of *Sex and the City* was beset by production problems because the stars squabbled over the amounts that they were paid (which in every case ran into several millions of dollars).

 ✔ Many professional sports players have and exhibit an attitude of 'I'll play if/when I feel like it.' And if anyone questions these players' attitudes, the players assert that they're looking for other jobs, teams or competitions.

Positive attitudes and values in situations where you may expect negative attitudes and values:

 ✔ British Airways' cabin crews have clear expectations, hierarchy, performance and tasks that they carry out – with a consistently agreeable and positive attitude. The positivity comes from extensive staff training and recruiting only individuals who actively want these jobs.

 ✔ Dutton Engineering, which makes office furniture and computer, video and television hardware, has shifted its quality assurance and customer support functions to its manufacturing teams. Work teams are allowed to set their own production schedules (subject only to customer deadlines), and the manufacturing teams must have full confidence in each other at all times. The result is that the company has no discernible absenteeism and a managerial hierarchy of four people (indeed, these are the only employees not involved in production and sales activities).

You can get more and more out of your people as the result of the attitudes and values you instil, provided that these can be harnessed to the work in hand. Furthermore, the power of positive attitudes has nothing to do with the nature of the work itself – otherwise all footballers would play their socks off at all times, whereas you would always struggle to get a smile, let alone a coffee, from cabin crew staff.

Seeking out sources of power and influence

Organisation culture is rarely simple or straightforward. People often come to work with negative attitudes and lack of loyalty. Groups and individuals jockey for position. And many organisations encourage departments, divisions and functions to compete for rewards and resources. In short, many people in organisations seek to gain, develop and use power and influence – sometimes for the good of the organisation but always, always, always for the good of themselves.

Whatever the benefits, power manoeuvring is always expensive and time-consuming to manage. It takes resources away from productive tasks, and puts them into managing and resolving conflicts.

You therefore need to know and understand where power and influence lie in your organisation. The main sources of power and influence include:

- ✔ **Expertise:** Teams, groups and individuals seek to regulate and influence their relative positions within organisations based on their capabilities and the ways in which they deliver results.

- ✔ **Group membership:** Professional groups, special interest groups and other lobbies (including professional associations and trade unions) seek to exert influence that serves their own interests.

- ✔ **Peer pressure:** Some groups seek to influence others within their location or area of activity.

Any of the preceding groups can cross the line in exerting their influence. Instead of reasoning and persuading, they may start to bully, victimise or ostracise those who don't fall in with doing things their way. This behaviour is more than unacceptable – it is illegal, and damages are unlimited in proven cases. So when you come across these forms of behaviour, remove them and remove the perpetrators!

- ✔ **Patronage:** Teams and individuals seek the support of powerful and influential individuals.

- ✔ **Victimisation:** Groups and individuals seek to denigrate others for some reason (sometimes to do with their work capability, often to do with their gender, race, religion or other personal characteristic).

- ✔ **Heredity:** Individuals seek to gain positions as the result of kinship ties within the organisation.

- ✔ **Rank and status:** People use their positions in the organisational hierarchy to influence others to coincide with their points of view.

The preceding forms of power and influence (with the exception of patronage and victimisation) can be a force for good or ill. And regardless of good or ill, power and influence are always going to be part of any organisation – they're simply part of human nature!

If you're going to stay competitive, you need to look at ways of harnessing each of the preceding sources of power and influence to serve the best interests of your organisation, its products and services, its customers and clients. Therefore, you need to use *your* influence to make sure that you channel all sources of power for the good of the organisation.

Begin harnessing sources of power and influence by ensuring that you are, and remain, actively involved in all aspects of your organisation's collective behaviours. Reward instances of power and influence that benefit your organisation and discipline anyone who tries to use position or expertise for his or her own ends.

One sure way to identify a declining or under-performing organisation is to look at the prevalence and influence of special interest groups and powerful individuals. Organisations that spend a large part of their time fighting amongst themselves are always going to lose their competitive edge to those that have a strong measure of cohesion.

Establishing your culture

You have a whole lot of things to bear in mind as you go about designing your organisation's culture: the attitudes, behaviour and performance that you need and want, the structures you need in place and your ongoing processes for assessing and managing problems and issues.

Regardless of whether you're in charge of IBM or a small group of people, others take their lead from you. You create the culture and give life to the standards. So:

- ✔ If you're sloppy, others will be sloppy.
- ✔ If you're late, others will be late.
- ✔ If you miss deadlines, other will miss deadlines.
- ✔ If you bully people, others will bully.

'Do as I say, and not as I do' is a good old English maxim – but it's very bad managerial practice.

You establish the culture – the way things are done here – in terms of your standards, attitudes, values and behaviour. Always seek to be:

- ✔ Strong, not weak
- ✔ Inclusive, not divisive
- ✔ Positive, not negative
- ✔ Dynamic and progressive, not inert or frozen

Power and influence in the NHS

In April 2008, the NHS published a survey stating that fewer than half of the medical staff believed that treating patients was the organisation's top priority. Asked what they thought the top priority was, many responded that it was to stay within budget or to respond to the latest political issue.

The NHS went a step further and identified three clear sources and locations of power and influence in the organisation, including:

- ✔ **Medical staff,** who used their expertise to try and influence the organisation's direction based on their understanding of priorities.

- ✔ **Managerial staff,** who used resources to try and meet the latest political demand or to manipulate finances so the organisation stayed within budgets.

- ✔ **Political personalities and elements,** who used rank and status to try and gain a reputation for delivering some form of progress, which the wider world deemed the response required.

Some doubt that the NHS can ever integrate these three power sources into a top-quality, focused organisation, one that delivers the services for which it was (ostensibly) designed. Each power source remains determined to fight its own corner and meet its own agenda:

- ✔ Medical staff remain fiercely loyal to their professions but many have little loyalty to the NHS as an organisation.

- ✔ Managers need to meet targets in order to continue developing their own careers; and so in the absence of other direction, career development and narrow self interest become the driving forces.

- ✔ Politicians need to give the appearance that services and the NHS as an organisation are 'getting better' (whatever that may mean).

Unfortunately, the overall result is that the NHS is treating fewer patients, at a greater cost overall. This trend is certain to continue until the three main sources of power and influence agree to a clear set of objectives and use their expertise, rank, status and resources to deliver them.

Passing on attitudes and values

Your attitudes and values need to be positive, dynamic, inclusive – and must transfer to others in your organisation. In order for people to buy into your attitudes and values, you need to demonstrate to them that following your lead is in their own interests. For example:

- If you want people to work hard, you must reward hard work.

- If you want people to turn up on time, you must punish or sanction those who are late.

- If you want people to dress in a particular way, you must send people home to change if they haven't complied.

Sounds simple, right? Unfortunately, few leaders do as much as they can to reinforce the attitudes and values they desire. For example:

- Tackling problems of lateness or dress code breaches is awkward and uncomfortable. You can sound petty. But if you're seeking standards in these areas, you must reinforce them. Otherwise, people think that you don't care.

- If you require people to work hard but reward something else, they quickly learn to concentrate on the 'something else.' Once again, you're saying one thing and doing another.

Encouraging behaviour

As with attitudes and values, you also have to set standards of behaviour and performance. This, in a nutshell, means:

- Establishing what you want to be done
- Establishing how you want it done

The 'what you want to be done' is the easy part:

- 'I want this finished by Friday.'
- 'I want you to be part of a team that produces 100 cars per year.'

Using technology to gain a competitive edge

Part of your efforts to foster an inclusive and dynamic culture include encouraging your people to embrace technology and seek new ways of working. If you succeed, you give yourself the best possible chance of advancing and developing as new technology becomes available.

Yes, technology has resulted in many job losses as well as opportunities. So if the technology that you propose to introduce is going to result in job losses, tell your people early and give them as much time as you can to find other work. Not only does this openness reinforce your integrity, it's much more cost effective to have people using what would otherwise be productive time, wondering where their future truly lies.

But overall, properly introduced and installed technology consistently delivers numerous advantages, including:

✔ Improved production speed, quality and accuracy.

✔ Faster, easier access to the information via the Internet and intranets.

✔ More efficient communication and interaction via email and mobile phone technology.

✔ Greater security for data and financial transfers and transactions.

All great means of honing your competitive edge!

But there's a catch: you must take whatever time is necessary to train your staff to use the technology fully and effectively. Otherwise, you end up wasting money and damaging your competitive edge by having employees trying to work equipment that they don't fully understand.

The 'how you want it done' is harder. You've some basic choices to make:

✔ Do you need or want hourly, daily or weekly progress reports – or are you going to leave people to get on with things in their own ways? Either choice can be right – providing that you actively choose your process and can justify your choice.

✔ Are you going to keep your hands directly on everything that's going on – or are you going to delegate to more junior managers, supervisors and team leaders? Again, the choice is yours.

You actually have a fine balance to strike. Even if you leave people to do things their way and delegate as much as you think fit, you still need to have an active and positive identity with the staff. Whatever your choice, you must always walk the job as often as you can – just to see that all is well (and of course, to say: 'Hello' to everyone!).

Providing opportunities

The world changes, people change and their expectations change. But if you create a positive, inclusive, enthusiastic and committed culture, they can see all the turbulence in the world and change in your organisation as opportunities, not threats. This shift in perspective ought to lead to all sorts of things for everyone in your organisation – regardless of position, rank or status!

Ideally you want people looking out for things for themselves – and then coming to you with ideas and proposals. You can foster an innovating, entrepreneurial spirit by encouraging it. Get into the habit of asking your people what they think and then taking on board the things that they suggest.

Brazilian businessman Ricardo Semler once said, 'We have prospered by refusing to squander the greatest asset that we have – our people.' Semler's company, Semco, has grown great by asking its people what they think at all times, and then not just taking on board the things that they suggest but by always going with them unless a compelling reason exists. (See Chapter 18.)

Rewarding performance

You have to deliver rewards to your people for what they achieve. The following are some rules to remember about rewards:

- ✔ You have to be able to deliver financial rewards, including pay rises and enhancements, that people expect.

- ✔ Everyone expects at least an annual pay rise, and you need to be prepared and willing to deliver if you possibly can.

- ✔ You have to be able to deliver intrinsic rewards such as opportunities for growth and development, in addition to financial rewards.

- ✔ You need to offer praise and recognition when people do a good job.

- ✔ You have to be able to reward and recognise exceptional performance (which means that you – and everyone else – need to know and understand what exceptional performance truly is).

- ✔ You have to deliver what you promise.

All these rules are vital. Rewards are, after all, a large part of what keeps your people coming to work for you. And your people, after all, give life, energy and effectiveness to the core of your competitive operations.

Of course, the world isn't as simple as this. You must also be able to afford to deliver what you promise. If times are tight and less is on offer than in the past, you need to be able to explain why. Your ongoing policy of personal honesty and integrity is crucial here! That way, even if the staff don't like what you tell them, at least they understand why and they believe you.

Giving Structure to Organisations

All organisations must have structure. Quite apart from anything else, people need, and want, to know where they stand (whatever that may mean). To be fully competitive and effective however, you must demonstrate and deliver a clear division and integration of work, giving clear lines of authority and responsibility. Furthermore, you need to know and understand where resources are being apportioned and consumed, and where value is being gained and lost through the work itself.

The following sections explore options for structuring an organisation, as well as important principles that underpin any structure – authority, responsibility and accountability.

Considering various structures

Congratulations: the choice of organisation structure is yours! The main structure options available include:

- **Hierarchy:** Includes individuals' rank, title, status and occupation. Standard organisation charts (still more or less universally expected) typically reflect this type of structure.

- **Linking pins:** Demonstrate both the autonomy of working groups and the key relationships (or links) between groups.

- **Federations and virtual organisations:** Means by which teams and groups (and also specialists and other organisations) pull together for specific projects and ventures.

- **Propellers (or hub-and-spokes):** You have a core at the centre of activities, and key primary operating and specialist functions that connect out from the centre.

So choose your structure, but keep some caveats in mind – people like to know where they stand. If you don't deliver a ranking hierarchy, you must present something else, or at the very least be able to describe clearly to others where their positions are in the overall scheme of the organisation.

Dispersed organisations

Dispersed organisations – those that have many different locations, customers and supplier bases, as well as different products and services – have advantages and disadvantages.

The great advantage of dispersed organisations is the range of opportunities and interests present for anyone who's prepared to follow her ambitions. People in leadership and managerial positions can also re-schedule and re-order priorities in order to deliver products and services in the right ways and at the right prices and volumes.

Dispersed organisations do, however, have some notable challenges, including:

✔ Whether you pay and reward people the same, regardless of location – or you vary pay and reward according to local conditions and going rates. (See Chapters 10 and 17.)

✔ How much autonomy you give each location.

✔ How to structure effective reporting relationships between locations and the central office.

✔ Whether you're going to allocate specific activities for the entire organisation (such as accounts payable or customer service) in a particular location.

✔ How you coordinate and control activities and interactions between locations.

✔ How to ensure that you give comparable attention to the activities in remote locations and in the locations that you see every day.

✔ How to deal with specific cultural issues that are important to particular locations. This applies to specific school holidays in parts of the UK as well as social and religious customs around the world.

Defining authority

By paying attention to how people behave, their attitudes and values and how you manage and channel their power and influence, you define the nature of your authority and how you intend to exert it.

As a leader or top executive, you *must* exert your authority. After all, the organisation depends on you to do so in its quest to remain competitive! However good the organisation's products and services, you won't be able to implement any strategy unless you have the authority to do so.

People look to you to exert your authority in the name of the organisation – and in the name of implementing effective strategies, proposals and ventures. They look to you to have both moral and managerial authority in dealing with other stakeholders, the media, outside influences, financiers and backers.

Base your authority on your expertise and credibility, as well as your position. If people don't believe that you have authority, they'll take no notice of what you set out to do. Only by knowing and understanding how people think, believe, behave, act and react can you effectively define your own authority.

Taking on responsibility

With power and influence comes responsibility. If you're placed in a position of authority, everyone around you expects you to take responsibility for everything that's done in the name of the organisation. They look to you to set in place structures and allocate resources so that the organisation delivers the right results – particularly the right products and services to the right markets.

Everyone in your organisation needs to know that you, as leader or a top executive, are accountable for what is conducted within your sphere of influence. Everyone likes to be responsible for the successes, good things and triumphs. Accepting the responsibility for failures, errors and mistakes, however, takes character and courage.

Total accountability is part of any executive position. If you don't want to accept responsibility and accountability for the good *and* the bad, you shouldn't take an executive role at all. Furthermore, you cannot take a halfway or diluted position on this matter – you need to be totally accountable, or abdicate your accountability.

Creative structures and titles

Many organisations have tried to avoid formal structures and titles for workers. For example:

✔ The Disney empire calls its staff 'the cast'.

✔ Ryanair calls cabin staff 'the crew' – this term is familiar enough in the airline industry, but it's a mark of status at Ryanair.

✔ One manufacturing organisation allows its people to choose their own titles, but they ran into difficulties when people kept coming back to have business cards reprinted. Every time one person thought of something that sounded more important, the rest of his colleagues simply followed suit and changed their titles also.

✔ A computer company in Silicon Valley allowed people to choose their own titles – but even they had to take a more sober view when one staff member took to calling himself 'staff fleet commander'.

The result – and the lesson – is that, in many cases, you're forced to take the line of least resistance and meet people's needs and wants in this area. And taking a non-traditional approach to titling frees up an awful lot of time and resource that you can spend more usefully in getting on with competing.

You don't want to be known as an abdicator (someone who ducks problems when they arise) or an absconder (someone who runs away at the first whiff of trouble). Yet you'll be branded as one of the two if you don't tackle problems when and where they arise. And remember: the earlier you tackle a problem, the less of a problem it often turns out to be.

Those who abdicate their accountability normally find outlets for mistakes and errors by blaming others, through victimisation and *scapegoating* (finding someone to blame for all your misfortunes). Nobody wants to work in an organisation where these activities occur, so make sure that yours isn't one of them. Apart from anything else, victimisation is against the law in the UK; if someone sues you for victimisation and wins, damages are unlimited.

Creating a structure that works

People make up organisation structures and hierarchies – and people like to know and understand where they stand in the scheme of things. Your organisation's structure directly affects your ability to compete. People quickly become unsure of everything when they don't know:

- The opportunities ahead for them
- Their prospects
- The context in which they work
- The nature of ranking orders (and everyone especially likes these!)

Part of creating a structure is therefore meeting people's expectations. Organisation theorists can say things like, 'Oh, you can't make structures and pyramids out of people.' But people prefer structure. They understand structure (or think that they do). And they like to know and understand where they may be promoted and for what reasons. So you must provide something that meets this very human need.

Playing with the patterns of work

The days of 9–5 working where everyone had a steady and assured job were actually a myth. Although lots of people did (and some still do) indeed work like this, in truth lots more never did. There have always been flexible patterns of work – in healthcare, transport, energy, mining, water supply, telecommunications and many production activities.

All that's happened in the last decade or so is that the boundaries have been pushed back, giving greater flexibility and affecting more and more industries and sections. And much of this is the result of technological advance.

Call centre effectiveness?

You must weigh work-pattern flexibility and technological innovations within the context of your competitive strategy. For example, many people have received what they considered poor customer service from call centres located elsewhere in the world. Although overseas call centres may be efficient in cost saving, they can be ineffective in dealing with customers. Much of the problem stems from overseas staff who don't fully understand what is important and of value to the customer. So if your organisation uses these types of facilities, ensure that you have a proper cultural as well as operational fit.

This means that you can now be much more flexible and accommodating in the approaches that you take. By providing computers, mobile phones and even some production technology, you can have all sorts of work done:

- ✔ By your own staff, wherever they happen to be – in the car, at home, hotel rooms, business centres – even the office!

- ✔ By anyone else on your behalf anywhere in the world.

Wherever your people happen to be, you need some way to supervise and manage them. You need to see and know what they're up to – and they need to know and understand that they're not working in total isolation. An email once a day and a phone call once a week are the minimum contacts that you should have. In practice, if this isn't possible, find something that meets the twin objectives of checking progress and maintaining a connection.

Working with teams and groups

Creating and instilling positive attitudes, values and behaviour provides the crucial basis on which you structure your work teams and groups, and your departments, divisions and functions. See the section 'Creating a structure that works' earlier in this chapter for more on organisation structures.

Creating effective teams and groups and instilling positive attitudes, values and behaviour requires that you pay attention to all the following:

- ✔ **Task management:** Setting work methods, timescales and working relations.

- ✔ **Process management:** Developing integrated activities and ensuring that everyone makes her maximum contribution.

✔ **Communications:** Sharing information effectively within work groups, and also between work groups.

✔ **Attention to individuals:** Allowing individuals opportunities and freedom to develop (within the organisation's overall purpose, of course).

✔ **Management and supervisory style:** Establishing processes that are positive and dynamic, open and transparent.

✔ **Harmony of objectives:** Integrating individuals' aims and goals within the organisation's overall purpose.

✔ **Team spirit within groups:** Isolating and dealing with recalcitrant behaviour or attitudes quickly and effectively.

A major part of ensuring high-quality work from people, and therefore staying competitive, depends on relations between work groups and departments, and top and senior management. So make sure that your people see you, know you and can contact you at any time. Quite apart from creating effective groups and delivering top class work, you'll earn the respect, confidence and trust of the staff.

Team time: Some dos and don'ts

If you want to get the best possible performance out of your teams and groups (and you need to do so in order to remain competitive), follow these basic rules:

Do

✔ Provide meaningful work.

✔ Allow flexibility and equality in arranging work patterns.

✔ Provide training and development for all.

✔ Ensure that everyone has ready access to top and senior managers when necessary.

✔ Tell people everything important that's going on.

✔ Acknowledge crises or problems as early as possible – and ask for everyone's input to solutions.

✔ Tell everyone as soon as possible when any radical or contentious moves are afoot, such as a merger, takeover or redundancy.

Don't

✔ Make teams and groups compete with each other for resources, bonuses and results.

✔ Have favourites and victims.

✔ Avoid confronting problems.

✔ Encourage elites and 'bunker' mentalities, in which the actions and thoughts of some groups are deemed fireproof, always right, and therefore untouchable and un-criticise-able.

✔ Be afraid to re-energise groups when they seem to be running out of drive or output.

Chapter 13

Doing The Right Things: Ethics

In This Chapter

▶ Defining ethics and standards

▶ Establishing a work ethic

▶ Setting and maintaining standards

▶ Mixing ethics, competition and profit

A lot of misunderstanding surrounds the meaning of ethics and standards in business and management. Critics of ethics continue to take the view that an ethical approach to business – setting high and distinctive standards of attitude, conduct, behaviour and performance – affects your profit levels. This is quite true of course – but setting and delivering high standards in all areas puts your profit levels *up*, not down!

Think about ethics from your own point of view – do you prefer to deal with people who say what they mean, do what they say they'll do and deliver what they say they'll deliver? Or do you prefer to be unsure about the standards of products and services that you're going to get? Of course, you prefer the former, and your response says all that you need to know about the importance of setting and maintaining your own standards.

If you don't set standards for your staff, they set their own (see Chapter 12). Do you want to leave to chance the ways in which they behave and conduct themselves in their dealings with each other and with customers – or are you going to make sure that you get this right?

So if you're ready to discover the benefits of doing the right things, read on.

Taking Positions: Ethics

Every organisation must have standards; these form the basis of your organisation's collective attitudes, conduct, behaviour and performance. Standards set the face of the company and affect production, product and service delivery, design, workplace relations and dealings with customers, suppliers and backers.

Customers and clients need to be sure of what they're getting when they buy from you or do business with you. If you haven't set distinctive standards, how can they be sure? Eventually, these customers and clients are likely to gravitate away from you (from something they're not sure of) and towards something of which they *are* sure.

You can look at ethics in the realm of business and management in several ways, including:

- ✔ **An absolute position of right and wrong.** You establish clearly the things that you do – and the things that you don't do.

- ✔ **A set of positive values.** Ethics underpin your organisation's collective attitudes, conduct, behaviour and performance.

- ✔ **Culturally influenced expectations.** Ethics inspire you to meet the expectations of everyone concerned – staff, backers, customers and suppliers – without compromising your absolute standards of integrity.

- ✔ **A reflection of your moral and professional fibre.** Ethics govern how you conduct your business affairs.

- ✔ **Acceptance of responsibility and accountability.** Ethics back up everything that you do – and also everyone associated with the organisation.

- ✔ **The basis of your business relationships.** Ethics inspire you to deliver your products, services and activities to the best of your capabilities to your customers, suppliers, backers and staff.

Finding your absolutes

If you're going to establish your ethics correctly – and give yourself a competitive edge in the process – where exactly do you start?

You start with the absolutes, and you commit yourself now to leading by example (see the sidebar 'Stellar standards' for some examples of exceptional business absolutes in action). Business aspects on which you need to take absolute positions include:

- ✔ Your established quality of products and services.

- ✔ The ways in which your staff behave towards each other.

- ✔ The ways in which your staff behave and conduct themselves in the name of your organisation.

- ✔ The way you deal with the press, media and public at large.

- ✔ Your attitudes towards some key specific issues, especially waste and effluent disposal, organisation appearance (whether it's smart or scruffy), health and safety and financial reporting.

- ✔ Your attitudes to problems and issues (especially whether you sweep problems under the carpet or deal with them in a timely manner).

- ✔ Your attitude towards unacceptable staff conduct, especially activities such as bullying, victimisation, discrimination, harassment, fraud, vandalism, violence and falsifying company information.

Of course, strong ethics are so much easier when your organisation already holds a collective positive attitude, when you have harmonious employee relations and when people actually want to come to work in the first place. Positive attitudes are founded in mutual interest, trust, respect and value. If you don't put these in place, you can never maximise or optimise your competitive advantage, however good your products and services. (See Chapter 12 for more on organisational attitudes.)

Stellar standards

Ethically strong organisations take absolute stands on issues they determine as essential. Consider the following examples:

- ✔ On his day off, an employee of Coleman's food company in Norwich went into his local supermarket to shop. Scanning the shelves, he noticed that two trays of one of the company's products were badly labelled. He bought them all and when he returned to work the following day, he took them into the company's public relations office. He explained his action as: 'I saw them and couldn't bear to leave them on the shelves.'

- ✔ Walker's Camping Equipment Ltd was having problems with one of its models of

camp cookers, which wouldn't turn off. The product management team got together to discuss the problem and determine what to do. After a few minutes of discussion, the product manager jumped to his feet and said, 'So we've got goods out there that don't work. Call them all back, refund people their money – and find out why!' The meeting duly broke up.

In both cases, a standard was absolute to the individuals involved. They were completely committed, so they had nothing to discuss or debate. The products were wrong, and so they had to be removed, recalled and replaced. And in both cases, the result was that the company cut straight to the chase, got the products back in and replaced them.

Defending ethics

Some critics of workplace ethics say that ethics create laziness. But part of the creation of a positive, respectful, harmonious – and yes, ethical – place of work is giving people work to do! Whatever their jobs, people will beat a path to your organisation's door if they know that the work is worthwhile, demanded by the organisation and reasonably rewarded.

By offering worthwhile, valued work, you lay the foundation stones for your organisation's attitudes and standards – and in turn, you create the basis of your organisation's work ethic. If you extend your organisation's attitudes to topics like employee relations, collective and individual conduct, attitudes, behaviour and performance, you can eventually create a positive, cheerful and committed attitude throughout the organisation. Ultimately, by instilling a positive ethical attitude you give your organisation its best chance for success.

Addressing the tough stuff

When establishing your organisation's ethics, you must take on several tricky issues, including:

- ✔ What you do and don't do
- ✔ Right and wrong
- ✔ Survival
- ✔ Corporate social responsibility
- ✔ How you do and don't do things

I cover each of these issues in detail in the following sections.

Deciding what you do – and do not do

As the leader of an organisation, you have some choices to make, including:

- ✔ The kinds of products and services that you do and don't produce, deliver and sell.
- ✔ The customers and clients that you do and don't serve.
- ✔ The locations in which you do and don't work. (See the sidebar 'The ethics of location' for more on this topic.)
- ✔ The ways in which you do and don't deal with waste disposal and pollution.

Who do you want to work for?

The organisation that has the longest waiting list and largest volume of unsolicited applications as a percentage of its staff total in the UK is the BBC. Yes, it has locations and activities in all parts of the country and is permanently before everyone as a broadcaster and entertainer. So its top spot makes sense.

However, the UK's other highly desirable employers may surprise you. Other popular companies include:

- British Airways, particularly for its cabin crews.

- Ryanair, for cabin crew and sales staff.

- Nissan in north-eastern England, for assembly line positions.

- Virgin, because of Richard Branson, where many people will take any job, just so that they can work for *this* company.

And other than the BBC, the queues are essentially for supposedly mundane jobs – serving food and drinks, selling tickets, assembling cars. And of course, those who advocate against ethics and standards will say: 'Ah yes, but these are unskilled jobs for people who will take any job, and they have to take these jobs because they are not clever enough to do anything else.'

This attitude stinks of course (as well as being false). First these companies, and others like them, do not have to take anyone – indeed they only take people who want to work for them. Second, if you are still in any doubt, compare these waiting lists with the shortages in other, and supposedly much more worthwhile or glamorous, areas. In particular, you should note the continuing chronic shortage of doctors – a supremely worthwhile occupation which cannot attract or retain people because they are not sure of the standards demanded in UK healthcare. And you've surely been to sporting events where some of the highest paid individuals in the world plainly cannot be bothered to perform.

So note and take on board the examples of mainstream employers enjoying considerable success in attracting potential employees. If you value the people working for you, others will beat a path to your door, pestering you for any chance at all to work for you!

The preceding are just abstract, theoretical concepts – they crop up in real problems that real businesses confront every day. For example:

- If you're an independent grocery store, do you sell alcohol and cigarettes to all? Do you sell to customers who you know and believe are going to hand them on to children under 16?

- If you're a mortgage broker or finance house, do you sell sub-prime products at all? Do you sell to people who you know and believe to be unable to make repayments?

✔ If you're an armaments company, which governments do you deal with, and why? Do you deal only with governments – or do you deal with brokers also?

✔ If you make foodstuffs for the retail sector, what deals are you willing to strike with the dominant supermarket chains? And how does this decision affect your dealings with local and independent grocers?

✔ If you own a bar or restaurant, are you responsible for deciding when somebody has had enough to eat or drink?

✔ If lots of people desire to do business with you, at what point do the gifts from salespeople or suppliers cross the thin red line from inducements and sweeteners into bribery?

Distinguishing right and wrong

What's right? And what's wrong? Up to a point, your answer is – whatever you think it is!

In particular, right and wrong are fairly subjective in terms of the components of your products and services, the prices that you charge and the ways you conduct yourself in your dealings with others. You simply have to be able to justify your take on matters – in public if required. When in doubt, follow the principle, 'Do as you would be done by; do unto others as you would have others do unto you'.

The ethics of location

Location can be an ethical as well as an operational issue because location informs your attitudes towards where you choose to work.

The location of customers and suppliers used to drive decisions about where to set up business. For example, if your product gained weight during production, you typically located your business near the markets, whereas if your product lost weight during production, you typically located your business near the suppliers of raw materials.

Everything nowadays is much more complicated. People can choose to locate wherever they choose! Thus, for example:

✔ Manufacturing activities have been relocated to areas known for supplying cheap labour, premises and technology. Is this the morally right thing to do? In the light of rising fuel, transport and energy costs, should a UK company maintain overseas investments?

✔ Financial services and telecommunications have gone through periods of restructuring, during which they outsourced technology development and customer service functions to parts of the world where high expertise is available for a lower cost (than in the West, anyway). Some companies say that moving these services overseas has helped them establish business activities in the new locations. But many customers complain about the service, citing varying service quality and a perceived lack of value placed on the customers themselves.

So if for example you think that any of the following are right, all you must do is be prepared to stand up in public and justify why it's okay to:

- Dump toxic effluent in a river.
- Throw confidential patient records on to a public rubbish dump un-shredded.
- Allow a hospital to cause 90 patients to die from hospital-acquired infections.
- Fail to bolt down railway lines, thus causing a fatal crash.

If you're not prepared to stand up in public and say that these events were right, you must:

- Acknowledge that they're wrong.
- Set your own ethical standards high enough to eliminate the possibility of these kinds of events ever happening in your organisation.

Some things are just plain wrong, For example, it is wrong:

- Not to comply with the law.
- Not to create and maintain the healthiest and safest place of work possible.
- To allow bullying, victimisation, discrimination and harassment in any circumstances.
- To condone vandalism, violence, theft and fraud.
- To use untried and untested product components and ingredients.
- Knowingly to sell unsafe products and services to your customers.

It's also always wrong to look at the law from a negative, protective or otherwise unacceptable point of view. To use a response like, 'We comply with the law' as your stock answer to all questions of possible malpractice or negligence simply gives the impression that you're abdicating responsibility (and you probably are). People always remember your lack of integrity and honesty. So you need to make up your mind to deal honestly with everyone. If, for any reason, you can't tell the truth, then at least tell no lies. After you're caught lying, retrieving your reputation can take years.

Don't make financial gains the principal aim of your organisation's ethical strategy. Do the right thing because your organisation seeks to be held in high regard as a contributor to people and society – not just as a protector of its bottom line.

Surviving

Ethics are more than niceties – they're the standards by which your company or organisation lives or dies.

Survival itself is an ethical issue. You have enduring responsibilities to your staff, customers, suppliers and shareholders as well as the locations and communities in which you do business. You must design and live by standards that enable your organisation to have the greatest chance of fulfilling its obligations. For example, if you offer lifetime employment (as many companies and organisations still do), or if you offer lifetime product and service guarantees, you've a duty to be around to deliver your promise.

At the core of your survival is your ability to deliver *enduring value* – value that your customers and clients expect and are willing to pay for. Companies and organisations that set and maintain high standards of conduct and performance are much more likely to deliver enduring value.

Never underestimate the relationship between ethics, survival and profitability. And never underestimate the capability of an organisation to fail if it doesn't set and maintain its own absolute standards.

Ways and means

Right and wrong become more complicated when you factor in *ways and means,* or how you do things. For instance, you can do:

✔ **The right thing for the right reason:** Hopefully, this is the case for you, all the time! Everything that you do is honest and above board – and it serves your customers well at all times.

✔ **The right things for the wrong reasons:** You sell goods and services (the right thing) to those who can't afford to pay, just so that you can meet your sales targets and profit quotas (the wrong reason).

✔ **The wrong things for the right reasons:** You keep obsolete product lines going (the wrong thing) for an enduring but dwindling band of customers who still use them (the right reason).

Other examples of doing the wrong things for the right reasons include making redundancies and lay-offs to preserve stock market confidence; outsourcing activities overseas to preserve credibility and standing in the industry sector; and selling assets to raise short-term funds during times of difficulty.

✔ **The wrong things for the wrong reasons:** Although narrow performance targets in education and healthcare don't work and lead to poorer, slower service, these organisations continue to set targets regardless. These targets do nothing to help develop the services (the wrong reasons). Furthermore, these targets gain a life of their own. As a result, everyone works towards them, in spite of a collective understanding that they're wrong (thus the wrong reasons gather strength).

Standards and survival

The Body Shop shows just what you can do when you set yourself high and distinctive standards – and keep to them! The Body Shop was created and developed in 1974, during a period of high inflation and rising unemployment. The company produced a range of distinctive cosmetics, skincare products and high-quality, premium-price gifts. At the time, these products were the last thing that the market rationally needed. There were more than enough companies in the cosmetics sector, and people were spending less on gifts and presents.

Nevertheless, the company was able to develop a reputation and brand because of its distinctive ethical position. It also quickly became known for its work ethic – the distinctive and especially committed ways in which shop staff presented themselves and served customers. Additionally, many consumers valued, and were attracted by, its ethical stance against animal testing.

So The Body Shop supported and reinforced its position by attracting and retaining staff who were driven to work for a company with high and distinctive ethical standards, as well as a strong and unique work ethic. (And while others have emulated The Body Shop's practices, the company remains a beacon for high and distinctive standards all round.)

Railtrack plc. was established in 1989, following the privatisation of the UK rail network. Railtrack was responsible for maintaining and developing the railway lines themselves and also the network's property portfolio – the stations, goods and freight yards, and other loading and unloading facilities. To ensure that Railtrack remained viable, all the train operating companies paid a levy (which the train operators added on to passengers' ticket prices).

Railtrack held a captive market and was assured of sufficient revenue to carry out its activities. It was, therefore, a monopoly. The company's priorities soon became clear as it paid out surpluses as dividends to shareholders and bonuses to top and senior managers. In particular, a divide existed between individuals responsible for doing the actual work on the railways and individuals responsible for running and operating the rail network.

Furthermore, the company had no distinctive or unifying work ethic. The result was chaos – subcontractors and work groups set their own standards and were able to concentrate on their own narrow interests. So, even through Railtrack had assured finances and a captive market, the company went bankrupt in 1999 – due in large part to the fact that it had no distinctive standards or a collective or cohesive work ethic.

Considering corporate social responsibility

Corporate social responsibility (CSR) is a reflection of the overall attitude an organisation develops towards its obligations and duties to society at large.

The idea of CSR is not new. The great trading organisations of the 18th and 19th centuries – the East India Company, W.D. and H.O. Wills, the Players, Cadbury and Rowntree families – all took the view that they were trading and earning fortunes for the good of society and their communities, as well as for themselves, their staff, their backers and their bankers. And while many were (and continue to be) criticised for corporate colonialism, the standards that they once established continue to be held in high esteem.

Much has changed. Over the past century, drives for instant returns on investments, short-term share price rises and market dominance have led companies and organisations to concentrate on their own narrow interests rather than those of society as a whole.

And now things are beginning to come full circle: legislation in specific areas (finance, advertising, product performance and trade descriptions) is beginning to underline a more general enlightenment and regard to collective social interest that's essential for the wellbeing of society as a whole, and to collective and individual prosperity. For example:

- ✔ Advertising and marketing regulations have been tightened to prevent the exploitation of children and other vulnerable society groups.

- ✔ Products aren't allowed to claim benefits that they don't actually deliver. For example, food products cannot claim that they make you thinner; cosmetics may not claim that they make you younger.

How you do – and do not – achieve standards

The preceding ethical aspects all lead you to set your organisation's standards – how you will, and will not, do things and the ways in which you accept and carry out your responsibilities.

You need to be very clear about the reasons for the standards you set and how people should behave and perform in the light of your standards.

You're so transparent

Financial transparency has been at the heart of recent corporate problems, calling into question organisations' responsibility in sharing financial details with investors and the public.

Some of the problems surrounding financial transparency were inflicted on organisations and their managers by large corporate shareholders who didn't want the world to know what they were actually investing in. And some of the problems were brought on by a generation of managers and shareholders who didn't fully understand the complexities of their financial structures and obligations.

But most serious of all have been corporate collapses brought about through fraud or negligence, for example:

- ✔ **Enron,** the energy distribution company based in Texas, collapsed in 2001 after a series of internal transactions conducted by and on behalf of its Chairman and Chief Executive Officer, as well as other top and senior managers.

✔ **Northern Rock,** the UK regional bank, collapsed in 2007 as the result of expanding its mortgage operations into the sub-prime market far too quickly, leading to loss of confidence and lack of funds required to meet obligations to its core customers.

The Enron case especially, led to the US passing the Sarbanes–Oxley Act in 2002. The Sarbanes–Oxley Act in practice has set a more or less universal standard for all company and financial reporting and transparency. The act requires that all companies and their directors and managers:

✔ Keep financial records up-to-date and make them available for inspection at any time.

✔ Provide full transparency, including lists of assets and liabilities and rationale for labelling items as either.

✔ Clearly and accurately state the value of items on Balance Sheets and Profit and Loss accounts, as well as the rationale for all valuations.

✔ State the value of items not included on Balance Sheets and in Profit and Loss accounts, as well as the reasons for not including them.

And responsibility for this transparency doesn't just fall on the shoulders of organisations. Under Sarbanes–Oxley, outside auditors also have much greater responsibility to check the details of everything that companies tell them.

You may well ask why any of this is necessary! The answer is simple: companies and organisations – and their top and senior managers – were not carrying out any of these activities fully or adequately enough. As a result, companies and organisations were abdicating rather than carrying out their responsibilities and obligations. The lack of transparency allowed anyone who needed or wanted to engage in dishonest or opaque business practices to do so fairly easily.

Your responsibilities and obligations for your standards extend to everyone with whom, and for whom, you work. You don't want your standards compromised by a lack of clarity or transparency on the part of business partners, suppliers, customer groups and financial interests. (See the sidebar 'You're so transparent'.)

When you're planning to enter into a long-term business relationship, be sure to also discuss the deal's ethical dimensions. Doing so is safer for all parties and helps preserve your competitive edge and profitability. And of course, makes sure that the standards of others involved are as high as your own!

Making a Profit – Ethically

Establishing your personal and business ethics isn't just right and moral, it's also profitable. You need to be looking at the standards that you set for your products, services, conduct and performance in terms of the results that they deliver, not just as a soft or woolly option.

An ethical approach is never a soft or woolly option. Think of all the times at work when telling an outright lie would have been easier than facing unacceptable or unpleasant truths. And think of all the people who you've worked with who do lie to get out of difficulties. Do you respect them, trust them or even employ them?

Ethics play a key part in your competitive edge, providing a major point in your strategy. They're one of the foundation stones of profits and profitability. Barry Bugden, previously sales director at Mars UK, has his own very distinctive take on business ethics. He assesses every new project that drops on his desk by asking the following questions:

- ✔ Does it work?
- ✔ Is it right?
- ✔ Does everyone benefit?
- ✔ Is it profitable?

The following sections address Bugden's final question in various ways.

Gaining a competitive edge based on your standards

'Say what you mean and mean what you say' sounds like good advice, but why should you follow it? Well, if you promise something but don't deliver it, people stop trusting you.

If you promise high quality and then charge high prices, there's nothing wrong with this. (Indeed, there's everything right in many cases!) Just be certain that you can and do deliver what you say. For example:

- ✔ Many people expect to pay more for Marks & Spencer sandwiches than those available at other outlets. As long as the bread and fillings are fresh, and the content is substantial, then a higher price reinforces your standards and promise. But woe betide Marks & Spencer (or anyone else who takes this approach) who sets a high standard but then doesn't deliver a high-quality product!

- ✔ Direct Line, the motor and domestic insurance company, doesn't give out its service data or prices on insurance price comparison websites. Direct Line is more expensive than many because of some clear promises about the quality, coverage and completeness of its service. For the quality and peace of mind these promises are expected to bring, customers are prepared to pay premium prices. Direct Line, and others like it, will lose their reputation and value (and the strongly ethical component of their brands), if they start to gain a reputation for haggling over fine detail when people make legitimate claims on their policies.

At the other end of the scale, supermarket value lines must not be cheap or shoddy. They must be good value (and a world of difference exists between 'cheap' and 'good value'). So:

- ✔ Value line milk must still be milk
- ✔ Value line bleach must still clean your surfaces
- ✔ Value line meat must still be tasty and substantial

Building trust and confidence

All the time that you set particular and distinctive standards, you're building trust and confidence for yourself, your staff, your organisation and its products and services.

Business gurus once called these activities *relationship management* – anything that creates and develops a physical and (more importantly) psychological bond between an organisation and its staff, as well as the organisation and its customers, suppliers and backers.

Trust between all parties and confidence in one another provide the basis for any effective business relationship. Specifically:

- ✔ **Staff** expect to have full confidence in the organisation and its leaders, directors, managers and supervisors. They also expect to have confidence in their colleagues. They expect the processes and practices developed by the organisation to act in the best interests of everyone.

- ✔ **Customers** expect to have confidence in the integrity of products and services, as well as the value that they deliver.

- ✔ **Suppliers** expect the organisation to keep its word and stick to supply-side contracts.

- ✔ **Shareholders and backers** expect the organisation to make its profits from legitimate use of their funds.

Ongoing dilemmas

You're always going to have dilemmas to face, address and resolve. And these dilemmas are not straightforward or clear cut.

- ✐ At present, the branded clothing garment and leisurewear companies continue to make healthy profits. However, many of them at different times have been charged with using child or slave labour in their factories (or those to whom they have subcontracted their production demands).

- ✐ Many of the world's large oil companies dump into African river deltas the toxic waste and effluent from their extraction and refining processes, because doing so is much easier and cheaper than disposing of their rubbish effectively.

- ✐ In spite of the credit crunch, many retail banks and finance houses are still targeting the sales of loans and the provision of credit cards to those who are least able to afford to repay them.

In each of these situations, who is doing the wrong thing? And what, if anything, is being done wrong? If you were in charge, what would you do? The issues are complex. However:

- ✐ The use of slave labour is certainly wrong – full stop. If you're going to use slave labour, eventually you'll be called to account for this. So just don't – do something else!

- ✐ The dumping of effluent or anything else for that matter, simply because you're big and powerful enough to do so, is wrong.

- ✐ Selling people loans and credit cards that they can't afford to repay is, at best, 'the right thing for the wrong reasons'.

Eventually, of course, it's you who has to decide, and you'll live or die by your decision. But in every case where real and perceived wrongs are being perpetrated, it only takes a combination of a quiet news day, and a cameraman with some extreme images, to put you out of business. So be very careful – always!

Earning loyalty

Loyalty isn't a right. Organisations and managers must earn it from their staff, customers, clients, suppliers and backers. As you build relationships (see the preceding section), you begin to develop real and understood mutual interests. If you eventually grow to trust people, a *loyalty bond* – a position of mutual interest as well as trust and respect – starts to exist between you and the other groups.

Without any smugness or boasting, try to figure out why your staff and customers are loyal to you. Identify where your strengths lie, and build on them. If your staff or customers aren't loyal to you, work out why this is the case. (Just be sure to avoid using any of the following blame-based phrases: 'cut-throat competition', 'poor wages' or 'Tesco is too big for its boots'.)

You build and reinforce your loyalty bond with customers through your own demeanour and actions. People prefer to do business with you (and therefore you become more profitable) when you cheerfully do what you say you plan to do. Happy, loyal customers tend to come to you for other things, which can in turn lead to further business development.

Developing an ethical stance

Everything I discuss in the preceding sections combines to form your organisation's *ethical stance* – the standards of conduct, behaviour and performance that you set and deliver.

Your ethical stance sets the tone for how your organisation as a whole acts and reacts in its environment and its markets. It's reflected in the standards and quality of your products and services, and the ways in which you deliver them. And it also sets out your staff's work ethic. (See the earlier sidebar 'Standards and survival' for more.)

Handling complaints

From an ethical point of view, handling complaints requires some standards and some consideration. The following sections look quickly at various types of complaints your organisation may encounter, and how you can respond ethically to such complaints.

Everyday customer complaints

You set your own standards and processes for handling complaints – you must also meet your obligations. So, if you give guarantees or make statements about replacements and upgrades, you must deliver.

You never win a fight with a customer. Yes, you're going to end up replacing goods and services even if the customer complains falsely to you or about you. But doing so is better and more cost effective than bogging yourself down in expensive and damaging fights over individual products and services.

Serious customer complaints

If customers make serious complaints to you about, for example, a major malfunction of one of your products or services, you must go to the heart of the matter as quickly as possible. You have no other standard to apply! If something has genuinely gone wrong and you're negligent, the fallout can cost your organisation its life.

At the very least, assess the situation for yourself. If subsequently you find that the customer was misusing the product or had misunderstood the service on offer, make sure that you write provisions for this possibility into subsequent sales and product- and service-performance literature.

Staff complaints

You also need to have an ethical view about staff complaints. Staff can complain about anything if you let them! (Actually, most staff only complain about things long after they should have brought particular matters to your attention.)

If and when staff complain, you must treat the matter with the utmost respect until it's proven or demonstrated that the matter is trivial. And remember: even if the matter turns out to be trivial, it was nevertheless important enough for the staff member to raise with you. So, you must respect it.

Many staff engage with you in complaints about trivial things – and in many cases, this is to test you out and get you talking, as a prelude to telling you what's really bothering them. So again – always listen!

You must also treat seriously any staff complaints about bullying, victimisation, vandalism, theft, fraud and violence. Investigate these complaints immediately and do everything necessary to get to the bottom of the matter. And if, having followed a rigorous disciplinary process, you find that members of your staff are indeed at fault in these areas – then the only thing that you should do is dismiss them.

Encouraging openness and honesty

By building an ethical stance for yourself in the ways I describe in this chapter, you're developing a position of openness and honesty with which everyone can be comfortable.

In addition to business virtues and profits, you're also demonstrating your own humanity. If you can show that you're a human organisation as well as a hard-working and profitable one, producing excellent products and services – then people will indeed continue to beat a path to your door.

Chapter 14

Wrangling with Risk

. . . .

In This Chapter

▶ Understanding the nature of risk and risk management

▶ Anticipating and minimising risk

▶ Dealing with difficult situations

▶ Creating a culture of risk alertness

. . . .

*L*ook at the business pages of any newspaper today and you find numerous references to risk and risk management. A 2007 Chartered Management Institute survey states that 85 per cent of companies and organisations now have risk management policies – up from 35 per cent in 2001.

Although everyone seems to be talking about risk, many don't manage it well. For example:

✔ In July 2007, the Northern Rock bank failed with debts of up to £30 billion.

✔ In June 2006, EADS announced it was not able to deliver the A380 super-jumbo airliner on time.

✔ In December 2007, the NHS stated that the cost of its fully integrated IT system would be £25 billion, rather than the £2 billion forecast.

✔ The 2012 London Olympics was originally budgeted at £2.3 billion. In 2008 the stated budget is £19 billion and is certain to rise.

In each case, the risk of getting things wrong was well-known in general terms. However, nobody attended to the *specifics* of what could go wrong:

✔ The Northern Rock bank assumed that historically bad debtors would nevertheless continue to pay up on their mortgages and loans.

✔ EADS assumed that production and delivery schedules wouldn't be disrupted by anything.

- ✔ The NHS assumed that its IT project would experience no glitches, and made no provision for transferring handwritten data to computers.

- ✔ The original budget for the London Olympic Games was guessed; and to date, the £19 billion remains an estimate rather than a detailed forecast.

So there's plenty of evidence that things can go spectacularly wrong at exactly the time that risk and risk management are organisational and managerial priorities. You therefore need to look at what risk actually is and how you can manage it most effectively – which is exactly what I do in the following sections.

Knowing the Unknown: Risk and Uncertainty

Certainty is when a set of circumstances or outcomes can be fully predicted or known. Uncertainty is when nothing is known or understood about a set of circumstances or outcomes. In between certainty and uncertainty is *risk* – a place where you know and understand some things, but not the full set of circumstances.

You therefore pay a premium (a fee) as a hedge against your lack of knowledge and understanding. You must also take steps to develop, as fully as possible, your knowledge and understanding of the given set of circumstances so that your fee is as low as possible. For example, you don't know precisely *when* you're going to have accidents and emergencies, but you do know that these things are bound to happen at some time. You insure (pay a fee) for when they do happen, so that you can cover yourself and your obligations when the time comes.

One way of looking at risk is that you can insure against risk; you can't insure against uncertainty. Stated another way, you *can* insure against accidents, as with the preceding example, but you *can't* insure against what you absolutely don't know (and which is therefore uncertain). You have to be able to give an idea of what risk you and the insurer are facing!

Your drive when confronting risk must therefore be to fill in the gaps in your knowledge and understanding as far as possible so that you:

- ✔ Know and understand as much as you possibly can.

- ✔ Know and understand what you're insuring against.

- ✔ Can decide whether the risk is worth insuring against.

The core of *risk management* – knowing and understanding what can, may and does go wrong – is to assure you and your organisation that you can implement your competitive strategy, undertake specific ventures and respond to opportunities with as much certainty as possible.

Looking at key areas

Effective risk management is based on thorough and frequent environmental scanning and analysis (see Chapter 5). Constant examination of what's going on inside and outside your organisation yields a lot of useful information about risk.

You're looking for early warnings about changes in any or all of the following (be prepared, this a very extensive list!). Ask yourself, 'What can possibly go wrong?' about each of the bullets:

- The availability of finance, and related costs of finance (interest rate, exchange rate changes and so on).

- Changes in market size and structure.

- Changes in customers' spending power, tastes, needs, wants and demands.

- Changes in technological capacity, especially whether such changes are going to affect your competitiveness or cost base.

- Overall information technology and data processing capacity.

- Changes in the labour market, especially the price, value and relative security of workers with specific expertise, knowledge or skills.

- Entry of new players into your markets and the strengths and weaknesses that they bring.

- Exit of existing players from your markets and the extent to which you can fill any gaps that they leave – or whether their exits in fact destabilise the whole sector.

- The stability and security of your internal operations, specifically your ability to protect confidentiality, secure finance and identify theft and fraud.

- Staff management issues, especially behaviours such as bullying, victimisation, discrimination and harassment,

- The effects of staff relations on overall organisational performance.

As you go through the list and try to identify possible problems, try to look at risk in directly practical terms, from the point of view of what can possibly go wrong in a specific area. Some specific questions may be:

- ✔ What are the consequences of computer/technology/IC/IT system failure or crash?

- ✔ What are the consequences of doubling or halving supply-side prices?

- ✔ What are the consequences of fraud, vandalism or sabotage?

- ✔ What are the consequences of negligence or ineptitude?

- ✔ What are the consequences, as well as the opportunities, of taking particular decisions about going into (or stepping out of) particular ventures and proposals?

If your people are still producing bland or general answers to the preceding questions – or worse, saying things like, 'Nothing can go wrong; this is foolproof' – you must ask and ask and ask again until they get to grips with the details.

Pondering the wild and wacky

In addition to asking what can possibly go wrong with all the garden-variety aspects of your business, you also need to develop your knowledge and approach in order to ensure that you address the wild and wacky – the things that you think can't possibly ever happen.

Three reasons for taking the wild and wacky into your risk consideration are that:

- ✔ It enhances your capability to think; and therefore the scope of your quest for knowledge and understanding.

- ✔ It means that others have to lift their horizons and broaden their outlook.

- ✔ Many of the wilder and wackier things do indeed come to pass!

Some examples of wild and wacky considerations include:

- ✔ Who would ever have thought a few years ago that oil prices would reach $100 a barrel? The result is that many companies and organisations are now making projections based on $200 and even $300 a barrel – not as a wild and wacky idea, but as a serious aid to understanding how their business may need to change if oil prices escalate.

> ✔ Who would have thought that a year or two ago, the value and confidence of large banks would be corrupted and skewed – by their own traders colluding with others in the financial services sectors to cause a run on confidence and share values?

And of course, the original wild and wacky consideration:

> ✔ Who ever thought the Titanic would sink on its maiden voyage?

The point of considering truly offbeat scenarios is simple: each generation has to keep learning and re-learning to expect the unexpected. Your priority should be to instil this kind of inquisitiveness and quest for understanding in yourself and others.

Learning from previous events

Companies and organisations that seek to be competitive must examine, analyse and learn from previous events and actions. Analysing risk-related events that have already happened inside and outside your organisation isn't a history lesson. Your goal is to retain the knowledge gained and to apply these insights to future risk management. For example:

> ✔ In 2003, the World Health Organisation announced an impending global epidemic of bird flu that would place restrictions on trading patterns. The WHO further stated that if flu crossed over to the human population, a major epidemic would result. Several years have passed, but the problem (the risk) hasn't gone away! Organisations need to consider and build into their risk management strategies to cover the likely and possible range of effects and restraints that may result if bird flu (or indeed any other disease epidemic) comes to pass.

> ✔ In 2007–8, the global banking sector lost billions of pounds, dollars and euros in speculating on the values available in the world's sub-prime (high-risk) property markets. The immediate effect of this made finance much more difficult to come by – and also more expensive. Going forward, organisations need to know and understand the likely and possible effects of further hikes in the availability and price of finance for the future. (And in order to be prepared, you need to consider the wildest and wackiest prospects – what if the price of finance rises to 50 per cent of its value (so in order to borrow £100, you actually have to pay £150)?

You can anticipate specific events and prepare responses. You may not be able to predict events in full detail – for example, you can't predict that the next epidemic will be smallpox/TB/HIV/bird flu. But you can predict that an epidemic of something will occur at some stage. And this predicted information is enough for you to put your response in place.

Taking cues from human behaviour

Of all the reasons for things not being addressed in organisations, the two most common are:

- ✔ Nobody thought they were important enough.
- ✔ Nobody got around to them.

Either or both of these conditions are invariably present when disasters occur. For example:

- ✔ Nobody thought it was important enough to have enough lifeboats for everyone on the Titanic.
- ✔ Nobody thought it was important enough to clear the ice off the wings of the planes involved in the Munich air disaster of 1958 or the Potomac crash of 1990.
- ✔ Nobody thought it was important enough to shut the bow doors of the 'Herald of Free Enterprise' before setting sail.
- ✔ Nobody thought it was important enough to have clean hospitals in the NHS until it became clear that thousands were dying every year as the direct result of hospital-acquired infections.

Each of the preceding events is clearly an extreme example to drive home the point that human reaction and response has many lessons to offer about potential risks.

Every organisation has equivalents of these well-known disasters. In all organisations diseases occur through air-conditioning systems; computer systems crash because of inadequate staff training; people lose life and/or limb because of inadequate safety training. All happen, and all prove to be very expensive to deal with.

Most importantly, far fewer of these types of events would occur if, at a strategic level, organisations thought that such events were important enough to prevent in the first place. And each time they do occur, resources have to be diverted from primary purposes into remedying errors.

Commit yourself to believing that risk issues are important enough and worth getting around to. Train everyone in your organisation about risk management, explaining that things can and do go wrong. Reinforce ongoing risk management in your organisation by ranking it high on organisational priority lists and by undergoing thorough inspection and appraisal processes. (See the sidebar 'Upon closer inspection' for more information.)

REAL WORLD EXAMPLE

Upon closer inspection

Business activities can go wrong when they aren't properly or thoroughly inspected. With everything that you do, you have to commit yourself to adequate inspection processes and practices.

The immediate problem related to inspection is that it adds to your initial costs, increasing the level of outlay required and potentially cutting into your returns and ability to compete. Nevertheless, you must carry out inspections, whatever the cost.

Adequate inspection could have been better in all the following situations:

✔ The Northern Rock crisis would have been flagged up in 2005 rather than 2007.

✔ The 2012 London Olympic budget would have been addressed immediately.

✔ With the delays to the A380 airliner, EADS, the parent company, would have been forced to increase the production of components, or to strengthen its transport networks.

✔ The doors of the 'Herald of Free Enterprise' would have been closed as a matter of routine before setting sail.

In each case, the losses were compounded by the fact that the organisations involved assumed that everything was in order and gave the activities and the individuals involved clean bills of health; some organisations even went so far as to pronounce that they were satisfied with the strength of their inspections and the effectiveness of their actions.

When you're conducting your own inspection, you need to step back and make sure that you're not taking anything for granted. Continue to look closely at every aspect of your organisation and its activities for things that can possibly go wrong.

Looking at untargeted projects and proposals

Other areas that organisations need to be aware of in risk management include untargeted projects and proposals – and this includes vanity projects!

Vanity projects are often activities considered the baby or brainchild of a top, senior or powerful executive. These projects are supposed to give the company some kind of prestige or status (even if they lose money, as often happens).

Untargeted projects and proposals gain credence in organisations because of their sheer technological or design brilliance, or because they seem exciting. Often these projects rise up from think tanks, are tossed around and quickly gain lives of their own. Because the project is believed to be so brilliant, any projections as to how it may perform quickly become fact. (See the sidebar 'The untargeted Millennium Dome' for an example of a particularly notable untargeted project.)

You must work to find specific targets for everything that you do (see Chapters 1, 3 and 4). Targets include specific customer bases and segments, locations and outlets, new market development or new products and services for existing markets. Failure to obtain specific understanding based on real information lays you open to the risk of compromising the value and integrity of everything that you currently do, which in turn is likely to damage your reputation (or at least give you a reputation for inertia and slow movement).

Defending your reputation

Everyone makes mistakes. This is a fact of life and it applies to all organisations, their products, services and activities. Your customers, clients, suppliers and backers accept mistakes quite willingly, providing that, when you do make mistakes, you put them right – and don't repeat them.

Failure to address your mistakes eventually compromises your reputation. As well as losing faith in your products and services, people begin to lose their confidence in you. Rightly or wrongly, you then begin to gain a reputation for being an organisation that:

- ✔ Delivers bad products and services (regardless of whether this is true).

- ✔ Delivers bad quality and customer service (again, whether true or not).

- ✔ Is dishonest and expedient in its dealings with customers, suppliers, the media and even the world (again, whether true or not).

When your reputation crumbles, customers turn away from you, suppliers begin to wonder about the value of their contracts with you and backers question the value of their investments. Your staff also begin to look elsewhere for jobs.

Failure to manage your reputation and to assess the risks involved in compromising it therefore leads to decline in business volumes and turnover, and to products and services being delivered by poorer quality staff, less effectively.

So obviously, building up and protecting your reputation needs to be part of your ongoing consideration of risk. The following section explores specific ways in which you can minimise the risk of damaging your reputation.

REAL WORLD EXAMPLE

Sub-prime performance, indeed!

The so-called sub-prime mortgage crisis actually represents multiple failures by multiple organisations to correctly and completely assess risk.

Some mortgages were extended to non-creditworthy customers and then 'sliced and diced' – cut up into an almost endless number and variety of parcels or *tranches*. These bits were often then re-assembled into complex, exotic financial securities.

Sound complicated? Well, it is!

But few thought to unravel these complex combinations and look at the actual risks of the bad mortgages within. In some instances, these securities simply contained too many pieces to try to examine! In others, so-called 'neutral-risk managers' dared not alienate the salesmen in their organisation by saying 'no', lest the managers, in turn, be sacked.

As a result, many organisations came to rely on outdated statistical assessment tools that were not designed to deal with these new risks. The result? Look at the FTSE in 2008, especially bank shares!

Avoiding wrong actions

You lose both money and reputation if you become associated with managing matters incorrectly. Although every organisation has to make its own distinctions between right and wrong (see Chapter 13 for more on ethics), some absolutely wrong actions include:

- **Breaking the law:** This includes trading law, product and service delivery law, advertising and marketing standards, employment law and more.

- **Inadequate health and safety procedures:** Failures in these areas increase the regularity, frequency and severity of accidents, chemical leaks, effluent management issues and more.

- **Financial wrongdoings:** These include managing your share price through insider trading, *ramping* (buying and selling your own shares to ensure that you maintain a certain share price) and many other underhanded schemes.

- **Excessive compensation:** Paying large bonuses to top staff for mediocre, average or declining performance is simply wrong.

- **Legal wrangling.** Using the legal system to block or delay investigations that you know to be legitimate is wrong.

REAL WORLD EXAMPLE

The untargeted Millennium Dome

The Millennium Dome was commissioned in 1995 as a monument to everything good about the previous thousand years and as an icon to herald in the next millennium. At first glance, the Millennium Dome looks targeted. But in practice, anything as vague as this project must always ultimately remain untargeted.

In the case of the Millennium Dome, the following factors further compromised the venture:

- The venture's religious significance (which was after all the basis for the Millennium itself) was never made clear.

- The nature of events and exhibitions to be held within the Dome was unclear, untargeted and uneven.

- The location was wrong – in the middle of a London suburb, rather than in central London.

Still, the project quickly took on a life of its own. For example, planners drew up visitor projections that indicated that 26,000 people per day for each day of the year were required for the project to break even in one year. This project immediately became *assured* – assumed to be capable of being met – and then quickly it was certain to be met!

The idea of celebrating the Millennium was first proposed and explored in 1991, and the Millennium Dome emerged as the only thing that anyone could really think of doing! Each year from then onwards, the Government had ample opportunity to cancel the project and replace it with something genuinely targeted. In particular, the change of government in 1997 offered an opportunity to cancel the project but by then the Dome had taken on a life of its own – and so the project was allowed to progress.

No one ever explored ways to use the project as a focal point for regenerating the south-east London area. No one ever fully established costs or a clear return on investment. Furthermore, no leader, director or project champion was appointed. (Not until the Dome had been open for nearly six months did Piet Verhayen take up his position as its operational Chief Executive.)

When the Dome opened on 31 December 1999, everything that could go wrong, went wrong. The Queen and the assorted VIPs were kept waiting outside in the cold for two hours. The entertainment was under-rehearsed. The public had difficulty reaching the Dome because the transport network was inadequate. And the firework display that was to usher in the new millennium was poor as well.

And so it went on. The exhibitions and entertainment that were presented during the life of the Dome in 2000 were deemed to be adequate or average but not outstanding. Many people did indeed go and visit, but not in the numbers demanded. And so the Dome gained a reputation as something of a national embarrassment.

When it closed on 31 December 2000, nobody was sure what to do with it. Some wanted it turned into a super casino. Others proposed dismantling it and re-developing the site for housing. Others wanted to turn it into a sports arena.

Finally, in 2006, the Millennium Dome was handed over to an entertainment consortium for £1. This entertainment consortium developed the O2 arena as a concert venture; and because it now had a clear and targeted purpose, it subsequently became a success.

The admitted cost to the public purse was £700 million; the actual cost very much higher.

If you see any of the preceding things in action, know that they're just plain wrong! You must intervene by using any influence that you have to stop them immediately, and put right whatever the issue happens to be. Nothing else will do here!

Dealing with stress

Another major element of risk management that you need to be aware of is stress. And stress is more complex than is usually understood. You need to be aware of two main forms of stress:

- **Physical stress,** including repetitive strain injuries, back pain and physical damage to the body.
- **Mental or psychological stress,** leading to feelings of pressure within individuals and groups.

So stress includes factors relating to workloads, working practices and occupational and personal health. Stress is a disease (or injury in the case of physical stress) brought on by bad or conflicting working practices, lack of clarity of objectives, lack of training and understanding, extreme overwork (and – rarely – extreme under work), adversarial working relationships and bullying, victimisation, discrimination and harassment, especially in management styles and practices, and group relations.

Stress-filled work environments always lead to conflict, mistakes and errors – as well as serious health problems for the individuals involved. The worst cases can lead to physical and verbal threats and violence, and to drink and drug problems. If stress-related cases ever come to court, they're expensive to settle and can damage your reputation (see the preceding section 'Defending your reputation' for more on reputations). Something you definitely want to avoid!

You can also see stress in terms of 'stress on systems and processes.' This kind of stress occurs where, for whatever reason, your systems and processes can't cope with what people are asking the systems and processes to do. Examples include:

- Your technology and IT systems don't have the capacity to work at maximum effectiveness and efficiency all the time.
- Your website crashes when it receives too many hits at the same time.
- Your supply and distribution networks can't be effective in the local prevailing traffic conditions and transport infrastructure.
- Your people aren't able to get to work easily – or you can't attract people to work for you because of your business's location.
- You can't process your invoices and liabilities quickly enough to meet your obligations.

The aqueduct

A large specialist civil engineering contractor was engaged to construct an aqueduct from the reservoirs in the Pennines in the north of England to deliver water supplies to the urban populations of Manchester and Leeds.

The company had a reputation for medium quality work: normally only a month or two late in meeting deadlines and exceeding budget by 5 to 10 per cent. For many years, this level of work was an acceptable standard in the industry. And because of its specialism in aqueduct work, the company's order book was always full.

However, the company's assured and dominant position led to complacency. With the aqueduct contract, mistakes crept in. During construction, the contractors allowed gas pockets to build up. When an electrical fault occurred and produced a spark, a fire ball travelled the length of the aqueduct and blew up a pumping station on the outskirts of Manchester. Two people were killed.

The point? An assured market position and a full order book never provide an end in themselves! You still have to attend to all the things that are of fundamental importance, including your continued ability to do the agreed-to work, your commitment to health and safety, your promise to produce high-quality goods and services and ongoing recognition that anyone can make mistakes (even companies with full order books and dominant positions).

In this particular case the company went bankrupt, and was bought by a Dutch multinational. And in this case, the company's success or failure was in its own hands. It failed because of insufficient attention to risk management.

All the above situations place stress on the organisation, and consequently on those who work there. Frequent, long-term and extreme stress on the system can eventually damage your business, your reputation and everyone's overall confidence in you.

In all the preceding examples, failing to recognise the risk of any or all of these stressors happening at a given time (or at the same time) is certain to damage your business, product and service output and quality, cost effectiveness and efficiency – and therefore your competitiveness.

Eliminating risk

Of course, eliminating risk is impossible! What you can do – what you need to do – is to take every possible step to *minimise* the risk of anything that's potentially negative occurring. You should, after all, know and understand that they do happen – you've seen them elsewhere and identified potential problems in your own organisation.

To minimise risk, you must attend to each of the following:

✔ **Market and sectoral trends:** Gain as much knowledge as possible of the present and unfolding state of the markets, and the position of your products and services within it. (See Chapters 3 and 4.)

✔ **Likely and possible entrants to the markets:** Know and understand what you may need to respond to. (See Chapter 6.)

✔ **The actual nature of transport and technology infrastructures:** Be able to take remedial action when barriers and blockages occur.

✔ **Staff management practices:** Be able take remedial actions where bad or unacceptable working practices are affecting output; focus on training and developing staff appropriately in order to avoid bad work practices altogether.

✔ **Operational aspects:** Know and understand everything that's going on within your organisation in the delivery of products and services so that you can take remedial actions when barriers and hold-ups occur. (See Chapter 12.)

✔ **Manage financial aspects:** Ensure that your invoicing, billing and accounting procedures are watertight.

✔ **Manage staff involvement in financial activities:** Minimise the risk of fraudulent activities. I would love to say 'eliminate' – but in practice, people take advantage if they can; so you must maintain constant vigilance (see Chapter 8).

✔ **Constantly assess the capability and potential of your workforce:** See that they're constantly being trained, developed, improved and re-energised.

✔ **Constantly appraise the capacity of your technology:** Ensure that your technology is being made to work as cost efficiently and effectively as possible; and that you upgrade it when required.

✔ **Deliver your products and services on time and within budget.**

✔ **Deliver your products and services to the quality and volumes demanded by the markets that you serve.**

The end result is that you create an accurate and informed assessment of the risks in your particular sector that everyone involved knows and understands. It also means that you can make contingency plans and have funds available to meet problems and issues when they occur.

Making efforts to minimise risks doesn't mean that you don't take risks! You simply know what you're letting yourself in for and can take steps to improve your knowledge and understanding – therefore minimising the risk of things going wrong.

Responding to Real Risks

Anticipating risk is important. But you must also pay attention to what can, and does, occur in organisations on a daily basis. You can look at what I call *real risks* from several points of view.

- ✔ To tolerate risks is unacceptable, so you must tackle them when they occur.
- ✔ Being unaware of these risks is acceptable – once! And if you're caught short, you make sure that this never happens to you again.
- ✔ If you don't tackle risks you do lasting damage to collective and individual morale, thus damaging the effectiveness of your business and activities.

If any of the real risks that I address in the following sections are allowed to persist, they're certain to do damage to your business overall – including your effectiveness, your reputation and your integrity.

Negligence

Negligence – paying insufficient care, concern or attention to things – can, and does, occur anywhere and everywhere, and not always for the worst of reasons. We're all guilty of 'never having quite got around' to doing something that needed to be done. Nevertheless, you have to tackle incidents involving negligence and incompetence when they do become apparent.

You begin by tackling negligence in terms of making sure that everyone knows and understands where her priorities lie and then making sure that they follow them. For example, if you know that some part of your organisation's work is never quite done, find out the reasons why.

And if you discover that the part of the work doesn't get done because it's dirty, boring, difficult or demeaning, make it clear that you're all in it together, and if it's appropriate, take your own turn at it also.

Make sure that you engage the entire staff in the process of identifying and explaining incidents involving negligence. This is a function of your own commitment, energy and enthusiasm. And if they still don't grasp the message – put them through poor performance procedures.

Incompetence

Incompetence – the lack of capability, skill and expertise necessary to do what you need to do – is a serious risk because it means that you've placed people in positions without fully checking their capabilities. In many cases therefore, incompetence is not the fault of the individual.

Where incompetence becomes apparent, you need to make sure that staff receive the full training and development that they need. You also have a common law duty to make sure that people are capable in what they do in any case! If staff members still cannot do jobs despite all your best efforts, consider reassigning them to other duties. And if they turn out to be unwilling rather than incapable, they need to be disciplined.

Fraud

Fraud can't be committed accidentally. You need therefore to take every possible step to prevent it from happening within your organisation in the first place – and to deal with it in full when it occurs.

Fraud can, and does, happen anywhere (see the sidebar 'Fraud in action!'), so you need to be constantly aware of the possibilities. If you ever find discrepancies in your financial statements or reports, always check them. And whatever the causes turn out to be (fraud or anything else) tackle them immediately.

Bad behaviour

The risk to your organisation of deficiencies in behaviour affect your reputation and your pocket. After others find out that you don't punish unacceptable behaviour, they come to believe that you actually tolerate it.

Think of all the excuses that people make for bullying, victimisation, harassment and violence. You know the sorts of things:

- 'Oh, but he's always like this.'
- 'Well, she's a larger than life character.'

Anything, in fact, rather than confront bad behaviour.

Fraud in action!

Instances of fraud in business are legion. Some particularly notable recent examples include:

- **Enron:** The largest corporate collapse in business history was that of Enron, the US energy trading company. Essentially, the problems at Enron started out as making full use of a legitimate business tactic – placing some assets and liabilities 'off the Balance Sheet'. This practice means that the fundamentals of the company are represented on the Balance Sheet, but problem areas are not. Enron's biggest mistake was basically its failure to recognise that it would eventually need to address these 'off Balance Sheet' items. As the situation worsened, the company resorted to setting up subsidiaries, over-valuing them and using the over-valuation to support (on paper) its borrowings and share issues. The whole thing turned especially nasty because directors pocketed the profits on share issues created in the described ways and left the rest of the company's employees responsible for Enron's massive debts.

- **Aero Engineering:** A major manufacturer of aero engines was caught colluding with one of its suppliers in a price-fixing arrangement. Now, price fixing is hardly unusual! But in this case, the prices were fixed so as to generate specific levels of business revenue that would in turn guarantee bonuses for those engaged on both the purchasing and also the supply sides.

- **Leisure facility fires:** Every time a funfair, seaside pier or other ageing tourist attraction goes up in smoke, everyone becomes suspicious! People concentrate their attention on what could have happened and why in particular sets of circumstances – and then look to the insurance valuations of the particular buildings and facilities.

The lessons you can take away from these sample cases include:

- The Enron case caused the collapse of the company and wider loss of confidence in the energy trading industry. Widespread collapse happens in any sector where such fraud is discovered amongst one of its major players.

- The Aero Engineering fraud was able to persist for many years before being discovered (and one of the companies tried to hush the matter when it finally came to light). However, when the authorities were called in, the chief investigator reported, 'I suppose at last we have been called in to investigate the parts scam'. So in fact everyone knew what was going on anyway.

- The facilities fires indicate how people tend to think when certain things do occur. Although in many of the cases a disaster has a clear and legitimate reason for happening, people nevertheless do often point the finger of suspicion somewhere – regardless of whether doing so is justified.

When you allow negative behaviour to persist, the situation goes beyond one of risk and becomes a matter of reality. People can and do go home and tell anyone who'll listen that you put up with bad behaviour, tolerate it and even encourage it.

By not nipping bad behaviour in the bud and dismissing the perpetrators where proven, you're actually damaging your own reputation, as well as that of your organisation. And although you may not see the effects in terms of lost sales, you see:

- ✔ Your good staff leaving and being hard to replace (which adds to your costs).
- ✔ Costs incurred when staff who are on the wrong end of the bullying, victimisation or violence then sue you.
- ✔ Adverse media coverage.

And there's no maverick, laddish or work hard/play hard culture that can justify truly bad behaviour, nor the fact that you do nothing about it. Indeed employers have a legal duty to deal with bad behaviour.

Product and service problems

As I discuss in Chapter 13, problems with your products and services are ethical factors. They're also risks. For example:

- ✔ Do you want to be the one who has to face the courts because you know that your product was a fire risk/health hazard/prone to explosion, but did nothing about it?
- ✔ Do you want to be the one who has to face the courts in order to explain why you placed investments in a fund that you knew to be unstable?

If scenarios like either of the preceding examples – or dozens of other situations – happen to you, you must realise that you'll be on your own. Your organisation does its best to disown you. Colleagues suddenly emerge from the woodwork to state that they knew about the faults all along.

Security issues

Ask yourself just how secure are your data, IT systems, company and organisational secrets, HR and financial information? And just how secure are your premises and your staff physically? Can anyone possibly rob or defraud you?

You probably all work in an organisation with rigorous security systems – CCTV, computer scanning and email scrutiny. However, even with all of this technology, you can never make anything totally secure. What you can and must do to alleviate the risk is ensure that you have *fallback positions* for when crises do occur. For example:

✔ Major airlines back up all their company and customer data three times.

✔ Universities have central, as well as individual, file stores.

✔ Factory premises have personal and organisational recognition and security systems that individuals must go through before making deliveries.

✔ Airport staff have to go through security just the same as the travelling public before being able to work on the other side of any security checkpoint.

So, as with behaviour problems, security is in your hands. You must determine how secure you want to make your activities and the steps that you need to take to protect your assets and your interests.

Accidents and injuries

Rationally, in most places of work, the risk of accidents and injury is minimal. Health and safety procedures are in place and, where necessary, specialist equipment (for instance, gear for working in very hot, cold or dangerous conditions) is always provided. And yet, 2.5 million industrial injuries are reported every year in the United Kingdom. So accidents must still be happening somewhere!

However mundane it may seem, you must keep an active watch on everything that goes on in your organisation. When you spot potential hazards, tackle them immediately.

'However mundane it may seem' **is** unfortunately the attitude that many take to health and safety, accidents and hazards. You need to change this kind of attitude whenever you encounter it. Doing so is important both to you and anyone who has an accident. And where accidents are proven by official inquiries or by the courts to have occurred as the result of negligence or inadequacy of procedures, damages are unlimited.

Disasters

Serious incidents at places of work are thankfully relatively rare. However, you need to be aware of their potential for happening and the damages that you can incur when they do.

To minimise your disaster-related risk, you need to concentrate on two aspects:

✔ The extent of the disaster that would occur if you lost all your company data or information from electronic systems.

  ✔ The extent of the disaster that would occur if you experienced a serious physical incident, such as a fire or explosion.

  ✔ The extent of the disaster that would occur if you were to experience an earthquake, tornado or hurricane.

Getting Everyone Involved in Risk Management

As you take time to consider all the risks that I cover in this chapter, what you're beginning to do is to develop your own basis for risk management. Additionally, you can start thinking about how to develop a *risk-aware culture*, one in which everyone plays an active part in minimising and managing risk.

The positives of having risk management plans and a risk-aware culture include:

  ✔ You have an early warning system for spotting things that can go wrong.

  ✔ You have an immediate and effective response system when things – anything – go wrong.

You also need to make up your mind now that you don't want to be caught in either of the following risk-related traps:

  ✔ **Benign neglect.** You (forlornly) hope that if you don't tackle a risk, it'll go away or sort itself out. Of course, nothing ever goes away! And especially things that present risks to you, your company and its wellbeing. Don't fall into this category.

  ✔ **Seeking a victim for whatever has gone wrong.** If something turns out to be your fault, you must take the blame. If the situation turns out to be the fault of someone else, then tackle it and learn from it. And if it was fraud, violence, bullying or victimisation, dismiss the perpetrators when the case against them is proven.

Creating a full understanding of risk

By learning from your own misfortunes and the mistakes of others and by seeing those things that went wrong, you're enhancing your own expertise in the area of risk management, as well as your general knowledge of the organisation as it operates in its environment.

Blowing the whistle

Whistle-blowers are those who quite legitimately find that they have no choice but to make public their problems. Whistle-blowers fall into two categories:

- Individuals outside the organisation
- Individuals inside the organisation

Whistle-blowers outside the organisation are much easier to deal with. Suppliers, customers and clients who know or believe that they have had a raw deal from you simply go public when they choose – and you can do nothing about it. You're left with no choice but to acknowledge your faults and put them right, and make sure that the things never happen again. And if you truly committed no wrong, you also can eventually explain this in public.

Internal whistle-blowers are much harder. If they have any sort of a case, they're going public on something that you should have put right before – and haven't!

So what to do? As when dealing with outside whistle-blowers, you must publicly acknowledge the situation and put things right – and then follow up by making sure that the problem never happens again. The difference with an internal whistle-blower is that you have to re-build the relationships that have undoubtedly been damaged within your organisation. In practice too, if someone has a complaint against you, everyone else then knows about it.

So you have to take it on the chin – and make sure that you learn from it and that it never ever happens again! And remember: you can't sack people for whistle-blowing (or if you do, you'll find yourself paying unlimited damages for doing so!).

And from this expertise, you can begin to develop a more dynamic approach to risk. Thus, you and all your colleagues can begin to concentrate on minimising the chances of anything happening in the first place, rather than putting them right afterwards.

Start off by involving everyone. You need to include risk management at the induction stage of employment, when you cover emergency and fire drill procedures and introduce any particular organisational or occupational hazards, technology and materials. You're likely at this stage also to cover things such as what to do about general security, computer crashes and systems failures.

Assessing risk – actively and constantly

By doing everything I discuss in this chapter, you're building risk awareness and an active approach to risk management on the part of everyone right from the outset of their employment. You reinforce risk awareness procedures by the ways in which you and your colleagues conduct yourselves and in the overall attitude to your business within its environment. Doing all this gives you the best possible chance of minimising the risk of anything going wrong.

You can't eliminate risk. What you can do though – what you're seeking to do – is to minimise the risk of things going wrong. You're attending to all those areas that you know can and do go wrong and doing your very best to remove them from your particular equation.

And when the genuinely unforeseen does occur, you learn from this, add it to your fund of knowledge and so generate an even greater risk awareness all round.

Part V
Looking Towards Your Future

'So you think you were born to be
a leader, Maulverer?'

In this part . . .

In order to enjoy a successful future, you need to be constantly aware of and looking at the key things going on in the world today. I highlight trends in expansion, outsourcing and opportunities for new markets and globalisation.

Chapter 15

Venturing Into Mergers, Acquisitions and Takeovers

*O*f all the things that are supposed to reflect the effectiveness of a strategic and competitive approach to business, mergers, acquisitions and takeovers come very high on the list. Effective and successful mergers, acquisitions and takeovers enhance share values, provide synergies and economies of scale and gain you new markets, products and services very quickly. What better reflection is there of strategic and competitive acumen than pursuing such business deals?

As always, the truth is both different and also more complex. In this chapter, I examine all the major steps – and obstacles – you encounter when pursuing a merger, acquisition or takeover. I also look at what happens when you're being taken over (regardless of whether you want to be!).

Going into Strategic Ventures

You read stories of mergers, acquisitions and takeovers all the time. So they must be good for everyone – as well as simple and straightforward to carry out – right? Well, not quite. In fact, most don't deliver as planned, turn out to be more expensive or end up introducing a fresh sets of problems. (See the sidebar 'Mega-venture success?' for more.)

Essentially, all the venture types I discuss in this chapter interrelate, but you need to note some distinctions:

- **Mergers** involve two or more companies coming together and combining operations on basically equal footings.

- **Takeovers and acquisitions** involve one company buying up another (or others).

- *Mega-ventures* are mergers, takeovers or acquisitions on a large scale. These deals require lots of finance to happen and then lots more finance to continue working.

Although many organisations and their executives go into mergers, acquisitions and takeovers with the intention of increasing share values, experiencing dynamic synergies and gaining new markets, products, services and customers, many others unfortunately go in for a host of inappropriate and potentially damaging reasons, including:

- The prestige and kudos that come from being part of a mega-venture.

- Shareholder pressure, in which a dominant backer asks (or demands) that the organisation gets involved in the venture because doing so is likely to lead to short- or medium-term share price advantage.

- A presumption that the businesses involved will achieve vaguely appealing 'synergies and economies of scale,' rather than an accurate calculation or detailed forecasting of what the deal can actually achieve.

- An us-too mentality. 'Everyone else in our sector is doing it, so we must also' has been the rationale between legions of horrible business decisions.

So you have to bring your full expertise to bear as you're considering one of these mega-ventures. You need to ask detailed questions such as:

- Who benefits from this immediately – and who will benefit from this in the longer term?

- Who loses out immediately – and in the longer term?

- Who wants the venture? Why do they want it? Why do they really want it?

- Who does *not* want it? And why not? What are the reasons for not going ahead?

- How will such a venture benefit customers and clients? Will they continue to use and trade with the new organisation? If so, why? If not, why not?

- What will be the attitude of suppliers to dealing with a merged, larger and more dominant organisation? Will they be happy to carry on, or will they see the new organisation's size as a threat?

Mega-venture success?

Research from the late 1980s reveals that more than two-thirds of all mergers fail, based on the criterion of a return that exceeds the risk-free rate at the time. For non-related acquisitions, the success rate is even worse – only about one in ten of unrelated deals succeed based on this criterion. And yet, mega-ventures continue to dominate the business headlines. Interested parties (particularly bankers and intermediaries who are typically only paid when these deals occur) are always going to push for the deals, regardless of value or reason.

In 2001, the Chartered Management Institute produced a survey and data which stated that 87 per cent of all mergers, acquisitions and takeovers failed or fell short of full success. The reasons for failure were:

✔ Lack of attention to the cultures and structures of the newly merged organisations.

✔ No consideration of how to merge and integrate workforces.

✔ No consideration of how to integrate technology, communications and information systems.

✔ Removal or loss of key positions in the old organisations, thus losing critical expertise.

✔ Loss of leadership and clarity of direction.

✔ Loss of confidence in the new organisation on the part of the staff of the old ones.

✔ Inaccurately projected performance for the newly merged organisation (invariably wildly optimistic).

✔ Focus on short-term interests, especially enhancing share price.

✔ No knowledge or understanding of what 'the synergies' or 'economies of scale' were actually supposed to deliver.

A 13 per cent (or 1 in 8) chance of success looks little more than a bet! You must know and understand what you're letting yourself in for if you want to give yourself a much better chance of success. (For more, pick up *Value Management* (1991, McGraw Hill) by Peter Clark – or read my summary of this classic book in Chapter 18.)

Obviously, you have a lot of groundwork to do before you get to the nub of the issue, which is a detailed and accurate projection of:

✔ The costs of the merger, which include things like harmonising staff, combining terms and conditions, integrating technology and standardising products and services.

✔ The benefits of the merger, which include the stated and accurate economies of scale that you intend to achieve. (See the section 'Economies of scale' later in this chapter for more on this topic.)

Chapter 20 features my ten essential strategies for completing successful acquisitions and mergers.

Lining Up Resources and Finance

To engage in any merger or takeover activity, you must have money – capital and revenue resources. You need to know and understand how much money the venture requires and where it's to come from. You need to know and understand the costs of capital and revenue finance, as well as the benefits. And you need access to *contingency funds*; you must have some idea of where you can acquire additional funds, if necessary.

In general, your sources of funds include:

- ✔ **Share capital and rights issues**, in which you ask the existing sharehold- ers of one, both or all the organisations involved to raise extra capital to fund the merger or takeover.

- ✔ **Private equity**, in which you secure arrangements with individuals or finance houses to fund and underwrite the activities.

- ✔ **Loans and mortgages**, in which you offer a whole or a part of the organi- sation and its assets against the repayments that must be made, thus eating into any future benefits.

- ✔ **Deficit finance**, in which you fund everything on overdraft-type loans through your own institutions or those of your backers. (This option has been popular with private equity-supported ventures in the recent past.)

So you have choices, and each of these choices comes with its own caveats and risks.

- ✔ Share capital and rights issues can and do mean that you're likely to have to concede a measure of control and influence over the direction of the venture. In particular, a dominant or controlling interest may want to take the venture in its own direction – and you may have no choice but to follow.

- ✔ Private equity means that you concede control and influence to an indi- vidual or small group. If they choose unilaterally to change the rules of their engagement, or pull out altogether, you're going to have to take immediate remedial actions to get the money that you still need to com- plete the venture successfully.

- ✔ Deficit finance – whether your own or provided by private equity – is at its most effective when currency values and financial resources are steady and assured, and when the markets for commodities, products and services are rising. Deficit finance is at its most vulnerable when the costs and charges associated with finance are high, sources of finance scarce and expensive and commodity, product and service prices and volumes are falling.

Furthermore, the risk that you incur when using deficit finance is that the money may come with strings attached – not just at the outset, but also and especially later on, when things may get even tougher!

Corporate raiding and asset stripping

Within the terms of business law and practice, you're completely within legal rights to take over another company or organisation with the stated and express purpose of selling off some of its parts, streamlining it, enhancing its share value, and then selling the remaining organisation at a profit. Of course, this practice certainly is morally questionable in many cases. And even for companies that do this, the risks present in all takeover activities still apply. For example:

For many years, the Butterley Brick Company Ltd., was a successful, effective and profitable supplier of house bricks and other building materials to the UK house-building sector. It produced large volumes of high-quality bricks and sold them at premium prices throughout the UK. Because of its reputation for quality, the company was able to build in premium prices and delivery charges to its activities.

Without a doubt, Butterley was not as effective or profitable as it could have been. Nevertheless, each year the company generated a substantial profit volume. Based on reliability, trade confidence, product quality and assured delivery services, everyone who used the company as a supplier was happy.

The building recession in the UK in the early 1990s was clearly signalled several years in advance. In 1988, Butterley Brick was taken over by Hanson, a finance company. Hanson assessed the value of the company and its activities and determined those operations that were profitable and those that were not.

Hanson curtailed production. The company identified a core market in the West Midlands, near Butterley's main location. Hanson closed and sold off other production, distribution and wholesale depots. The transport fleet was reduced by three-quarters. Deliveries were no longer to be made on demand but would be agreed according to schedules and timetables proposed by Hanson.

Hanson realised some substantial revenue from the sale and disposal of assets. However, Hanson was disposing of these assets, so the prices of these assets went down. Hanson also managed to turn the company from a national provider into a specialist regional provider and was able to charge premium prices from those elsewhere in the UK who still wanted to buy Butterley bricks. However, the industry as a whole started to look for substitute and alternative products (such as specialist localised and distinctive bricks from many different locations in Great Britain), and so this part of Butterley's operations went into decline.

During the 1990s, Butterley was able to withstand the building recession better than many other brick manufacturers. However, when the building industry took off again, the company didn't have the capacity to respond quickly or effectively, so it lost market share to other manufacturers that had started to provide substitute and alternative products.

So the moral of the story is this: be clear about what you're letting yourself in for and make sure that the takeover is not an end in itself. You must have plans for managing the new organisation in a changed, as well as present, set of circumstances.

Of course, nobody ever goes into mergers and acquisitions to lose money. But you do need to know and understand what can possibly go wrong and so derail your plans. And so – however great the prospects currently appear – always consider the opposite point of view.

The other key matter to note at this stage is that if you find yourself in a jam with finances, you know how to get yourself out! Extricating yourself from a financing deal is certain to come at a heavy price because everyone bailing you out seeks maximum and assured returns, including measures of control, as conditions of being involved. So have the finance and resource issues, warts and all, clear in your own mind before you proceed.

Approaching Mergers, Acquisitions and Takeovers

Two main approaches to mergers, acquisitions and takeovers exist – those that are hostile and those that are friendly:

- ✔ **Hostile bids** are made by one company for another, even though the second company wants to retain its independence or not to be taken over by the first.

- ✔ **Friendly bids** can arise from all kinds of sources – shareholder propositions, meetings between managers and executives, getting someone out of a jam, logically extending a deal into a joint venture, needing a local or regional partner or securing a reliable supply and distribution network.

Making a hostile approach is, in a way, more straightforward than a friendly one because everyone knows and understands where they stand in a hostile bid. Situations in which everything is supposedly friendly still require you to put a structured, orderly and strategic approach in place very quickly, otherwise you lose focus and impetus, and the deal-making process becomes more expensive.

Whether you engage in hostile or friendly activity, you need to be absolutely clear about your objectives so that everyone knows and understands where they stand and so that you can provide a clear basis on which you're going to seek any backing and resources that you may need.

Figuring out why

You must get to the core of the matter: why are you pursuing this specific merger, acquisition or takeover? Why are you involving yourself in something that statistically gives you a mere 13 per cent chance of success?

Short-term share price rises

Rumours of merger and takeover activity frequently fuel rises in the share prices of the parties concerned. In order to keep interest high, the players in these potential deals often carefully release information. Releases focus on the desirability of the shares. After all, someone clearly wants to buy them! Thus, the shares become desirable – and the prices rise! Then, after weeks of speculation about whether the deal will happen and what may be the value of the shares, the crunch comes. A formal statement about the venture must be made – that it will, or will not, go ahead.

When things don't go ahead and there's been a great deal of excitement, some undoubtedly benefit from the short-term rising share price before it settles back to normal.

If you have such a proposal in mind, make sure that you fully think it through before you get everyone excited about it. You don't want to become known as 'the nearly person,' get dragged into something because of rumours and half stories or lose your credibility for when a venture comes up that you *have* thoroughly considered.

Also, fuelling rumours of dramatic deals to ramp up the share prices of those companies involved is illegal. So don't!

Your objective is most likely one or more of the following:

- **Seeking a greater market share:** You need to be able to state which market and what share – as well as why this venture is the right way to achieve your aim.

- **Securing a key supplier:** You need to be able to state why this venture is so important and how this deal improves and shores up your competitive position.

- **Access to distribution channels:** You need to be able to identify the detail of the improvements that you seek.

- **Entering a new market or location:** You must state why and how you intend to succeed in the new area, and in what way you can offer additional benefit to the customers, clients, staff and backers.

- **Acquiring a particular technology that is of value to you:** You need to be sure of the value that you place on the technology. Are you indeed getting 'value for money' by acquiring it in this way?

- **Acquiring expertise:** You must know and understand how and why the desired expertise is of value for acquisition in this way.

- **Acquiring particular customer and client bases:** You must know specifically which markets and locations you're gaining entry to – as well as the value of new customers and clients.

✔ **Acquiring industry-specific assets:** You must know what you're really acquiring and what it's worth. For example, in the airline industry, companies often take over others in order to acquire specific route networks, landing slots and access to specific airports.

You need also to be clear if any of the following motivate your interest in a mega-venture:

✔ **Prestige, kudos and triumphs for your organisation and/or its top and senior managers:** If a venture is for prestige, be clear about it because these types of venture invariably carry considerable costs in terms of staff and systems integration, and product and service performance, at least in the short to medium term.

✔ **Excitement and adventures:** Everyone loves adventures – especially at someone else's expense. If you're buying up a supplier or service provider in an exotic location, make sure that you can cover the costs that you may incur if anything goes wrong.

✔ **Short-term share price advantage:** Yes, when rumours of mergers and takeovers pop up in the media, the share prices of all parties tend to rise. When the dust settles though, you're still going to have to do the hard work of re-branding products and services, and integrating staff conditions, technology systems and performance.

Understanding your competitive drives

Whatever the precise objectives of getting involved in merger and takeover activities, your key point of reference has to remain: how does this venture benefit your organisation in terms of retaining, developing and enhancing your ability to compete and be profitable?

This question is absolutely critical when looking at the benefits that you expect to accrue – synergies, economies of scale, sales of assets and liabilities, divestment of products and services and divestment of property (all topics I cover in the following sections).

If you go into a venture with any of these expectations, prepare for a major test of your strategic and competitive expertise.

Synergies

Synergies occur where you can create a combination of resources in which the whole is greater than the sum of its parts. All companies love synergies, because they look like they're getting really good use out of their resources.

We gotta sell!

The social services department of a county council in southern England implemented a policy of 'Care in the Community' for its most vulnerable clients. The policy meant that people with learning disabilities, the elderly and children in care were now going to be cared for in their own homes, or else in small units provided by a consortium of private sector providers. The policy therefore became a merged or partnership activity between the council and private/commercial providers.

To pay for the transition and support venture initially, the council decided to sell off some of the premises that it had previously used to provide institutional care for these groups. These premises included:

- A large secure unit in its own extensive grounds valued at £12 million.

- A regional council headquarters valued at £11 million.

- A city-centre day-care facility location valued at £6 million.

The council needed to raise £18 million, so leaders anticipated that these value figures more than covered impending costs.

The city-centre location was soon snapped up for £7.5 million, but no one came in for the other two sites. The council had to raise money to meet financial targets as well as to pay for this particular venture; and eventually the council blinked. Property companies that were waiting in the wings now entered into negotiations. Eventually the other two sites were sold off – the secure unit for £900,000, and the regional headquarters for £3.5 million.

After a promising start, the venture was now running at a serious deficit. The council had to use more resources trying to re-negotiate its arrangements with the commercial providers. Eventually, it had to raise the council tax to ensure that the venture was fully underwritten.

The case illustrates what happens when someone knows that you've got to sell. And the one example of price collapse – the secure unit dropping from £12 million to £900,000 – also illustrates in extremis what can, and does, go wrong sometimes.

However, synergies don't always work out as planned, in practice. Always test your assessment of synergies thoroughly, including projected operational and cost savings. Synergies most frequently occur when you:

- Integrate technology and staff.

- Reduce headcount by removing duplicate functions and activities.

- Harmonise and integrate supply and distribution activities.

- Sell premises, capital equipment and technology that you no longer need as the result of integrating organisations.

Here are some strategies for maximising synergy benefits:

✔ When people know, understand or believe that lay-offs are in the future, the best staff take matters into their own hands and find other jobs. Thus, you're left with individuals who can't or won't find alternative employment, who are determined to stick it out or who are not the best members of the workforce.

✔ When people know, understand or believe that redundancies and lay-offs are coming, they spend work time talking about these matters rather than doing anything productive, so both productivity and morale go down.

✔ When people know, understand and believe that lay-offs are coming, they seek the best possible severance terms for themselves.

✔ When you want to sell off technology, premises or capital equipment, buyers try to negotiate the prices of each with you, which invariably means that you must lower your expectations. See the sidebar 'We gotta sell!' for a particularly dramatic example.

✔ When you need to sell off technology, premises or capital equipment, the prices collapse.

Of course, if you do the work in detail in advance, you know and understand all the preceding items. You can be fully aware of what you're letting yourself in for, the effects on your competitive position and your ability to remain effective and profitable. It also provides the basis on which you need to secure the critical resources that you may need to develop your position.

Make sure that you test all figures to destruction, and that everyone's clear:

✔ That at least the worst projected outcome is achievable.

✔ What the consequences are if the worst projected outcome isn't achieved.

Economies of scale

People talk about economies of scales, but they generally have little idea about what they really are. *Economies of scale* are based on the concept that:

✔ You get more out of a large organisation than a small one.

✔ You get more out of combining resources than operating them separately (similar to synergies, see the preceding section).

✔ You better use resources in larger organisations because you dispose of duplicate activities during the merger process.

REAL WORLD EXAMPLE

When children's charities don't mix well

Active Kids was a children's charity providing adoption, fostering and special needs education services in the rural Home Counties of England. Cityscape was a children's charity providing a similar range of services, including family support, in the outer London Boroughs. The top management of the two organisations got together and worked out a merger that was seen as in the interests of both, enabling each to benefit from the professionalism, understanding and strength of the other. As resources became increasingly tighter in the sector, the combined organisation was able to raise capital by selling off the two office and administrative buildings that Cityscape owned in Sidcup and Greenwich.

The status of the 'merger' became that Active Kids would de facto take over Cityscape. Excited by the venture, everyone got eagerly to work. But then the joy was killed.

The HR Director of Active Kids found anomalies in pay, perks and terms and conditions of Cityscape employees at all levels. He proposed full consultations with all staff and the trade union recognised by Cityscape, after which he would structure a proposal that bought out all the anomalies. This, he estimated at the outset, would be a one-off charge against the newly merged organisation (about 20 per cent of total annual payroll).

The CEO of Active Kids overruled. The merger was to go ahead straightaway. Staff terms and conditions of employment were mere details. And in any case, he reasoned, these organisations did charitable work, so nobody would raise objections.

Unfortunately, the merger quickly became chaotic. The Cityscape premises were indeed sold; and the office staff moved to the Active Kids offices. Many people who were doing the same jobs were now working side by side – on vastly different terms and conditions of employment. The disparities led to staff losses on both the professional childcare side and also from within the administrative and managerial functions.

In the end, the merger took nearly five years to resolve, under a series of disputes, grievances and tribunal cases. The CEO of Active Kids left the merged organisation after three years. His successor, a woman who joined the organisation from a similar function in local government, stated in one unguarded moment: 'To date, the merger has cost nearly 70 per cent of payroll.'

If you're going to merge, you have to do it properly. And although the figure of '20 per cent of total annual payroll' may seem very high, you ignore this perception at your peril. And if you're still in any doubt, you should work out in the same amount of detail what the alternative is actually going to cost. At least then you can make an informed choice.

So if, for example, you're going to merge two sets of head-office activities, you need to be able to project where the economies of scale are available in full detail. For example, if Company A in the venture has 18 finance staff and Company B, 30 finance staff – do you need all of them? If so, why? If not, how many are to be lost, where from and by when? What is the cost of doing all this? Will there be compulsory redundancies or natural wastage?

Automaker mismatch

There was a major merger between two of the world's largest and most famous and prestigious car manufacturers. One of the companies was Chrysler, the American company from Detroit; the other was Daimler-Benz, the German motor giant, based in Essen in the Rhine Valley.

The merger strategy was quickly made clear. The companies would work together, use each other's facilities to produce each other's ranges of models and share their distribution networks to ensure that both makes of cars were sent to market in the volumes demanded.

They proposed an interchange of staff at all levels to ensure that everything came to pass. In the interests of developing a new working culture, staff would come to learn and understand each other's technology, designs, assembly methods and ways of working.

The due diligence was very thorough. The American top management duly arrived in Germany to seal and celebrate their achievement – and what a disaster that turned out to be! The German hosts put on a celebration as only they knew how – plenty of food and drink, beer and champagne, a raucous atmosphere and scantily clad dancers. By contrast many of the visiting Americans were teetotal, modest and devout Christians. Matters came to a head when the German CEO picked up a bottle of champagne in one hand, a dancer in the other and stated he was going back to his hotel room.

Furious diplomacy behind the scenes ensured that the merger stayed on track. However, the venture never fully worked and many parts of the joint activities have subsequently been de-merged or sold off.

The lesson is that you should never underestimate the effect of cultural differences on the success of a merger, acquisition or takeover. Always seek to know and understand how people behave in particular circumstances as a precondition for your ability to do business with them.

If you don't create economies of scale correctly, you end up with diseconomies of scale. In diseconomies of scale, the merger or acquisition goes ahead, but the new organisation is more expensive and cumbersome to operate than the previously independent ones!

In addition to staff questions, you also need to ask:

- ✔ Are the financial systems compatible? If so, how do you integrate them? How long will this take? Are there any questions of capacity?

- ✔ And if the systems aren't compatible, how are you going to replace them – and when, where and with what? Do you have the expertise to do this – or must you buy it in? Do the existing staff have the expertise to use what you envisage? If so, fine; if not, where are you going to find the expertise?

And so on, until you calculate in full detail every aspect of the envisaged venture. If you approach a potential deal this thoroughly, you can achieve some fairly detailed figures. Then add it all up and subtract it from the savings that the economies of scale are supposed to deliver. And then you have some real figures to work with.

You won't be popular if you carry out this detailed type of financial analysis. Not everyone wants to be involved in this – it's far too tedious! But you're being professional and making clear (to yourself at least) what you're truly letting yourself in for.

Staff culture

Managing the transition of staff cultures and patterns of behaviour is the most neglected part of all merger and acquisition activity. Dealing with staff cultures is messy and unpredictable. You never quite know how people are going to respond to these initiatives until they're actually faced with them. (The failure to create a new corporate culture is one of the most widely cited reasons for lack of performance of the new organisation, as I note in the sidebar 'Mega-venture success?'.)

However, some mergers and acquisitions don't go ahead because the individuals driving them decide that the cultural fit between the organisations involved is insufficient. Merging organisations and creating a common culture for the future is simply not worth the candle (or the financial commitment demanded).

However, if you're going to go ahead with a venture, dealing with two or more staff cultures is a major issue to tackle. You need to know and understand in detail:

- The strengths of the existing cultures and the effort required to give a new identity to the combined staff.
- Where equivalent, matching and mismatched positions exist.
- Where the differences are in terms and conditions of employment. You need to know this because you're going to have to arrive at a view on:
  - The terms and conditions on which you engage new starters in the newly merged organisation.
  - How you go about addressing existing anomalies in pay and working conditions (including buying them out).
  - How you're going to meet obligations such as pensions and healthcare.
  - Any status symbol differentials (for example, which grade of employee is entitled to what make of car).
  - Where the wage and salary differentials lie.

Nonsense, you may be saying. Maybe you think that you can sort out arrangements through natural wastage and gradual re-positioning over the next five to ten years.

Five to ten years? If you take this long to achieve an integration, you'll not only be buying out people, you'll also be paying heavily through your operational HR effort in resolving individual and collective grievances and disputes as they arise.

So the choice is truly yours – to buy out up front as a strategic initiative, or to pay anyway over the long term. But never doubt that you'll pay – one way or the other.

Everything that's to do with securing economies of scale and managing the staff and organisation culture during the process affects your competitive strength and position and your ability to secure the returns on the venture. All the time that people are being diverted by the cloudiness and woolliness around these issues, you're not focusing on your competitive strengths and position.

The Chartered Management Institute and the American Management Association both state that only 13 per cent of mergers and acquisitions work as fully and effectively as they were intended. Of those that don't work fully and effectively, the biggest problems that organisations fail to recognise are: over-estimating the returns, underestimating the costs and paying insufficient attention to staff management issues.

Securing Other Critical Resources

Knowing and understanding your competitive drives in the area of mergers, acquisitions and takeovers also makes easier the securing of critical resources that are additional to finance – technology, expertise and capability.

You need to choose the expertise to fit the venture unless you have absolute confidence in the overall value that you can deliver using regular staff and advisers. Clarity of purpose is everything:

✓ If you're going into a venture to secure economies of scale (see 'Economies of scale' earlier in this chapter), you must engage experts who understand economies of scale, and you must seek backing from individuals who have experience in underwriting these types of venture.

✓ If you know and understand that integrating staff and technology is a priority, you must then secure this expertise, as well as the finance and backing to underwrite this type of venture.

✔ If you need knowledge and understanding of a particular location, you must engage people who are familiar with the particular area, and you must seek financing from individuals who understand the pressures of operating in a specific location.

Even if you're going into something for reasons of share price advantage or asset stripping, you still need to make this goal clear because you must secure the services of specialist stockbrokers or expert investment managers.

Whatever resources you may need, you're going to have to pay for them. Include these costs and charges in your calculations as part of the overall value and integrity of the venture. You don't want things to fall apart because you failed to make allowances for small but critical issues along the way.

Leadership

All merger, acquisition and takeover ventures need clear, expert and committed leadership. Indeed, leadership involved in these ventures requires strategic expertise based on the clear statement of purpose that the organisations make when seeking to enter into the particular venture.

You must choose the people who you want to lead these matters on the basis of their expertise and commitment. You need these leaders to be engaged for the duration of the venture. You can't guarantee that anyone will stay with an organisation or with a venture or project for any length of time. But you can remove many of the barriers that prevent people from staying by giving them clear tasks, paying them well, supporting them fully at every stage and making adequate resources available. If you can't, or won't, guarantee to provide and deliver all this support, you're going to have trouble in securing quality leadership during the venture.

Saying no

Everything I look at in this chapter is part of an effort to help you know and understand what you may be letting yourself in for with a merger, acquisition or takeover.

If you go through all the details I discuss in this chapter, you'll have all the evidence and support you need if you decide to say no to a venture and decide not to proceed. Using this chapter as

your guide, you can have the strength you need to argue your case against those who still want to go ahead. After doing a lot of groundwork for a particular venture many organisations want to press on regardless. But if your own expertise requires that you say no, then no it must remain – at least until somebody persuades you that your line of reasoning is wrong.

Any venture leader must be credible with all stakeholders. Staff, shareholders and backers, suppliers, customers and clients are all going to have legitimate concerns over what's going to happen, and they're going to expect these concerns to be addressed and answered.

Contingencies

Things go wrong! The truly unforeseen can and does occur! People indeed up-sticks and leave! Consultants and experts let you down! So you need a pool of back-up resources – experts and technologists, specialists in all parts of merger and takeover activity – on which you can call (often at very short notice) when these things do happen.

If ever anyone says to you, 'We've thought of everything' or 'Nothing can possibly go wrong,' argue with him till he changes his mind – or run away as fast as you can! Nobody can possibly think of everything. You have to prepare for contingencies.

Outsourcing

Outsourcing occurs when a company buys up another organisation for the purposes of creating an independent or semi-detached entity that delivers one particular product, service or function in return for an agreed and assured budget. As long as the agreed and assured budget is adequate – and as long as the product, service or function capability, value and quality can be assured – this particular form of acquisition activity is both effective and profitable.

✔ The parent company secures a key part of its operations for a figure that's known, assured and predictable.

✔ The subordinate company has its own specialism, funds, technology, equipment and ways of working.

Where outsourcing goes wrong is when the parent company uses the deal to drive costs down to the exclusion of all else in relation to the particular product, service or function. This is a recipe for disaster, and in recent years has led to several notable failures:

✔ British Airways found itself without a catering supplier for its long-haul flights after it drove down the costs too far, and therefore drove its outsourced caterer out of business. As a result, British Airways had no long-haul flights for three days until it secured alternative supplies.

✔ General Motors was without a range of engine parts after it tried to default on payments to its own wholly owned subsidiary manufacturer. GM eventually received the parts – more than six weeks late.

The motivation for outsourcing deals is cost knowledge and assurance, not a way to hammer the supply side. (Hammer too hard and you can hammer them – and yourself – out of business.)

Chapter 16

Getting the Big Picture: Globalisation

*F*or many business leaders, joining the elite of the world's largest, most prestigious and prosperous companies is both a driving ambition and a fitting recognition of their excellence at everything that they do. And if you can sustain this position, everyone's happy – customers get good products and services, shareholders enjoy a company that's clearly highly profitable and staff have lots of opportunities for growth (and good salaries and bonuses too).

So companies strive for this position – for the recognition, status and prestige that being a globally successful organisation brings. For those organisations that do succeed, the rewards are truly enormous.

However, you must be a bit realistic. You have to know and understand that in order to be truly global, you need resources, expertise, technology, suppliers and distribution channels that you can command and dominate wherever and whenever you need. This authority isn't always straightforward – even for the biggest and most established companies. Even global leaders have to operate within the economic, social, political and legal constraints of their particular locations.

For those wanting to expand, grow and become international, some hard and expert work is therefore demanded. This chapter examines this work in detail and offers you the essential advice you need if you plan to grow your organisation into a global success story.

Going Global

Joining the elite of international companies and organisations is hard work, as well as a mark of status and prestige. As with any ambition, going global comes with costs as well as benefits.

You need to be clear that attempting to expand your organisation to a global level is going to be commercially viable, as well as prestigious. You need to be clear about where the resources to do this are going to come from, and what the effects are going to be on the rest of your business (which is, after all, the core business on which you built the capacity for this expansion in the first place).

If you go down the globalisation route through vanity or because everyone else is, make sure that you're also following a business opportunity that can accommodate you and deliver sustainable profitable activities. Otherwise, you're simply following the sheep!

Preparing to expand

Whenever and wherever you expand, you need to be able to gain, maintain, sustain and develop a viable presence, which means that you need:

- **Finance and resources.** All expansion requires investment. Your decision to invest in going global affects the levels of funding you're going to need. Establishing and developing a truly global or international position requires high levels of funding and command of other resources (especially technology), which you can command and deploy at any time (often at very short notice). See the following section 'Acquiring global finance and resources' for more information.

- **Expertise.** You must be able to engage people with expertise and executive authority to be able to travel to particular locations, assess the opportunities quickly and effectively and then give proposals, projects and ventures the go-ahead or else reject them. See the following section 'Acquiring global expertise' for more information.

To have a viable global position, you must be able to finance, support and sustain activities in the *axis of globalisation*, which Figure 16-1 illustrates.

REMEMBER

Global? Says who?

If you Google 'global companies and organisations,' you get up to 30 million responses. Just because you describe yourself as global, doesn't mean that you are. As an example: when one very senior manager of a UK civil engineering company went to seek contracting work from the Malay government, he was asked to name the five main indigenous contractors with whom he would be competing for work. When he couldn't, the Malay government official said: 'That's fair enough. Because I can't name five UK civil engineering contractors either'. So if you think you're global, in most cases you need to think again!

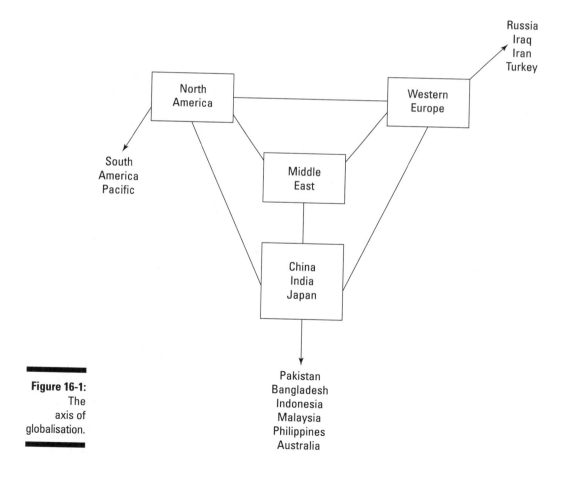

Figure 16-1:
The axis of globalisation.

REAL WORLD EXAMPLE

npower and Brazil

Following a tendering process, npower, the UK electricity generating company, was awarded a contract to develop the electricity supply infrastructure across six states in Brazil, including remote locations in the centre of the country.

The contract value was £250 million. The company considered the deal an opportunity to sell and develop its expertise all over the world, as well as a nice easy venture in a friendly country. npower hoped to use results and publicity from the venture to demonstrate the assuredness of its global capability.

Staff from the company duly arrived in Brazil to start work. But it quickly became clear that life wouldn't be quite so simple. The Brazilian hinterland was difficult to access, and the road network uncertain. Communication networks didn't always work. The sheer distances were awesome.

Furthermore, the ability to recruit and retain specialist subcontractors as well as unskilled labour, a detail not researched during the deal-making, turned out to be very difficult. The company had no prior knowledge or understanding of Brazil's working and social culture. Most importantly, the Brazilian people, including the wider political and social institutions, viewed the company as just another foreign company coming in to the country to take what it could and then clear off.

The venture quickly ran into difficulties and ultimately failed. npower sold the contract for £1, and wrote off the £250 million as a one-off charge against its accounts.

As you see in Figure 16-1, the main points of the axis are the EU, USA and Japan. The figure also indicates the *sub-axes* (which are strengthening almost by the minute). The sub-axes include the Middle East (still the centre of the oil industry), Russia (with its huge reserves of energy and mineral resources) and China. Additionally, you need to note the sheer volume of population that exists in China and its neighbours – India, Pakistan, Bangladesh, Malaysia, Indonesia and the Philippines. And you should note also the parts of the world that remain to be developed, above all Africa, Central America and South America.

Establishing a physical presence is one part of going global and international. Other things that you need – and that you must be able to pay for – include:

- ✔ **Global reputation:** You need to develop expanded reputation and confidence in your products and services, and the integrity of your activities and practices must transcend international boundaries.

- ✔ **Global technology:** You must be able to connect to any part of your empire at any time.

- ✔ **Global expertise:** You need people in top, key and executive positions who know and understand the main issues in particular locations, and who also have a clear grasp of your organisation's overall strategy. See the following section 'Acquiring global expertise' for more.

- ✔ **Global reach:** You must be able to set up, anywhere, effective and profitable activities that fit your strategy and competitive position.

- ✔ **Global networks:** You need a complete team of suppliers, subcontractors, specialists and distributors, so that your products and services are fully assured wherever they're demanded or required.

You must underpin all the preceding items with a unified attitude that you take to each of your activities and locations. You need to be absolutely clear about your goals and purposes. You benefit no one if you state one thing and then do, or attempt to be, another.

If you've the resources and finance necessary to operate on a global scale and the drive to do so, clearly you're going to be powerful and influential enough to go into any location for your own reasons. But you must make up your mind to be clear in advance about the approach that you intend to take. If this approach is a bit contentious or extreme – if you're frankly going into the location purely to exploit it – you must have the courage to say so.

More generally, you need to be clear about any of the following conditions that you may seek to fulfil as part of your globalisation efforts:

- ✔ **A long-term presence** in order to gain a stable and assured position as a provider of products, services, employment and other facilities.

- ✔ **A short-term presence** purely because doing so is in your present interests.

- ✔ **A short-term presence** using local partners and facilities to supply a range of activities.

- ✔ **The ability to carry out detailed evaluation of other opportunities** that may become available in the future.

These conditions, in turn, determine some key operational priorities including:

- ✔ Whether to have universal employment standards, hours of work, terms and conditions, wage and salary structures – or to vary these according to location and activities.

- ✔ Whether to charge universal prices for your products and services – or to vary these according to local pricing opportunities.

- ✔ Whether to set universal product and service standards – or to vary these according to location and activity.

- ✔ Whether to have a universal technology basis – or to use what is common practice in particular locations.

- ✔ Whether to set your own absolute standards that transcend the legal and social requirements of everywhere in the world – or to meet minimum legal and compliant standards in particular locations.

Thinking and acting globally

Whatever you set out to do, you need to be aware of the responses that you're going to receive from the locations that you enter. These responses are certain to be a combination of:

✔ We welcome the investment because we need the work and jobs that this will bring.

✔ We know and understand that all foreigners and incomers are only here to exploit and take advantage of us.

✔ We welcome you – but this venture has to be a partnership.

✔ We welcome you and look forward to learning from you, so that we can then develop our own expertise and independence.

You must be aware of the basis on which you're going into particular locations and the basis on which they welcome you. In particular, if you're going to be a large or dominant force in the new location, you'll be resented if you don't also accept some responsibility for giving something back as well as taking.

You're essentially clarifying the basis of your own approach to globalisation. Although this topic is worthy of an entire *For Dummies* book, you have three basic choices:

✔ **Think globally/act globally:** You set your standards high enough to transcend any local customs or laws so that you always more than meet whatever is demanded locally. Or you use your command of finance, resources and technology to bludgeon a presence in your chosen locations.

✔ **Think globally/act locally:** You create a host of local and localised activities on an enduring partnership basis. Or you take advantage of local labour, land and technology rates and laws to create local activities that give you a particular opportunity.

✔ **Think locally/act locally:** You're most likely to find this approach in companies that continue to engage local executive management that is responsible for reporting to the global parent company. This approach works best when you marry local knowledge and presence with the overall standards and quality that the global parent organisation offers. The approach works less well when you use a strong local presence to impose your own ways of doing things, regardless of what the locality actually needs or wants.

At the core of your choice is your attitude, your own dominant position and how you're going to use these in your business dealings. Clearly in many globalised cases, you have the opportunity to exploit an area or locality if you choose. Clearly also, you can use your command of resources to secure a viable commercial position for the longer term.

All the preceding questions are complex and go a long way in establishing the extent to which you're going to 'act globally/think globally' or 'act globally/think locally.' See the sidebar 'Thinking and acting globally' for more information. Whatever you do, make your position clear to everyone in all your activities.

Acquiring global finance and resources

Whatever your chosen approach to globalisation and expansion, you need finance and resources to underwrite it. You need enough to be able to gain a presence, develop it and maintain it. (You may also need to finance a withdrawal; see the sidebar 'npower and Brazil.')

Seek to command finance and resources on terms that suit your purposes and that are acceptable to people in the markets that you seek to enter and develop. And you can only discover this information by going out, seeing for yourself and getting to know the particular locations.

You use these resources in any or all of the following ways:

- **Buying a physical presence:** You need resources not just to buy the premises but also to furbish and develop them in order to create a viable commercial presence.

- **Engaging in local partnerships:** You produce and deliver resources that are going to enable both you and your partners to develop the presence commercially.

- **Joint ventures:** You enter into a relationship with one or more organisations that already often have a presence in the region. In this case, you may have to pay well over the odds as the price of your entry and involvement (because you are, after all, taking advantage of someone else's expertise and experience to try and gain your own presence).

- **Taking over a locally established player:** In these cases, because the local player knows that you want in, the price of the takeover normally goes up.

- **Buying up a key resource or expertise in a locality:** This scenario plays out, for example, when you purchase the provider of a major mineral, technology or natural resource. Like taking over an established local player, if you're dealing with a key resource, the price goes up because others inevitably become interested as well.

First and foremost, make sure that you can afford what you set out to do. After this, you must commit resources to developing your presence and be prepared for your costs to rise along the way. For example:

- Wage rates in Bombay, India doubled between 2006 and 2008 in the banking and finance sectors as more and more Western organisations located activities there.

  ✔ Wage rates in the international shipping markets have risen as more and more transport organisations have sought the advantages of running their ships out of Panama and other flags of convenience.

  ✔ Wage rates in the European haulage industry have risen in what many considered to be the cheaper locations of Poland, the Czech Republic and Latvia as more and more transport firms locate in these areas.

If you think that venturing into a specific location is a good idea, others invariably have the same thought. Be prepared to pay in order to play. You need to be able to fund any competitive development that your presence and the presence of others may bring – establishing yourself in the location isn't an end in itself. Both local *and* international players will fight back against your initiatives and activities. Furthermore, you're going to be competing in the new locations for labour and resources as well as products and services. You must be able to compete according to local conditions.

Don't assume that because you're good in one place, you'll be good in others. You must pay and resource everything, so make sure that you know and understand everything about each place that you enter.

HSBC's bumps in the road

HSBC is one of the nearest things to a genuinely global retail bank with activities in 165 countries. And yet, even for HSBC, things don't always work out as planned.

Like many others in the banking sector, HSBC set out to cut costs by moving many of its UK and European customer service functions to India. The company stated that it would save by closing down its activities in the UK and Europe, selling off the premises and property and laying off its expensive European staff.

In practice, none of this happened. Further uses were found for the property that was vacated by call centre staff. All of the call centre staff were able to find other activities and opportunities within the HSBC company. And of course, HSBC found that labour, premises and technology were not as cheap in India as it had first perceived.

So the costs for this global initiative went up – not down. And although the relocation did indeed develop a presence in India, none of the other assumed or targeted advantages came about.

Of course, the fact that HSBC could immediately use the resources that were freed up by the move to India may be a tribute to the company's business development and staffing policy expertise. Clearly also, the company gained other advantages that it hadn't thought of or sought – especially using its existing staff on new ventures. But the entire endeavour illustrates how careful you must be if you seek one narrow target – such as saving money – as the driver of a global expansion.

Acquiring global expertise

Global expertise means just that – knowing and understanding everything possible about each and every location in which you seek to do business. And you have to go out and see for yourself. Making assumptions about particular parts of the world from the safety and comfort of an office in Great Britain, Europe or North America is meaningless. You must have, develop, acquire or purchase global expertise.

Global expertise combines hard skills such as:

- Economic and financial understanding of all the locations in which you operate.

- The ability to make, agree and enforce contracts in every location in which you operate.

- Understanding logistics, transport and other infrastructures in different parts of the world.

- Understanding how timings and schedules vary in each of the locations in which you work.

And soft skills including:

- A humanitarian and sympathetic or empathetic approach to the locations in which you work.

- Knowing and understanding social and religious customs, habits, norms and prejudices – particularly how they apply to places of work or affect the way you carry out work.

- Knowing and understanding the prevailing attitudes that people from particular countries and locations adopt towards foreigners – especially those from the West and Japan.

Most countries have some history of Western involvement. And unless you give these individuals cause otherwise, they pre-judge you as intending to behave exactly as Westerners who came before you. If people from the West behaved well in the particular localities, you've less of a problem. But if people from the West behaved badly, you immediately have your work cut out to change attitudes towards you – at least.

Pondering prejudices

All parties in global ventures bring prejudices to the bargaining table and global workplace. Examples of prejudices and norms that affect your ways of working in some parts of the world include:

- Men won't work for women.

- Women won't work for women.

- People won't work for someone younger.

- You can't conduct any business between 12 noon and 2 p.m.

- You can't get anything done during August.

- People like to know and understand ahead of time whether you're coming to meetings for work or on a 'jolly,' so they can sort out your visit accordingly.

And many others exist! You only gain the detail behind these kinds of prejudice by going to visit and seeing for yourself.

Ask non-threatening, non-judging cultural questions as you do your research. Preface your question with a quick explanation of what the norm is in your country or organisation. For example: 'My co-workers and I go out for celebratory drinks after a big sale. How do you and your co-workers celebrate?'

As I note elsewhere, if you're a truly global company, you may have the clout and resources to impose your will anyway, regardless of local prejudices and pre-judgement. If you choose to do this, at least make an effort to know what norms you're imposing on. Or you may even find that you're actually different from the others, that you can achieve much greater profits over a long period by engaging in the localities in which you find yourself working. Try it.

Expanding your business, expanding your views

So if you're thinking of expanding into particular places, the first thing that you need to do is go and see the locations for yourself.

Go and see what the place is really like. See how it works, where the blockages and hold-ups are, where the traffic jams are! Find out what the real attitudes (including prejudices) are towards foreigners and incomers. Find out how long it takes to arrange appointments with bankers, experts and specialists. Find your way around the wider locality as well as the specific area that you're targeting.

Seeing for yourself is, in truth, the foundation of global expertise. (And seeing for yourself actually applies to *any* expansion decision, regardless of whether you're expanding into a different part of your present location or half way around the world.) Think about it this way: if east and west London have different customs, habits and patterns of behaviour, shouldn't the same apply to east and west Cape Town, Caracas, Adelaide – and Tuvalu.

REAL WORLD EXAMPLE

A crash and Japanese custom

In 1986, a Boeing 747 owned by Japan Airlines (JAL) crashed into wooded hills as it made its way into Tokyo, causing serious loss of life. As well as a major disaster, the crash brought great shame on JAL and its top management. In order to put the situation right and alleviate its sense of shame, JAL had to discover the cause of the crash.

Engineering consultants from Boeing arrived from the USA three days later. Eager and determined to proceed with the investigation, they went straight to the CEO of JAL. But the JAL CEO refused to see them, stating that Boeing should have sent someone of his rank and status to deal with the matter.

Undeterred, the engineers and consultants made their way to the crash site – only to find that it had been made into a shrine by the bereaved. With great difficulty, the engineers managed to find and remove the pieces of the plane that appeared to be faulty and to examine them.

At this point, serious negotiations had to take place at the highest level between JAL and Boeing. The JAL CEO had to restore his own credibility and absolve himself from shame. In the end the problem was resolved by placing two top managers, one from each company, on the investigating panel. Effectively present only as observers, protocol was nevertheless satisfied when the top manager from Boeing handed the report findings and conclusions to the top manager from JAL – someone who JAL's culture allowed to report directly to the JAL CEO.

And the lessons? How you do things is often as important as what you do. Whatever your rationale of a particular situation, whatever the 'actual' drives and priorities that you may see, you need always to be prepared for others to see things differently.

And when these kinds of culture clashes occur in business, you need to have a very clear view – not just of the particular matter in hand, but also how the situation may affect working relations in the future.

So when you make an effort to see things for yourself, remember the following strategies:

- ✔ Discover what's important and of value to the society and the communities in which you seek to locate, as well as the economic details of the markets you're targeting.

- ✔ Find out how people expect to work and when they need to take time off.

- ✔ Investigate the social and religious pressures that impact on working hours and patterns of behaviour and attendance.

- ✔ Assess the technology that's present and decide whether this technological capacity is suitable for you.

- ✔ Understand how much you're really going to have to pay for expertise.

- ✔ Assess those who are competing with you for the same expertise.

- ✔ Determine what it will take to make people willing to work, as well as capable of working, for you.

- ✔ Be clear about how well transport infrastructure, telecommunications and distribution networks actually work.

Above all, you need to know and understand the value and importance of your products and services to the local markets. Just because you're introducing new products and services that may be successful in other markets, don't assume the same carries over to all markets. For example:

- ✔ The children's toys market in Romania, Bulgaria, the Czech Republic and Poland is very small because life is so difficult that the people can't afford them.

- ✔ Companies that have sought to sell birth control pills to areas of the world with population explosions have, in many cases, had great difficulty because contraception is often socially unacceptable in these areas.

- ✔ Companies wanting to export consumer goods to France have to deal with a strong national urge in France to buy French goods and services.

- ✔ The overwhelming reason why Japanese manufacturing and car companies gained a foothold in the UK is product quality and the high standard of working life offered by the companies as employers. The UK never wanted the companies or the products; the UK already had strong indigenous companies when the Japanese first established their presence. People would have preferred to continue to buy British, but the Japanese quality was simply overwhelming.

The cornerstone of your expertise and your ability to apply it universally is your capability to understand and assess every situation and every opportunity that comes your way – and to understand that these are indeed opportunities!

Considering the role of technology

On the one hand, technology (especially computers and ICT) gives you a universal presence. Anyone with an Internet connection can access your website from anywhere in the world. By the same token, you can also be in contact with anyone you choose. On the other hand, having a website or an email address doesn't make you a global or international player. (It may not even make you a local player.)

Transport

You probably already know that getting around places like London, New York or Los Angeles can take many hours each day. But keep in mind that travelling around many international cities can take a long time as well (for example, the ride from Bangkok airport to the city centre can take hours).

Transport can be a major hindrance to progress. (Transport problems costs the UK economy £30 million per week in terms of lost production and staff time – on the British road networks alone!)

Be aware that it can take days, or even weeks, to travel from a major airport to locations in the hinterland of particular countries. You need to investigate transport and travel costs for your particular set of circumstances.

As a global organisation, you're inevitably going to experience some very-expensive-to-sort-out problems – but you have to be capable and willing to take these on when they do occur. For example, a middle manager at a branded clothing company spent nearly a week travelling to a factory in rural Pakistan to address a manufacturing problem. Setting out from London, he arrived in Lahore in eight hours, but then travelling to the factory took five days. Because of bad weather, he ended up waiting nearly three weeks to make the return journey. The problem itself only took a matter of hours to fix at the factory, but it required the physical presence of someone with executive authority.

The test of whether technology makes you a global organisation is the extent to which technology allows you to do business anywhere in the world – together with the fact that people do actually conduct business with you as the result of your technology and its connections. Technology in organisations that are truly enterprises facilitates communications, takes and processes orders, tracks deliveries, manages the supply side and conducts marketing activities – everything that a global or expanding organisation needs.

Technology also allows you to take advantage of high volumes of skilled labour anywhere in the world. Thus, the well-known and understood examples of:

 ✔ Clothing and garment manufacture carried out by and for the branded clothing companies in Asia and central America.

 ✔ Call centre and customer service activities carried out in many parts of the world.

 ✔ Engineering manufacturing in China, Malaysia and Korea on behalf of Western organisations, as well as indigenous companies.

Although these activities haven't always been conducted with absolute probity (accounts in each of these sectors about exploitation, bullying, victimisation, violence and assaults against the staff have come to light), these examples do indeed demonstrate the possibilities that are available with the aid of technology.

The Birth of Swatch

Everyone pondering the possibilities of techno-logical and labour advantages to aid in taking an organisation global, needs to be aware of the example of Swatch.

In the 1970s, the Swiss watch industry had all but collapsed. It was unable to withstand the competition from cheap and accurate prod-ucts offered by Seiko and other Japanese and Chinese companies. Indeed at one point, the whole of the Swiss watch industry seemed about to be sold off to the Chinese.

However, the Swiss establishment hired Nicolas Hayek, a manufacturing expert, to reform and transform their industry. Hayek first established the specific markets in which the industry needed to operate. The industry would continue to produce top- and middle-brand watches, and it would also introduce a cheap watch that directly competed with Chinese and Japanese products. (The cheap Swiss watch was called 'Swatch.')

Hayek consolidated the manufacturing process into a series of factories. Set in the Swiss coun-tryside and employing local labour, the factories produced components and final products more cheaply and cost effectively than the Chinese and Japanese competitors, which enabled the Swiss watch industry as a whole to regain a large part of its competitive position. Above all, it was able to enter successfully into the low-cost/good-value end of the market.

Hayek's strategic leadership delivers two lessons:

✔ One way of tackling problems is to look at the ideal solution, and then work back from this.

✔ You don't have to go to the lands of cheap labour or technology to be cost effective and competitive. (Indeed, Swiss land and labour costs are the highest in the world.)

The other main opportunities that you have with the present range of technology are:

✔ Access to other organisations, markets, locations and expertise.

✔ Access to information from all parts of the world.

✔ Introductions to potential business partners throughout the globe.

✔ Greater choice and availability of information on the supply and distribution sides.

✔ Access to the kinds of detailed information that help to ensure that your risk management and forecasting are as effective as possible.

One major downside of technology is that it can lead you to believe that you can run a global organisation from the cosy comfort of your computer screen. But this isn't the case! You must go and see things for yourself. After you use technology to generate leads on ventures that may (or may not) turn out to be opportunities, you need to go visiting to see what the people, places, locations and markets are really like.

Outsourcing global expansion

In the context of globalisation and expansion, setting up joint ventures and contracted arrangements with outsourced providers lets you explore opportunities that may be present in the places where the outsourced providers are located.

As with all outsourcing and subcontracting activities (see Chapter 17), the quality, volume and assurance that the provider is going to deliver is much more important than its location. The last thing that you need or want is a bad provider of products, supplies and services that you can't easily get in touch with to sort out.

So, as with all expansion and globalisation – go and see potential outsourcing partners for yourself first! Meet with them and decide if you like them and if you have confidence in them. Contract with them if they're good, and not just because they're cheap or cheaper. If they destroy your reputation, these services are a very expensive way of saving money.

Applying Global Competitive and Strategic Principles

Clearly, you have some real choices that you need to make when deciding to take your organisation global. You must base your choices on true expertise in the fields of strategy and competition. The key choices are as follows:

 ✔ Is your competitive strategy and core position going to be the same in all markets and locations that you serve? Or are you going to have different core strategies and approaches for different markets and locations (for example, cost advantage in one and brand advantage in others)?

   The choice is yours, but you have to decide – and this means that you must know and understand the principles of competitive strategy in each particular context, whatever you choose to do. (See Chapters 1 and 2 for more on competitive strategy and core positions.)

 ✔ Are you going to treat all your staff the same regardless of location – or are you going to pay whatever 'the going rate' is in each location?

 ✔ Are you going to have global or local marketing campaigns? And if you choose to have local campaigns, make sure that you have someone local check your language and wording for sense as well as accuracy!

 ✔ Are you going to set the same overall standards for all your locations – or are you going to vary your terms and conditions of employment, hours of work, health and safety practices, wage and salary rates according to local norms and laws?

> ✔ Are you going to engage in the same trading practices regardless of location – or are you going to vary these?

For each of the preceding questions, the choice is yours. But this list does, hopefully, drive home the fact that you're considering a business venture – one with the potential to enhance your competitive edge and capability. And so you must make every choice and attend to each detail as if you were making decisions for operations at your own home base.

Whatever your choices in each of the preceding areas, if the language to be used is not your own – always, always take interpreters and translators with you. You don't want to place yourself in the position of President Kennedy in 1961. Addressing a crowd in West Berlin at the height of the Cold War, he said: 'Ich bin ein Berliner'. Intending to state that he was a true citizen of Berlin, the phrase actually translates as: 'I am a doughnut.'

A tough sell for ACN

ACN is a successful utilities company based in Chicago that provides water, gas, electricity and telecommunications services to many parts of the US. With deregulation of the water, gas, electricity and telecommunications markets in the EU in 2002, ACN cast its eyes across the Atlantic, seeking new opportunities.

The company did its own strategic and competitive analyses and decided to focus its overseas interests on the UK and French telecommunications markets. In each of these, by law, the main providers of telecommunications services (BT and France Telecom) had to provide the basis for competition by selling up to 30 per cent of landline capacity at wholesale prices. Also, many consumers perceived both BT and France Telecom to be relatively expensive in their retail activities.

ACN decided to set up its EU base in Amsterdam (located roughly in the middle of the two target nations and sent its representatives into the field to sell telecommunications products and services to customers. Priced at 5 per cent below the BT and France Telecom rates, ACN waited for the money to roll in!

Unfortunately, the whole thing failed. In the UK, ACN was entering into a market that was ripe for development – but developing very differently to how ACN envisaged. For example, UK-based sources of supply were already extremely well developed through computer and Internet search engines. Consumers already had many choices available, and the ACN provision wasn't sufficiently attractive to make people want to change.

In France, ACN's representatives were mainly English, but drawn from the expatriate community living in France. ACN had to address both the language barrier and a certain amount of anti-American prejudice. More significantly, ACN failed to recognise the very strong collective pull that French customers have towards French providers (for instance, the three largest car companies in France in terms of volume sales remain Citroën, Peugeot and Renault).

Additionally, ACN failed to recognise that although Amsterdam is close physically to both target markets, neither French nor UK customers were used to dealing with such things overseas. Consumers in both countries expected their telecommunication services providers to be located within their country's borders. Also, many UK customers were beginning to exhibit strong prejudices against customer services and call centres located overseas.

Finally, the price differential on offer was not enough to make people change their service provider. If the prices had been reduced to 5 per cent of BT and France Telecom levels (as Ryanair did with its ticket pricing when it first established itself relative to flag-carrying airlines), people would have been forced to take notice. However, because the price was only a little bit cheaper, nobody took notice.

ACN's foray into overseas telecommunications services is brimming with the kind of things that go wrong with global expansions. Every time you come to a rational conclusion (such as 'people will go with us because they don't like the present providers', or 'people will go with us because we're a bit cheaper'), you must question your conclusion from the point of view of people's real convictions and behaviours. Deeply held convictions and established habits and patterns of behaviour are as likely to damage you as bad products and services. And if people don't want your products for whatever reason – they won't buy them!

Chapter 17

Pointing Your Company Towards the Future

In This Chapter

▶ Pondering what the future holds

▶ Taking steps to ensure a prosperous future

▶ Seeking new opportunities

C ompetition and strategy are processes, evolving and changing all the time because you and your organisation don't stand still, and because your competitors' constant actions require that you be continually on the move as well. Your company or organisation must therefore always be looking at new ways of doing things, new products and services to introduce, new customers and clients to serve and new sources of supplies. In addition to this, you must always keep your eyes concentrated on the ever-changing economic, social, political and legal environment for any new bit of information that you may have to respond to – whether you like it or not!

In this chapter, I explore the many factors that govern the future of you and your company – regardless of whether you encounter difficulties ahead or keep marching on to success and profitability.

Figuring Out What Your Future Holds

The purpose of having planning and forecasting processes is so that you have the best possible idea of what the future holds for you and your organisation. You need, therefore, the best possible sources of data, together with the capability to analyse them effectively, draw conclusions, form judgements and take decisions.

You need to use these sources and then plan in detail for the environment and markets overall (see Chapter 7), as well as for each aspect of your organisation including:

- ✔ Costs that you can do nothing about, such as gas, electricity, water, fuel, petrol, transport and telecommunications. (For these types of costs, you need to plan based on the most rigorous information possible – see Chapters 7 and 14.)
- ✔ Finance costs – both capital and revenue.
- ✔ Staffing and labour costs and obligations.
- ✔ Changes and developments in the supply side, including the availability of new sources of supply of data, information, technology and expertise, as well as components and raw materials (These changes include losing major suppliers from any of these areas.)
- ✔ Changes in customer bases, locations and habits, including attention to competitors or alternatives that are taking away your customers.

You also need to include the consequences to your business, as well as the opportunities, of growing a major new customer base. If you do indeed do this, do you have the resources to fully service the new opportunity – or will you fail and hurt your own reputation (and, of course, profits)?

- ✔ Changes in your organisation's size, constitution and structure, which lead to new ownership or top managers imposing different priorities on you.
- ✔ Changes in direction as the result of changes in leadership and management.
- ✔ Changes in technology, capability and capacity, which can lead to changes in what you can deliver, the prices you can charge and the expertise required to make your organisation work fully and effectively.

Make up your mind that planning for your organisation's future is a personal, as well as a professional and occupational, priority. Make it your business to know and understand the prevailing trends in labour, products and service, finance and energy markets – particularly trends that influence availability and cost.

Building on present pressures and concerns

All organisations have their own present pressures and concerns in terms of capability, product and service demands and resource pressures and constraints. Knowing the finest details of your present conditions helps you build your strategy for future progress and challenges.

REAL WORLD EXAMPLE

Frozen fish

Helmont Ltd is a fish processing and cannery company located in the West Midlands. Helmont Ltd was a very successful and profitable company and supplied to all the main brands including John West, Bird's Eye and Ross. Helmont also supplied fresh, frozen, canned and processed fish products to the supermarket chains for sale under own-brand names.

Helmont Ltd took its supplies of fresh and frozen fish from Ocean-Going Trawlers Ltd, a fishing fleet based in Liverpool. Following new quota arrangements introduced by the EU in 2002, prices of the landed fish catches in the UK rose by 10 per cent. Accordingly, Helmont decided to look around for alternative supplies. Extensive research led Helmont to the port and fishing fleet of Cadiz, Spain. The catch prices in Cadiz were 53 per cent lower than those in Liverpool, and the full cost, including transport, worked out at 38 per cent cheaper than the Liverpool supplies. Figuring it had located a great deal, Helmont unilaterally cancelled its contract with Ocean-Going Trawlers and took up with Cadiz. What could possibly go wrong?

Needless to say, the venture did fail – because everything that could go wrong, *did* go wrong! Refrigeration units on the lorries broke down. There were strikes and disputes involving the border authorities between France and Spain, and France and the UK. As fuel prices rose, transporting catches more than 1,000 miles became more expensive. Helmont also encountered hold-ups on the Spanish, French and (especially) the English motorway networks.

In the end, the deliveries couldn't be assured, and this led to Helmont having to default on its own contracts. Accordingly, it negotiated its way out of the arrangements with Cadiz and returned to Liverpool, pleading for forgiveness!

All the elements of strategic management and competitiveness are contained in this case:

- ✔ The need to tackle costs – and the right way to tackle them.

- ✔ The search for cost efficiencies and cost effectiveness.

- ✔ The need to assure supplies.

- ✔ The need to meet and deliver your obligations.

Even more importantly, this case illustrates why you must take any decisions in full context. Even if your company needs to cut costs, a strategy along the lines of Helmont's isn't necessarily the way to do it. If you're faced with rising costs in one part of your business, you don't necessarily have to cut costs in that part of your business – you can cut them somewhere else.

Above all, you should never unilaterally withdraw from any agreement unless you're powerful enough to make your decision stick! In this case, Helmont was indeed welcomed back to Liverpool – but at the cost of paying a hefty premium to re-engage the contract, and stringent penalty clauses that would be invoked immediately upon any future cancellation.

TIP

Concentrate on successfully addressing these concerns as often as possible, so you develop the optimum customer and client base. That way, when you do have to make changes (especially when times get tough), you can keep as much of your business as possible.

This constant activity helps you know and understand the worst possible set of circumstances and trading conditions under which you can possibly remain viable. You don't want to receive a sudden financial hit and then have to take what many may perceive to be knee-jerk reactions to try (and often fail) to put matters right.

Defining growth for yourself

After trying, to the best of your ability, to predict what the future holds, you need to look at your strategy and your competitive position (see Chapters 2 and 4). So what do you find? Everybody wants to see growth!

Most people, especially investors, commentators and analysts, who say they want growth don't know why they expect you to grow – nor do they know by how much they expect you to grow. But nevertheless they still expect growth, growth, growth. And when you do try and pin down what exactly they mean by growth, they fall back on phrases such as: 'significant growth' or 'double-digit growth' – anything rather than explaining themselves fully.

Furthermore, some people's growth expectations are completely unreal. For example:

- ✔ In 2007, Tesco's expansion from 29 per cent to 30 per cent of the UK supermarket trade was described by media analysts as 'disappointing.'

- ✔ easyJet's passenger figures for 2007 rose from 29 million to 31 million; this was also described by the business press as 'disappointing.'

- ✔ In the football industry, Chelsea FC's growth from fashionable London football club to a major achiever in the sector was deemed unacceptable by the company's owner when, in 2008, it only came second in three of the four competitions that it entered.

The preceding expectations and subsequent critiques are clearly senseless, and you can see all growth in this light. No organisation can continue to double the market or its achievement if it's starting from a very high base already.

You need to see and define growth in terms of what's feasible and profitable for your own company, as well as what's actually achievable in the present circumstances. If necessary, you must be able to answer back those individuals who would otherwise want to see 'growth, growth and more growth'.

Find the strength to answer back by knowing and understanding how your strategy is to work and what your objectives are. Make all this information clear to people who want you to 'grow, grow and grow.' Back up your assertions with hard data; give these nay-sayers the simple and clear forms that even they can understand.

Establishing Your Future Strategy

Your future strategy must be as clear as the strategy you have at present. Start with a combination of your core position (see Chapter 2) and the competitive forces that presently affect you (Chapter 3), and then see where the opportunities lie and how you're going to take advantage of them from:

 ✔ Your present position.

 ✔ Your present position plus any changes you can make and sustain.

The core of your future strategy lies in developing your present strategy and primary activities. These are, after all, what have got you to your present position of success and profitability.

Planning for growth and expansion

Having considered and evaluated everything, if you do decide to plan for growth and expansion, you need to know and understand:

 ✔ Where the finance and other resources are coming from.

 ✔ Where the staff and expertise are coming from.

 ✔ Where the return on investment is coming from, specifically in terms of products and service sales.

 ✔ How soon you'll get your money back.

 ✔ What can conceivably go wrong.

If the preceding requirements sound like showering exciting plans with a dose of cold water – well, they are! You must check, check and check again your assumptions and projections. That way, if things do go wrong, you know and understand why. And if they go right, you also know and understand why.

You have two clear paths to growth and expansion: increasing how much existing customers spend when they do business with you or finding new customers in new locations (by taking them from your competitors and alternatives or else growing them afresh).

Whichever path you choose, you consciously make your decision and then evaluate your choice. Customers who may be perfectly happy taking one range of products and services from you, may prefer to go elsewhere for others, however good you are at providing them.

Choosing between organic or external

At the heart of the future development decision is the *organic versus external decision* – are you going to try and grow from within (organic) or look outside, typically by pursuing an acquisition (external)? Both paths have advantages and disadvantages:

✔ **The organic or internal path** is well-known, but the opportunities may be depleted, particularly if your organisation relies on ageing products or technologies. For example, traditional camera manufacturers have resisted 'going digital' because that isn't one of their strengths. But as customers quite literally die off, do these manufacturers have any choice except to look outside?

✔ **The external growth path** contains all the promises and all the risks associated with mergers and acquisitions (see Chapter 15). Almost half of all closely related expansion plans and acquisitions succeed. That may not sound very impressive, but that success rate is far better than expansion efforts into exotic new areas. Those adventures may be exciting, but the cost can be great.

Planning for other things

Even if growth or expansion aren't your goal, you still need to plan. You need some idea of how you're going to go about each of the following (because, in practice, each is certain to occur at some time!).

Consolidation

Consolidation means you take every possible step to ensure that your present customers stay with you and continue to do business with you in their present volumes. To do this, you ensure that your present customer base is as secure, loyal and happy with you as possible by ensuring the highest possible standards of service and responsiveness. Consolidation nearly always means having a continual stream of product and service quality enhancements, improvements and developments.

Withdrawal

Your organisation is always going to encounter times when you need to withdraw products and services from your markets or withdraw yourself from some of your markets.

When circumstances thrust either of these scenarios upon you, you need:

- A *contingency approach*, which is a combination of meeting your immediate obligations and providing public relations support regarding everything else that you do. Even if everyone knows and understands what you're doing and why, you're at least meeting people's expectations by confronting these issues when they arise.

- A *planned approach* to withdrawing products, product lines, services, markets and locations in phases. Like a contingency approach, a planned approach requires that you continue to meet your present range of obligations as well as taking steps to divest yourself of technology, information, facilities, premises and other equipment that you no longer require.

Of course, everything concerning withdrawals isn't always this straightforward. See the sidebar 'Withdrawal – right and wrong!' for some of the cloudier reasons for withdrawing.

Withdrawal – right and wrong!

Companies withdraw from things in all sorts of different ways. For example, the big supermarket and department store chains can and do withdraw from contracts with their suppliers – often giving only 24 hours' notice! Two notorious cases stand out:

- Marks & Spencer withdrew from its contracts with Scottish clothing suppliers and went on to source its garments overseas in China, Vietnam and Malaysia.

- In a week when suppliers announced large gas, electricity and energy price rises, Tesco went to one of its largest farming suppliers in southern England and announced unilaterally that the prices that it paid for milk and dairy produce would henceforth be 25 per cent lower.

Clearly, if you're big enough, you can behave like this. But be prepared to experience consequences if you keep doing so. You may find that people are unwilling to do business with you, however big you are. This practice is no basis for building a business relationship in which you're supposed to be serving everyone's interests.

Otherwise, of course, individual reasons for particular withdrawals always exist. For example:

- Accenture withdrew from its contribution to the NHS IT project because it couldn't pin down any clear objectives, deliverables or project and payment schedules from the NHS.

- Ryanair opened up 12 airports in Poland, in the advance knowledge that it would partially or wholly withdraw from those that didn't produce specified turnover and passenger volumes.

The key to effectiveness is your own line of reasoning! If you can justify and support your particular course of action, at least you have a basis on which to work. But remember that if you gain a reputation for being a 'sudden withdrawer,' people hesitate before doing business with you.

Seeing Where Your Opportunities Lie

As you see where the future of your company lies, you also see where the opportunities lie – the two are inextricably linked.

An opportunity is very much what you think it is! Your line of reasoning – and the expertise with which you back your judgement and evaluation – is paramount (see Chapter 7). What you see as an opportunity, others may see as nothing more than idle fancy if you can't explain and justify your position. Similarly, if others get excited about something that you see as a recipe for disaster, you need to be able to explain to them why you believe this to be the case. (See the sidebar 'You call this an opportunity?' for a particularly disastrous 'opportunity.')

Taking advantage

Seeing an opportunity is one thing; being able to take advantage is quite another. And the kind of advantage that you can take depends on many things:

- ✔ The speed and accuracy of your decision-making processes.
- ✔ The availability of finance, resources, staff and product and service delivery capacity.
- ✔ The effects on your existing range of activities.

Whether you take advantage of an opportunity also depends on who you are – the first or an early mover, or a latecomer late to the party (see Chapter 8 for more).

- ✔ **If you're first or very early**, you clearly have the opportunity to establish yourself. You also have the opportunity to make mistakes that others following you into the market can learn from. And if it is indeed a profitable opportunity, then others are certain to want to follow you.
- ✔ **If you're coming late to the party**, you need to make sure that you find out everything possible from people who are already in the market. Take with a pinch of salt any projection or forecast that you're going to take the new opportunity by storm, wiping out all the competition.

After you take advantage and establish your place in the new markets, simply staying in the market becomes one of your main activities. The excitement of the new quickly dissipates – but you've still got to commit to maximising and optimising the returns that you now need in order to make the whole thing worthwhile.

You call this an opportunity?

In 1997, the new Chief Executive of Marks & Spencer, Richard Greenbury, took charge of his first board meeting. He announced that the company was moving into the youth market. The youth market, he explained, was a fantastic opportunity. It was where all the money was, and youths had a very high propensity to spend. Accordingly, the company launched a large range of clothes and underwear targeted specifically at the youth market. The advertising and promotional activities used David Beckham as the core icon. (He was, at the time, England football captain, married to a pop icon, good-looking and all-round youth role model.)

With all this in place, Marks & Spencer waited for the money to start rolling in. And it waited and waited. Not only did the youth money not start rolling in, the core customer base of middle-class, middle-aged people (the real people with the real money) stopped using the store.

For the opportunity had turned out to be false. The youth market didn't want to be seen dead going into shops that were only used (in their eyes) by old people. And because of the emphasis on youth, shoppers aged 35 and over stopped going also. In the darkest days at the turn of the 21st century, the company depended for its survival on sales of its core food products, underwear and working clothes for men and women. It took the company nearly ten years to reach the market standing and profitability of the late 1990s.

Surveying new and emerging markets and activities

In general, the main areas for developing your strategy and competitive position come from the markets, locations and customer bases with which you're familiar. However, with all the caveats and pitfalls that I show and note throughout this book, you still have plenty of opportunities for entering new markets and activities.

One way of getting involved in new markets is to develop different designs and brands for your existing range of products and services, making sure that they're sufficiently separate and distinctive from the established. That way, providing that the product or service is of value to the new sector you're targeting, you can develop new markets for what are effectively your existing products. This can be a very successful strategy when you do it right. For example:

 ✔ Matsushita makes a range of commercial and industrial standard electronic and electrical goods under its own name, and also produces equivalent products for retail consumption under the Panasonic name.

- ✔ Electrolux makes washing machines under its own name that sell for high prices. Electrolux also produces very similar products under the Electra and Faure names that it sells for up to £200 less.

- ✔ Nokia produces branded ranges of mobile phone handsets for pre-pay customers and other branded ranges for pay-as-you-go customers – but the internal components are exactly the same.

Beyond these examples, take some time to consider three different areas where opportunities for developing your company and your markets for the future may be profitable:

- ✔ Public services

- ✔ Project work

- ✔ Outsourcing and collaboration

I cover each of these areas in the following sections.

Public services

The privatisation and restructuring of public services (those services that people expect taxation to provide – healthcare, education, policing and security), together with a shortage of public funds for capital investment, has led to many commercial companies and organisations taking advantage of the opportunities consequently available in delivering parts of what used to be paid for purely out of taxation.

Superficially, this situation is almost too good to be true! The Government guarantees you your fees. You have captive markets – customers and clients who need the services. If anything goes wrong, you can simply pull out and hand the service back to the Government.

Of course, it *is* too good to be true! Many companies and organisations that have gone in on this basis have gone bankrupt or lived to regret the damage to their reputations and finances.

So if you do go into providing public services, you need to remember that this is what it is – a service to the public. You need to know and understand that the public is coming to you because it needs you. You need to see this situation, not as an opportunity to exploit, but rather as a huge responsibility. Look at it in terms that as long as you provide a good service and make a reasonable charge (whatever that may mean), everybody is happy: the service is good, you remain commercially viable and the public is paying a fee that meets its expectations (and no more).

Captive audiences still have choices: PatientLine

Once provided free, telephone, radio and television services in hospital rooms have become fully privatised. PatientLine was the major provider across all NHS hospitals and other in-patient facilities in the UK. The company normally agreed a contract with NHS primary healthcare trusts. Subject to a minimum of two years, the contract could be of any duration, and some agreement contracts were as long as 15 years.

The charges made for these services were as follows:

- For a telephone call made by the patients: 49p per minute, subject to a minimum charge of £1.50.
- For a telephone call made to the patient: 12p per minute, subject to a minimum charge of £1.50 also.
- Television rental: £3.50 per day or part of a day.

Neither the telephone nor the television technology provided the quality or volume of services that many patients demanded. The telephone technology was never fully reliable, which led to patients being charged for telephone calls that had failed to be connected and calls made after the phone had been switched off and the handset returned. The television technology, normally related to satellite and cable sourcing, regularly broke down and disconnected.

The technology wasn't fully and comprehensively available to all upon demand either. There were never enough telephone handsets or television and radio sets to go round. This meant that not everyone could make or receive calls when it suited them; and this was found to be traumatic for those awaiting operations or on strict medical regimes, who had to make such calls at times that fitted in with their treatments.

The result was that, despite a captive market, consumers voted with their feet. Strictly forbidden by most hospital authorities, patients nevertheless brought in their own mobile phones and laptop computers. The result was that PatientLine found that NHS primary healthcare trusts were unilaterally cancelling contracts. The expected volume of business, together with the super profits expected to emerge from being able to dominate a market in this way, never materialised. Consequently, the company switched from being a service provider for a public sector captive market, to marketing, selling and installing technology for commercial customers.

So if you do try to exploit a captive market or take advantage of individuals presently using a particular public service, people can find ways around it. And above all – if your product or service is poor (or just a poor fit), they won't use you!

You don't want to gain a reputation for any of the following:

- Delivering shoddy building work on public facilities in return for large fees.
- Putting the elderly and disabled out of sheltered accommodation (as has happened when public fees have been inadequate to meet the demands of private care providers).

✔ Delivering inaccurate and inadequately marked exam scripts (as has happened with school attainment and A-level examinations).

✔ Putting up your charges by 400 per cent over a five-year period (as has happened with the UK gas companies).

Indeed, if you're preaching perfection, the ideal may be to engage directly with the public service providers and contract directly with them, rather than with the customers and clients themselves. That way, the whole situation is much less open to the abuses indicated in the preceding list.

Project work

One way of testing out new markets, locations and activities is to structure your initial effort as a project. Prior to this, you need to carry out feasibility studies and pilot activities, and produce detailed research. In order to develop this work further, in many cases, you can turn what you're proposing to do over to a project team.

Such projects normally produce a limited range of products or services with a view to testing a particular market, gathering intelligence and addressing future potential. At the same time, these endeavours limit the expenditure, so if you need to withdraw, you haven't done too much damage.

Examples of products and services successfully introduced on this basis include:

✔ The collectors' ranges of Barbie dolls, which were (and are) specifically targeted at those who buy the dolls as an investment.

✔ Sandals' family holidays, introduced as an alternative at different resorts to the company's main and exclusive holiday locations.

✔ Interflora, which simply required a telephone network when it was started up so that people could have flowers delivered to their nearest and dearest the following day, wherever they may be.

The project approach is presently being used on a commercial basis by such diverse organisations and industries as:

✔ **Building, construction and civil engineering,** as they try out new materials and technologies that aim to improve durability of facilities and reduce energy consumption.

✔ **The genetic modification of food,** to see whether some crops, herds and flocks can truly be made much more productive, effective and nutritious.

When things go well with project work or the initial effort, you may be tempted to think that all the hard work is done and future success is assured. Not so! You still need to do a full evaluation of why things went well, and apply all the lessons necessary to effectively expand your initial effort in the future.

Outsourcing and collaboration

You can develop your organisation's future and make an effective entry into new markets and activities through outsourcing and collaboration.

Outsourcing works in two ways:

✔ You hire a specialist contractor or provider to carry out particular activities. You ought to have at least half an eye on the opportunities that may be available to you in the new sector. And this applies even if you're outsourcing something as mundane as your security or catering services. After all, if you subsequently find out that security or catering (or whatever it is) is actually a hugely profitable niche, you may be persuaded to buy into it and develop it as a new field of activity – providing of course, that it doesn't impact on your core business.

✔ If you outsource in order to divest yourself of activities that others can do better for you, you also free up resources that you can put to other uses.

Look at collaborations, joint and *multi-ventures* (where you go into ventures with other partners on a cooperative and mutually profitable basis) as information-gathering exercises. You're going into something with others presumably because you all have expertise, resources, finance and commitment that the particular proposal demands. After you're in, obviously you need to deliver the venture to the best of your ability – but you must also always be looking around, scanning the environment for future opportunities in this field.

If you're working in a familiar field, you need to see how your partners and collaborators operate, what they do better than you and where else the collaboration may lead in terms of developing your own expertise and position.

If you're working in a new market and/or new location, you need to make sure that you take the opportunity to find out as much as possible about future opportunities that may be available.

Gaining entry into new markets and locations

The final aspect of assessing your organisation's present and future viability, strategy and competitive position is to make sure that you know and understand the resource demands that arise as a direct consequence of everything that you set out to do. In particular, you're certain to commit to some kind of finance. You must also always remember that you're putting your reputation on the line.

So whatever your strength and standing in your own area may be, you need to make sure that you can resource the new entry or development from the following points of view:

- ✔ Getting the new market used to the idea that you're now going to be present.

- ✔ Generating an active interest in the new market so that people want to try out your products and services.

- ✔ Managing people's expectations in advance of opening for business in the new market.

- ✔ Meeting people's expectations immediately. (The last thing you want to have to do is tell prospective customers that you're experiencing teething troubles and then go on and explain why you didn't think of them earlier.)

- ✔ Meeting people's expectations after the initial fanfare and fuss dies down.

Specifically, you need resources for:

- ✔ **The pre-phase:** You investigate the real possibilities of a location.

- ✔ **The start-up:** You establish your activities and open for business in a location.

- ✔ **The steady-state phase:** Everything is up and running. You conduct your business on a regularised and known and understood basis.

So make sure that you have enough resource, finance, technology and expertise at your disposal. Make sure that you examine everything in full detail and, where necessary, test everything to destruction. Also, your staff need to be trained in everything that you need and want them to do. You also need to ensure that people can get to and from your premises, and can access activities, products and services when you and they need. Then you need your own energy, enthusiasm and expertise to give life to everything that you're now going to go off and do! The rest (as they say) is up to you!

'Anybody who never made a mistake, never made anything'

–Napoleon

'Whatever you do, never give up. Never, ever give up.'

– Shane Warne, top Australian cricketer

Part VI
The Part of Tens

'Do we have a competitive strategy
in this company? — Why do you ask?'

In this part . . .

Because they're so easy to use – and just plain fun –
For Dummies books always end with a part of tens –
a short chapter with quick and concise bundles of
essential information. So as part of the long, proud tradi-
tion, I offer you ten of my top reading picks for stories of
competitive success, ten ways to effectively manage risk,
ten probing questions to consider before investing in
anything and a checklist of ten action items necessary if
you're ever contemplating mergers, acquisitions or
takeovers.

Chapter 18

Ten (Or So) Great Books on Competitive Strategy in Action

*I*f you're going to be a professional manager of anything, you need to go out and see what others are doing and how they do it. After reading even a few chapters of this book, you're better able to recognise what they're doing well and take heed of their mistakes.

So go out and see with your own eyes, but also be in the habit of reading. Evaluate everything that you get your hands on – delve in, see what others have to say about themselves, figure out what makes them tick and ponder why they succeeded or failed.

If you don't go out and see things, and if you don't read and read, you'll get left behind by people who do.

The following ten books are some of my favourites. So take a look – even if some are several years old. These volumes feature some universal and enduring lessons on strategically managing all types of organisations.

Any author who tries to blind you with jargon, sell you business models and convince you of some sure-fire, easy idea isn't doing you or your company any good. Commit yourself to reading, researching and doing the hard work that arises yourself.

Maverick

If you read no other book on business or management (aside from this one, of course!), you must read *Maverick: The Success behind the World's Most Unusual Workplace* (Random House, 2001). This book by Ricardo Semler focuses on the struggles of Semco, a Brazilian white goods and pumps manufacturing firm, to become competitive and deal with external pressures, including a national inflation rate of 3,000 per cent, staff opposition and an inept management team! Semler, who serves as company Chairman and Chief Executive, chronicles how he and his staff transformed Semco by paying attention to everything that's important and by working incredibly hard throughout the entire process.

Although Semco's stated strategic position is 'We have no strategy,' nothing is further from the truth. As the book clearly demonstrates, Semco is committed to serving niches (see Chapters 2 and 4) as a very high-quality, high-value operator. As a result, the company can charge very high prices for excellent product delivery and service support. Everything else – staff involvement, organisation structure, procedures, high ethical standards – is about ensuring that the company remains viable and profitable over the long term. So read it!

Ryanair

Ryanair: How a Small Irish Airline Conquered Europe by Siobhan Creaton (HarperCollins, 2003) is the story of how the Irish company transformed from a top-brand, exclusive and loss-making airline into the world's largest volume passenger carrier. The myths and legends of Michael O'Leary, the company's charismatic Chief Executive, are central to the story, particularly his personal and professional effect on the organisation. The book demonstrates the need for expert, as well as charismatic, leadership.

This book also strongly illustrates the importance of concentrating on a core strategic position (see Chapters 1 and 2) – which in Ryanair's case is cost leadership and advantage.

Competitive Strategy

You should read *Competitive Strategy: Techniques for Analyzing Industries and Competitors* by Michael Porter (Free Press, 1980; 2004) because of Porter's huge influence on the strategy process for leaders and managers. Porter's work has had a major influence on everyone's understanding of what strategy is and how to implement it. In particular, he laid the groundwork for modern business understanding of competitive forces (see Chapters 2 and 3).

This book has everything you need to know about competitive strategy from an organisational point of view, including the need to have a core position, the capability that you need and the actions that you can take to enhance your competitiveness. For Porter, strategy is a process. It's not a statement or an end in itself; it's the foundation of all business success.

This book (and all Porter's work) highlights the importance of clarity. If you aren't clear about what you're setting out to do – including why and how – you can't expect others to know and understand what you or your organisation stand for. You need clarity in order to deliver what you promise, meet expectations and provide value and benefits to your customers.

Management Stripped Bare

Management Stripped Bare: What They Don't Teach You at Business School by Jo Owen (Kogan Page, 2006) is a must for managers who have to implement strategy as well as design it. Jo Owen makes no bones about leaders and strategies: the first priority of all managers is to know and understand what is happening in their companies and organisations, and be able to influence the course of everything if, and when, necessary.

And Jo should know! He's the founder of TeachFirst, the pioneering organisation that takes the best graduates from the best universities in the UK, develops their character, courage and operational expertise by placing them in some of the worst and under-performing schools and eventually sends these young leaders into industry and commerce.

Dot.Bomb

Written by Rory Cellan-Jones, the BBC's industrial and business correspondent of many years' standing, *Dot.Bomb: The Strange Death of Dot.Com Britain* (Aurum Pres Ltd, 2003) tells the story of what happened during the not-so-distant dot.com era. The book examines a not-so-distant time when everyone was drawn into a craze, parted with life savings to invest in Internet companies and, by and large, lost a fortune. As the stock market overheated and the media went crazy, companies lost focus and direction – two essential qualities that companies needed if they were ever to stand any chance of survival.

The book has lessons for everyone. For starters, never believe your own publicity (see Chapter 6). Develop your competitive advantage based on a core foundation or generic strategic position (see Chapters 2 and 3). And always remember that you must have customers! Quite simply, many dot.com companies foundered because they didn't have any customers. That's a lesson for everyone.

Investment Appraisal

Investment Appraisal: A Managerial Approach (Palgrave, 2000), author Richard Pettinger – yes, the name does sound familiar! – looks at what really happens in investment appraisal, risk management and decision-making. These are all critical aspects of strategic management and developing your competitive position.

I produced this book because it fills a gap – specifically the relationship between how people really think about investing and how they really take decisions. So much decision-making is shrouded in financial calculations and presentations that demonstrate that one set of circumstances is bound to happen.

In practice of course, this never happens; decision-making is much more complex! People look at the figures – and then they choose to do what they want anyway, regardless of what the figures say! In this book, I show you where the pitfalls arise, and how to avoid them.

The Eddie Stobart Story

The Eddie Stobart Story (Harper Collins, 1996) by Hunter Davies is a story of growth – warts and all! The book tells how a single lorry transport operation turned into the UK's largest haulage company. Davies examines the pressures that were placed on the founding family (the Stobarts) and how they came through personal, as well as strategic and operational, difficulties.

The book also tells of how the company transformed its industrial sector by placing all staff (including drivers) on salaries and providing industrial, commercial and company training so workers became multi-skilled. This strategy encouraged (and continues to encourage) the drivers to accept a much greater involvement in company activities than is traditional in this sector. For example, Stobart drivers are now required to conduct the quality assurance functions, such as checking deliveries on and off the lorries and handling customer complaints.

Be My Guest

Be My Guest (Prentice Hall, 1991) was written by Conrad Hilton, the founder of the hotel chain of the same name. From its roots in 1906, Hilton Hotels transformed everyone's expectations of the hotel and accommodation industry (and left many sub-standard facilities at risk of bankruptcy and closure).

Hilton's promise was quite simple: to ensure that if you needed somewhere to lay your head at night, you'd always get good facilities at one of his hotels. Wherever in the world a guest ends up, he can be sure of a quiet and comfortable room with standard facilities. Over the years, Hilton has constantly upgraded the quality of these facilities so that accommodation now includes a private bathroom, television, tea and coffee facilities and a fridge/mini-bar.

In the beginning, however, Hilton set out only to ensure that individuals who came to big US cities on business had somewhere clean and tidy to go back to when they had finished their day's work. Once people knew what Hilton stood for and the quality that he provided, they began to flock to his facilities. He wisely used the profits from his early activities to build up the Hilton Hotel Group and to transform the ways in which everyone expects to settle down for the night when far from home!

The Rise and Fall of Marks & Spencer

The Rise and Fall of Marks & Spencer: . . . And How It Rose Again (Profile Books, 2005) by Judi Bevan is a shining example of what goes wrong when you lose concentration on your core foundation and generic strategic position and, consequently, your ability to compete.

This is a story of boardroom shenanigans, personality clashes, in-fighting and a lack of direction from the very top of the company. Indeed, the company's misfortunes can be traced back to the late 20th century when, within hours of the last member of the founding family leaving the Board, troubles began. Nobody quite knew how to proceed, so they fell back on to a series of guesses about the future, rather than concentrating on the things that they did well.

Marks & Spencer took nearly ten years to recover from this hiatus and to return to the profit and turnover levels of the late 1990s. If you want to know how *not* to run a company and *not* be competitive, then pick up this book! (The book also explores the hard work necessary to put things right when you don't run a company properly.)

Green, Inc.

Green, Inc.: A Guide to Business and the Environment (Island Press, 1995) by Frances Cairncross is an early, controversial and very stark study of the commercial drives that the environmental movement began. Cairncross examines all the key issues: asking people to change their behaviour; energy consumption; the generation of waste and rubbish; the controversies around packaging; and the enduring issues of fuel sources, genetic modification of crops and fair trading.

And, of course, the book exposes how many companies have hijacked these issues for commercial gain, changing the environmental movement to little more than a marketing ploy and enabling companies to charge ever-increasing prices for things that have no added value other than the fact that they're perceived somehow to be ethical and 'organic' (whatever that may mean).

Beyond the Deal

Beyond the Deal: Optimising Merger and Acquisition Value by Peter Clark (Longman, 1990) is a comprehensive study of all the things to pay attention to when seeking the best possible returns on investment and maximising your chances of success during merger or acquisition ventures (see Chapter 15).

Peter Clark worked for many years consulting on mergers and acquisitions for some of the world's best-known and most high-value management consultancies (as well as serving as the technical editor of this book). He specialised in mergers, takeovers and company valuations. His book is a detailed account of how to assess a company's value, taking into account not just assets and liabilities, but also where operations and activities gain and lose money.

Chapter 19

Ten (Or So) Questions to Ask About Any Corporate Investment

*A*t every stage of deciding, implementing and developing competitive strategy, you make investments – investments on which you expect returns. When you hear the word 'investment,' you probably think first of capital investments – production lines, equipment and the like. But keep in mind that many other forms of investment exist, including people and their expertise, new technology or the purchase of part of a (or an entire) company.

You must ask – and answer – the following ten important and straightforward questions about whether your investment opportunity is going to deliver the returns that you seek. The following sections take you through these questions and provide you with some direction on how to seek out the answers you need.

Why?

The most obvious of all the questions about an investment – and often the hardest to answer – is why? Why do I want to make a certain investment?

Always answer the question of 'Why?' in terms of returns, market opportunities, competitive position and the opportunity to deliver excellent products and services. Of course in practice, answers don't always focus on these specific aspects. If you can't come up with such direct answers, then be aware that the investment is likely to be problematic.

People invest in things for many reasons, including vanity, prestige, triumph, status and their own personal reputations. So be clear in your mind about the truth behind your answer to 'Why?' before you proceed any further with your investment decision.

When?

In the same way as answering the 'Why?' question, 'When?' can be hard to answer as well. So when is the best time to make an investment? Well, there's never a perfect time to do anything, so you always have to be on the lookout for opportunities. If the opportunities are legitimate (see Chapters 4, 5 and 6 – and also 15, 16 and 17) you need quality information and market analysis at your fingertips in order to make quick and effective decisions.

Ryanair bought a large proportion of its present airliner fleet at a time when orders for airliners were slumping and the main manufacturers, Boeing and Airbus, couldn't give the planes away. By being able to take this chance, Ryanair was able to maximise its investment in the planes, and so deliver the basis for working on its core position of delivering maximum passenger volumes at the lowest possible cost.

Where?

The simple answer to 'Where do I invest?' is that you invest in what you know and understand, what you can do and what you're good at.

The real answer, however, is that many organisations see the excitement of the new and unknown. They see themselves marching onwards into new fields, conquering all before them. But unfortunately, investments in areas that an organisation doesn't really know anything about invariably fail.

If you're going into an investment in the guise of being a pioneering company, find out everything you can before you go in. (See Chapter 17 for much more on doing proper and thorough location research.) This way you at least know and understand the environment that you're entering. You're not just guessing that an opportunity will be good for you.

How?

Answering the question 'How should I go about making an investment?' is a bit more complicated than Why?, When? and Where?

You can go into most ventures in several ways – alone, or as part of a joint venture with other partners. So during the 'How?' stage you need to assess your risks for each option.

The reason you assess your risks is because you need to take all the steps that you can, both to spread the risk and minimise it. See Chapter 14 for more on risk.

During the 'How?' stage, you also need to clarify the ways in which you're going to conduct yourself after the investment or venture is up and running. If you're going into something for the long term, make this clear. And if you're going into something purely to exploit it, make this clear also! You must have the strength of character to say what you mean and mean what you say. See Chapter 13 for more on ethical decision-making.

What Returns Are Available?

As part of your investment research process, you'll probably calculate a broad range of returns, based on various combinations of circumstances and eventualities. These calculations give you the basis on which to begin to evaluate your alternatives and make your investment choices. See Chapter 8 for more details.

You always have a complexity of factors to take into account, and you're likely to get some things wrong from time to time. So when you assess the likely and possible returns on your investment, always make sure that you consider your *nightmare scenario* – where everything that can go wrong, does go wrong! You don't want to blind yourself with the amazing possibilities of everything going well; you need to keep your feet firmly planted on the ground!

What Returns Are Really Available?

The answer to this question ought to be the same as your answer to 'What returns are available?' See Chapter 8.

Sadly, this isn't always the case. Asking about the reality of returns forces you to take another look at your organisation and identify corporate adventure-taking, those pioneering (and often phoney) activities that organisations claim as evidence of expansionary strategies, competitive effectiveness or forward-looking management, but which are, in practice, collective self-indulgence.

You pay for everything you do out of the profits that you make from the things that you do actually know and understand. So be careful and guard against having fun and games at corporate expense! You're most likely investing other people's money, so you need to invest in things that you actually know something – preferably a lot – about.

What Can Go Wrong?

You've surely been in meetings to discuss new ventures, products or services and ended up getting carried away with all the excitement of the chase! Proposals and ideas quickly gain lives of their own. Projections for market success can quickly go from an estimate to an accepted, absolute fact. And after projecting sales, you often quickly move on to making plans for what to do with the large income volumes that you're going to generate! And you're still in the planning meeting! And for sure you haven't even begun to consider nightmare scenarios (see the earlier section 'What Returns Are Available?').

Wildly optimistic ideas often indicate the first danger signs of an investment about to go wrong. Even if you're moderately successful, wildly optimistic ideas frequently lead to disappointment. And if things do go wrong, hold on to your hat. Senior and influential figures tend to withdraw from the investment decision, distance themselves from the situation and leave you to pick up the mess!

What Can Really Go Wrong?

The point of asking what can *really* go wrong is to make sure that you ask the question again!

When you ask this question again, you start to get into the details: the real costs of things, the real hold-ups and glitches that can occur, the real problems with supplies, the real issues with your staff. You must get people to think along the lines of what can possibly go wrong in the fullest possible detail, so that they get over the initial excitement and frenzy and move on to reality.

So get people thinking! And make sure that while the last thing that you want to do is to kill people's enthusiasm and commitment, everyone must get at the detail at the earliest possible stage.

Unfortunately, going into the details is where many people lose interest! The hard work required to turn an illusion into reality is of little interest to many. In many cases, people involved in the early stages of a project end up shifting the work and execution of the project onto lower-level workers – often with disastrous results. Consider:

- ✔ The Millennium Dome was conceived as a celebration of the new millennium and turned out to cost £700 million and celebrate nothing.

- ✔ The invasion of Iraq was conceived as a war of liberation and turned out to be totally destructive to the particular society.

- ✔ The sub-prime mortgage market was conceived as a way of getting high repayments on property debt and turned out to be a major cause of the falls in values of the property markets.

In each of these cases, no one questioned the original concept in the detail necessary. And in each case, the venture failed.

What's My Next Best Alternative?

Always look out for the next best alternative to any intended investment. Without a best alternative in mind, many companies risk becoming myopically focused on a single option, regardless of whether it's the best one.

Beleaguered American manufacturer General Motors is trying to develop a new hybrid car, the Volt. But with Toyota reportedly developing what may be a slightly superior, similar design in the same timeframe, an important question arises: has GM management considered its alternatives? How about simply buying another firm's models and re-badging them, rather than spending billions on an endeavour that may miss the market?

What's My Exit Strategy?

Viewing investments as a one-time decision is problematic. Consider the nuclear reactor manufacturers that faced insolvency because their business plans never took into account the cost of decommissioning old reactors and dealing with spent fuel.

Companies that don't prepare exit strategies may find themselves strangled in one later as old investments take up resources that they may otherwise direct elsewhere.

Do We Want to Invest?

You must ask and answer the question 'Do we want to invest?' and realise the effect of your response. Of course, legitimate responses (positive and negative) are possible for all proposals. These are based on a full evaluation of everything involved, what the proposal or venture is supposed to deliver and attention to detail.

But you also need to see the broader context:

- ✔ **If you don't want to invest,** you're likely to fall back on all sorts of corporate excuses: the money to invest isn't in the budget, times are hard, returns aren't proven, we have other priorities – anything to avoid making the investment.

- ✔ **If you do want to invest,** you find all sorts of corporate excuses to support the proposal or venture: this investment is a logical strategic progression; we have synergies and economies of scale to achieve; the market is presently being under-served – anything to make sure that the venture goes ahead.

In many cases, your answer to 'Do we want to invest?' is correct, but you must recognise personal aspects of decisions that are, after all, professional and corporate ventures.

What Next?

Investment is a process, not an individual event. If you're committing resources, you need to know and understand that you can't shut off your decisions from the rest of the world.

No investment decision is tidy, isolated or predictable. You're certain to need to draw on other corporate resources following a decision, perhaps unexpectedly. You must monitor for specific returns and make adjustments – both up and down – as circumstances change. In Chapter 12, I offer more advice on investment as a series of operations, rather than just as a strategic corporate development or a glamorous, pioneering activity.

Chapter 20

Ten Tips on Mergers and Acquisitions

In This Chapter

▶ Minimising the frenzy – and focusing on substance

▶ Asking yourself tough questions

▶ Knowing the deal in detail

As I discuss in Chapter 15, mergers, acquisitions and takeovers are certainly some of the most strategic activities that go on in today's business world.

When you face the prospect of merging with, acquiring or taking over another organisation – or having any of these actions taken on you – you need to follow a strategic approach. Without a strategic approach, you're likely to be driven by consultancy, legal fees and short-term share price advantages. These factors can be very attractive while you're setting up the deal but soon you're left with a whole lot of (often expensive) headaches, particularly integrating activities, product and service ranges, staff, supply and distribution networks and information systems.

'Synergies' and 'economies of scale' may be the buzzwords that drive mergers, acquisitions and takeovers, but what do these lofty terms really mean for you and your organisation? Don't jump into any of these high-level strategic deals without knowing and understanding in full what 'synergy' or 'economies of scale' actually mean in your precise business context.

So here are ten top techniques to make sure that you do indeed take a strategic approach when considering a merger, acquisition or takeover.

Clear Your Mind

At the proposition of a merger or acquisition, everyone gets very excited. You call in accountants and lawyers, consultants offer advice. Up goes the share price of all involved! Excitement and pandemonium reign! People work round the clock to make sure that the deal happens.

The first thing to do is to remove yourself from all this and clear your mind of all this floss. Relate the proposal to your core strategy (see Chapter 2), your competitive strengths (Chapter 6) and your organisational capabilities (Chapter 11). Make sure that the due diligence is thorough. Take a cold, hard look at what the real idea is, who is actually driving it and why. If you can't relate the proposal to enhancing your commercial or competitive position, you must question why you're contemplating it at all.

Assess the Target

You must assess the target – the merger or acquisition you're considering – from the point of view of what the deal can bring to you in terms of:

✔ Strengthening your core position.

✔ Strengthening your commercial capabilities.

✔ Ensuring the strength of one or more key elements of your business, which usually include finance, information, technology and supplies or distribution networks.

✔ Enlarging your customer or client base.

✔ Expanding your location or providing access to additional specific locations.

Acquisition and takeover activities provide a useful way of gaining a physical presence very quickly in new markets and locations, as long as you have the finance to buy up other companies in these ways. Acquisition is a key part of Tesco's expansion strategies in central and eastern Europe and the Far East, and Starbuck's across the USA and into Europe and elsewhere. The core of both companies' initiatives is clear commercial drive for new markets that each company believes it can profitably serve and compete in.

Weigh Assets and Liabilities

Your own expert judgement is vital when comparing the assets and liabilities associated with an acquisition or merger. Everyone involved in these deals holds a different view as to what the assets and liabilities actually are.

Someone or some group is likely to steer you in the direction of looking at the Balance Sheet and other figures in a particular way, telling you where the assets and liabilities are. They may even tell you that distinguishing assets and liabilities is simple – 'the figures speak for themselves'.

Of course, the figures don't speak for themselves. They're simply symbols on a page. Determining what amounts to an asset or a liability is both subjective and judgemental. You must rely on your ability to justify your own position in relation to how others see the same things. If something is truly an asset, you can find a way to demonstrate this value. And if you think that something is a liability, worry away and ask questions until you're satisfied with the answer that you receive. Go to Chapter 8 for useful ways to assess both assets and liabilities.

And never forget as you're making up your mind about assets and liabilities that although Balance Sheets typically use the legend 'sale of assets,' these documents invariably track the sale of liabilities.

Be wary of *winner's remorse*, in which management delights in praise from the business media on the day of acquisition, but the company's performance and reputation end up damaged when the deal turns out to be value-destroying (as two-thirds of all transactions are). Avoid winner's remorse and its consequences by anticipating it, even before you begin your merger and acquisition effort.

Set a Price

How much to pay for another company depends on how badly you want it, how badly someone else wants it and how determined you are to have it.

The most straightforward way of undertaking any merger or acquisition is when the present owners want or need to sell, and you're the only buyer. In this case you negotiate a price that's fair to all, or one side forces the other to accept a price.

Life is rarely so simple however. And if you get into an auction with one or more other bidders, expect to pay well over the odds, especially if the other bidders are equally determined to make the purchase.

If you end up spending a lot, you need a way to earn back your investment. You must improve the performance of the taken-over company or increase the value of its shares. Any plan must include one or both of these factors – or else consider withdrawing immediately.

Figuring out how high a price you should pay for another company is where your lawyers, advisers and accountants earn their money. If you're in a bidding war, your legal and financial experts must lobby and research what it will take to secure a deal with the target company. Otherwise the target company can simply sit back while its price goes ever upwards.

Identify What You're Really Paying For

Sure, you're acquiring or merging with another company, and doing so costs money. But what are you paying for? You can invariably come up with a range of answers to such a question, so you must be professionally disciplined and keep asking the follow-up questions: what are we *really* paying for?

Your answer needs to cover all the commercial advantages that you seek and have defined. Your answer, of course, must also fit your present core strategy.

If your questions don't yield answers that you're comfortable with, you need to check that you're not being drawn into the world of vanity purchases, short-term share advantages and unconsidered expansion – all of which are certain to cause you problems in the future.

So check, check and check again. And if you come to realise that the main drive behind a merger or acquisition isn't commercial, consider pulling out.

Know Why You Want the Deal

You should be able quickly – instantly! – to answer the question 'What do we want this deal for?' Are you seeking to strengthen your core business – or secure finance, technology, supplies or distribution? Good – so say what you mean!

To be certain that you get what you want from the deal, keep the following in mind:

- **If you're buying into a company for its locations or property portfolio:** Remember that the value of property can, and does, go down as well as up.

- **If you're buying expertise or technological capability:** Make sure that the people involved are going to be willing and able to work for you.

- **If you're buying a customer base or customer list:** Make sure that these customers can indeed deliver the value for you that they delivered to the target organisation in the past.

You need to have an effective integration plan in place before you finish any deal. Failure to smoothly and effectively integrate assets, IT, staff conditions or behaviour and employment terms can transform even a carefully planned acquisition into a nightmare. In 2008, Citigroup was forced to accept a bail-out from the US Federal Reserve. And a major contributing factor: a half dozen rushed acquisitions by former CEO Sanford Weill prior to 2008 had created an unwieldy company with multiple warring factions and cliques.

Consider Longevity

On the face of it, asking you how long you want the merger or acquisition to last is a silly question! Your answers may include 'forever' and 'how on earth should I know?'

And yet, you do need to know how long you plan to be involved with the acquired or merged organisation. Here's why: the longer you own the target company after you take it over, the more you must invest in it in terms of:

- Bringing facilities, technology and other equipment up to your own standards. If they're already up to your own standards, you still need to pay to integrate and use them.

- Integrating staff terms and conditions of employment (see the preceding section). These efforts can be very expensive if you have to buy out differences, quirks and anomalies or if they have, for example, superior holiday or pension entitlements.

Add – and Subtract – from Your Business

Many people think of mergers and acquisitions as strategies that only *add* to your overall business. Not so. Most mergers and acquisitions subtract more than you think!

For a start, if you have to bid for the target company against others, you're certain to pay more than you envisaged (and if the company was critical or desirable to multiple bidders, you may have vastly overpaid).

You're also going to have to pay, for example, for:

- ✔ Cultural and behavioural integration.
- ✔ Integration of trade union agreements, insurance arrangements, healthcare, pensions and other benefits.

Always look at a merger or acquisition on the basis that you'll have to pay, and not that you won't. The corporate world is littered with examples of companies and organisations that bought up others, tried to avoid costs and ended up in court being ordered to pay up. So always estimate the extent of your obligations high and treat any reduction as a bonus. (Setting your obligations low and then spending time, energy and resources on defending paying less is often an untenable – and ultimately expensive – position.)

And don't forget to consider what specifically the deal adds. You're surely aware of the expanded capability and capacity, the new locations, the synergies and economies of scale. But if you've gone wrong, you may also add the costs of a vanity purchase, excitement of the chase and personal ambition.

Be Realistic

Look at all mergers and acquisitions from the point of view of 'anything that can go wrong, will go wrong.' You're not being cynical – you're simply being realistic!

Your due diligence and detailed pre-analysis of any merger or acquisition deal is key. If you manage to retain clarity of thought, you're much more likely to identify all the problems that can arise and to take steps to ensure that they don't exist – or that if they do exist, you deal with them.

How the soon-to-be-merged or acquired organisation conducted itself before the deal is of paramount importance. Before you finalise the deal, you must ensure that you can introduce and implement standards of behaviour and performance that transcend what went on before and yet remain of value to the staff themselves.

This part of merger and acquisition activity is nearly always neglected – and is always expensive to put right. So you need to find out:

- ✔ What staff, customers, suppliers and shareholders view as important.
- ✔ What works well – and you can therefore keep and build on.
- ✔ What works poorly – and you need to reform or discard.

Let Go

In merger and acquisition deals, you can't control any of the following:

- ✔ How the customers and clients of the target organisation will behave towards you.
- ✔ How the suppliers of the target organisation will behave towards you.
- ✔ How the stock markets, media commentators and business analysts will view the merger, acquisition or takeover after it's implemented.

If you go into the deal because of the excitement of the chase and the resulting media frenzy, be ready for a backlash. Media that were only too happy to support, energise and give life to a proposal can turn on you very quickly when things turn out to be not quite as rosy. Under the media's spotlight, you may find yourself not only having to take all the remedial actions necessary but also justifying your actions along the way.

Work to identify everything that's outside your control with any deal and be prepared to deal with it. Being able to cope with uncertainty separates excellent managers from the rest. And nothing is more uncertain than the vagaries of the operating environment, and the ways in which the media behave towards you.

Chapter 21

Ten (Or So) Top Ways to Manage Risk

. . . .

In This Chapter

▶ Looking high and low for risk

▶ Responding effectively to risk

▶ Creating comprehensive risk management plans

. . . .

As I discuss in Chapter 16 and elsewhere in this book, risk is a major part of corporate strategy. The scarcity of resources, technology and expertise and the costs of finance, energy and transport mean that your organisation must have a risk awareness.

With the recent history of corporate failures, fraud and errors, you can't be too careful about anything or anybody. The recent wave of problems has happened at exactly the time that companies and organisations in all sectors are introducing risk awareness programmes and risk management policies.

You need a strategic approach to risk in order to ensure that you're fully aware of what can go wrong, that you understand why something went wrong and that you have steps you can take to deal with problems. Above all, doing this preparatory work – particularly attending to all the issues I highlight in this chapter – can prevent risk-related problems from happening in the first place.

Double-Check Yourself

As with many other important topics in this book, you must ask yourself a basic question about risks – twice. (Yes, this asking twice is becoming my mantra!) Specifically, in regards to risk, you must ask, 'What can go wrong?' And then you need to ask yourself, 'What can *really* go wrong?'

The knee-jerk response to this question is often, 'nothing.' Although this answer may feel a great comfort, you must question your situation and yourself until you're satisfied with your answer.

Risk is largely outside your control. Changes outside your organisation – changes in consumer confidence, transport and energy costs or finance availability – can and will affect everything you do. If you're an excellent provider of products and services to a large, loyal and active customer base, they'll nevertheless stop using you (or stop using you as much) if their circumstances change and they can no longer afford you. And although your customers may say something along the lines of, 'I love your products and services and have spent years doing business with you, but my bills have gone up and I can no longer afford you' may provide some comfort, that doesn't turn a profit.

Internally, risk is also often outside your control, but you can still look at the following to assess your risks:

- ✔ Prevailing attitudes and performance, staff satisfaction, staff absenteeism and turnover, injuries, accidents and disasters.
- ✔ How well your technology works.
- ✔ Financial strength and integrity.
- ✔ Where the cash is to come from.
- ✔ Staying within the law.

Assess internal risks by trying to pinpoint where things can and do go wrong. Keep your eyes peeled for the warning signs that all is not quite right.

Play a Constant Game of 'What If'

To help identify and examine risks, your immediate line of questioning needs to be, 'What if?'

Regarding external risk, ask yourself specific what-if questions such as:

- ✔ What if our energy bills double in a year?
- ✔ What if fuel costs go up 75 per cent?
- ✔ What if the road networks become even more clogged up?
- ✔ What if the government imposes new regulations on us?

For internal risks, ask yourself specific what-if questions such as:

- ✔ What if we lose a large customer base or a major customer?
- ✔ What if we suddenly lose 10 per cent of our staff?
- ✔ What if the information systems crash?
- ✔ What if the information systems lose their security?

The preceding what-ifs are just a start, but at least you're beginning to question the collective comfort that probably prevails in your organisation or section. After playing 'What if?' you're going to find many things to research further and address – whether to prevent disasters or to put things right as soon as possible before they become disasters.

Of course, you can 'What if?' yourself and your organisation into a complete state of neurosis, and this is not ideal at all! But you must get everyone thinking realistically . Besides, if you identify a problematic risk now as part of asking 'What if?', you've a chance to deal with things thoughtfully and on your own terms, rather than responding to an emergency.

Monitor Money

Any strategic approach to risk needs to start with the obvious, and money-related risks are universal.

Money risks arise from:

- ✔ Investment proposals that you don't think through properly – or don't cost or evaluate in detail.
- ✔ Lack of rigour in accounting methods and systems, which can include information leaks via your technology, filing and data processing systems.
- ✔ Fraud and theft, which go on in all organisations.
- ✔ *Insider share dealings* (using inside knowledge to gain financial advantages in the buying and selling of shares), which are widespread.
- ✔ 'Brother and Bob' trading arrangements, in which deals are brokered on the basis of friendship or kinship rather than corporate necessity.

You need structures and systems that prevent all the listed money-related risks from happening in the first place. Well-thought-out systems – such as tracking or clear paper trails – force money risks to show up instantly. And when these risks do show up, you need to have a reputation for swift remedial and punitive action.

Regard Your Reputation

In many cases, risks to your reputation lie outside your control. For example, Coca-Cola can assure the quality of its products, but it has little control over how its products are serviced by retail outlets. Or an airline may acquire a reputation for delays and baggage errors because of the actions of the airport authorities and airport baggage-handling staff.

Perhaps a particular business has gained a reputation for slow customer service or slow delivery; and this has only arisen because your backers don't want to invest in improving service and delivery (perhaps they just simply don't see the value). You have no control over this until you can persuade your backers to change their minds.

Or you may gain a reputation for late deliveries because of the vagaries of the motorway networks. Although you can't do anything about the traffic, you can schedule your deliveries at the quietest possible times (even if this means working at night).

Although you can't control these situations, you can *influence* them, if you choose to do so. Start by recognising that you can only work with what you've got, not what you would like. For example:

- ✔ Set your structures and schedules to keep damage to your reputation to a minimum. Perhaps you make an effort to get your lorries on the road at the times when hold-ups are likely to be at a minimum, thus improving your delivery times.

- ✔ Reinforce your damage-softening efforts with things that can influence your reputation, such as staff training and development or setting absolute standards of behaviour.

Now when you have to deal with the unexpected, you're dealing with the truly unexpected – not something that you've learned to live with.

Keep Things Honest

Of all the things that people everywhere hate, dishonesty comes very high on the list. An important aspect of assessing your organisation's risk means taking a close look at corporate, collective and individual dishonesty in an effort to figure out where the dishonest sources truly lie.

You reinforce your attitude toward dishonesty with the language that you use. For example, compare the following phrases. Which statement do you believe? Which do you not believe?

> ✔ There'll be no redundancies.
>
> ✔ We have no plans for redundancies at present.
>
> ✔ There'll be 38 redundancies effective on the last day of next month.

Many top managers use phrases such as the first two bullets in order to avoid personal discomfort only. (Personal discomfort when you enjoy a salary of £250,000 a year? You're in this position, so get used to the idea that you do have to do difficult things – and do them clearly and honestly!)

You create a culture of integrity and you minimise the risk arising from dishonesty when you deliver all your messages in clear, specific and simple language.

If you're ever caught lying, you'd better have a good reason. Nothing is as certain to damage your reputation as being caught in a lie and having no defence. And the defence for a lie? Not easy to find one, ever!

Set Standards

Risk is an outstanding reason for setting and enforcing your own standards of conduct, behaviour, integrity, probity and performance. If you don't set these standards yourself, people set their own, and in many cases, people genuinely believe that they're acting in the organisation's best interests, even when they do things wrong. If you don't set, maintain and enforce standards, people assume that they're doing all right. (Amazingly, 'not wrong' is often considered 'right'.)

You introduce and encourage risk when you fail to set standards, so set them and enforce them. Standards comprise one area that you really can influence as a business leader or manager. Be sure that your standards include specific references to money, theft, fraud, violence and conduct. (See Chapter 15.)

Assume the Worst

Nobody sets out to court disaster. Yet many companies and organisations take very different views of what they should do to prevent them. The air travel and nuclear energy industries, two industries where everything is subject to rigorous control and scrutiny, set standards for disaster management. Their approaches should guide everyone else.

But somehow when not flying at 35,000 feet or sitting next to a radioactive bomb, people slacken off. Instead of taking the same approach regardless of their sector, many people assume that nothing can go wrong.

Everything that can go wrong, will go wrong. For example:

- A stock market crashed in Japan because a trader hit the wrong computer key.
- Rail disasters occurred because nobody checked that the rails were bolted down.
- Banks collapsed because nobody checked what traders were actually doing.
- Medical disasters resulted because nobody checked what the surgeons were doing or that the hospitals were clean.

And all the preceding are quite apart from the vast numbers of workplace accidents, injuries and deaths that go unreported – additional bad experiences for which someone has to pay. If you end up at the centre of a managerial disaster, you risk your reputation as well as your bank balance.

Challenge Prevailing Risk Assumptions and Analysis Approaches

In part, the sub-prime mortgage mess occurred because of over-reliance on outdated, obsolete risk management analysis approaches that were never designed for exotic financial instruments such as credit default swaps.

If you don't have confidence in the methods for measuring risk in these things, why are you gambling your company's future? If your analysis tools aren't as advanced as the risk being measured, stay away!

Counterattack Violence

Vandalism, assault, bullying, victimisation, discrimination and harassment are all acts of violence. If anything causes moral outrage away from work, but in practice is allowed to continue more or less unchecked at work, you can consider it to be a form of violence.

Do you want a reputation for this kind of behaviour? Do you want a reputation as someone who tolerates it (and therefore de facto encourages it)? Or do you want a reputation for dealing with violence in all its forms immediately and completely wherever it arises?

In addition to the moral aspects, violence is also a serious risk:

- Nearly 500,000 assaults are reported at places of work every year (as well as assaults and other workplace violence that is never reported. Indeed there are hundreds of thousands of such incidents that aren't reported). These events have to happen somewhere.

- Financial compensation for victims is unlimited, and so you may find yourself having to pay out to victims. Furthermore, compensation rises when the evidence shows that you knew what was going on but did nothing.

- If – or more appropriately, *when* – a story of workplace violence reaches the media, reports always damage the reputation of the organisations involved.

Fortunately, you can minimise and eliminate workplace violence. For a start, after going through disciplinary procedures, you can sack the perpetrators and let everyone know that the firing was a consequence of the violence.

Walk the job to see where trouble may arise. Keep an eye on the habits, attitudes and temperaments of your staff. If you still need help, go to www.acas.org. uk. The Advisory Conciliation and Arbitration Service provides guidance on all aspects of workplace conduct.

Say No to Negligence

Granted, neglect is one of the more mundane aspects of risk management. But the main reasons why things don't get done at work are mundane! They include:

- I never got around to it.
- I didn't have time.
- I couldn't be bothered.
- I didn't like it.
- I was too busy.

If you have a truly strategic approach to risk management, you may find it very difficult to address negligence effectively. Everyone already has too much to do; and so of course, some things don't get done.

You reinforce negligence through poor performance policies and procedures – make sure that these are up to date, dynamic and enforced. Additionally, you minimise the negative impact of negligence by making sure that people know, understand and deliver their priorities. Make sure that they're fully trained and committed to your cause. And make sure that you tell them when they have done a good job; it reinforces all the positives that are the opposite of negligence.

And if people are still negligent, you should always have a poor performance policy through which you can take people if they still don't get the message!

Be Attentive and Alert

Like so much else, risk management is a process. So be vigilant! By remaining alert, you come across things that need attention, things that you haven't even thought of. There's nothing wrong with this – indeed, everything is right with it.

After you discover a new potential risk, however, you must make sure that you report it and add to your organisation's knowledge and understanding.

Be realistic. At least one major public body in the UK has complete risk management policies to counter terrorist attacks and chemical warfare – but has an inadequate stress management policy and up to 80 personal grievances against it at any one time. So while you can have all sorts of policies in place to deal with the unexpected, you need at the same time to concentrate your risk management activities on things that actually do occur on a regular basis.

Index

• C •

• *G* •

• *N* •

FOR DUMMIES®

UK editions

BUSINESS

978-0-470-51806-9

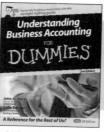

978-0-470-99245-6

978-0-470-75626-3

FINANCE

978-0-470-99280-7

978-0-470-99811-3

978-0-470-69515-9

PROPERTY

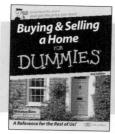

978-0-470-99448-1

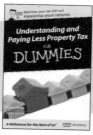

978-0-470-75872-4

978-0-7645-7054-4

Backgammon For Dummies
978-0-470-77085-6

Body Language For Dummies
978-0-470-51291-3

British Sign Language
For Dummies
978-0-470-69477-0

Business NLP For Dummies
978-0-470-69757-3

Children's Health For Dummies
978-0-470-02735-6

Cognitive Behavioural Coaching
For Dummies
978-0-470-71379-2

Counselling Skills For Dummies
978-0-470-51190-9

Digital Marketing For Dummies
978-0-470-05793-3

eBay.co.uk For Dummies,
2nd Edition
978-0-470-51807-6

English Grammar For Dummies
978-0-470-05752-0

Fertility & Infertility For Dummies
978-0-470-05750-6

Genealogy Online For Dummies
978-0-7645-7061-2

Golf For Dummies
978-0-470-01811-8

Green Living For Dummies
978-0-470-06038-4

Hypnotherapy For Dummies
978-0-470-01930-6

13902_p1

FOR DUMMIES®

A world of resources to help you grow

UK editions

SELF-HELP

978-0-470-01838-5

978-0-7645-7028-5

978-0-470-75876-2

HEALTH

978-0-470-69430-5

978-0-470-51737-6

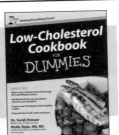

978-0-470-71401-0

HISTORY

978-0-470-99468-9

978-0-470-51015-5

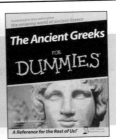

978-0-470-98787-2

Inventing For Dummies
978-0-470-51996-7

Job Hunting and Career Change
All-In-One For Dummies
978-0-470-51611-9

Motivation For Dummies
978-0-470-76035-2

Origami Kit For Dummies
978-0-470-75857-1

Personal Development All-In-One
For Dummies
978-0-470-51501-3

PRINCE2 For Dummies
978-0-470-51919-6

Psychometric Tests For Dummies
978-0-470-75366-8

Raising Happy Children For
Dummies
978-0-470-05978-4

Starting and Running a Business
All-in-One For Dummies
978-0-470-51648-5

Sudoku for Dummies
978-0-470-01892-7

The British Citizenship Test
For Dummies, 2nd Edition
978-0-470-72339-5

Time Management For Dummies
978-0-470-77765-7

Wills, Probate, & Inheritance Tax
For Dummies, 2nd Edition
978-0-470-75629-4

Winning on Betfair For Dummies,
2nd Edition
978-0-470-72336-4

FOR
DUMMIES®

The easy way to get more done and have more fun

LANGUAGES

Speak Spanish — the fun and easy way!
Spanish FOR DUMMIES
978-0-7645-5194-9

Speak French — the fun and easy way!
French FOR DUMMIES
978-0-7645-5193-2

The fun and easy way to start speaking Arabic
Arabic FOR DUMMIES
978-0-471-77270-5

MUSIC

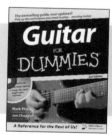

Guitar FOR DUMMIES
978-0-7645-9904-0

DJing FOR DUMMIES
978-0-470-03275-6
UK Edition

Piano FOR DUMMIES
978-0-7645-5105-5

SCIENCE & MATHS

Biology FOR DUMMIES
978-0-7645-5326-4

Chemistry FOR DUMMIES
978-0-7645-5430-8

Algebra FOR DUMMIES
978-0-7645-5325-7

Art For Dummies
978-0-7645-5104-8

Baby & Toddler Sleep Solutions For Dummies
978-0-470-11794-1

Bass Guitar For Dummies
978-0-7645-2487-5

Brain Games For Dummies
978-0-470-37378-1

Christianity For Dummies
978-0-7645-4482-8

Filmmaking For Dummies, 2nd Edition
978-0-470-38694-1

Forensics For Dummies
978-0-7645-5580-0

German For Dummies
978-0-7645-5195-6

Hobby Farming For Dummies
978-0-470-28172-7

Jewelry Making & Beading For Dummies
978-0-7645-2571-1

Knitting for Dummies, 2nd Edition
978-0-470-28747-7

Music Composition For Dummies
978-0-470-22421-2

Physics For Dummies
978-0-7645-5433-9

Sex For Dummies, 3rd Edition
978-0-470-04523-7

Solar Power Your Home For Dummies
978-0-470-17569-9

Tennis For Dummies
978-0-7645-5087-4

The Koran For Dummies
978-0-7645-5581-7

U.S. History For Dummies
978-0-7645-5249-6

Wine For Dummies, 4th Edition
978-0-470-04579-4

FOR DUMMIES®

Helping you expand your horizons and achieve your potential

COMPUTER BASICS

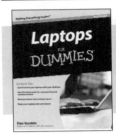

978-0-470-27759-1   978-0-470-13728-4   978-0-471-75421-3

DIGITAL LIFESTYLE

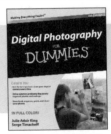  

978-0-470-25074-7   978-0-470-39062-7   978-0-470-17469-2

WEB & DESIGN

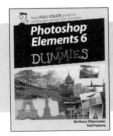  

978-0-470-19238-2   978-0-470-32725-8   978-0-470-34502-3

Access 2007 For Dummies
978-0-470-04612-8

Adobe Creative Suite 3 Design Premium
All-in-One Desk Reference For Dummies
978-0-470-11724-8

AutoCAD 2009 For Dummies
978-0-470-22977-4

C++ For Dummies, 5th Edition
978-0-7645-6852-7

Computers For Seniors For Dummies
978-0-470-24055-7

Excel 2007 All-In-One Desk Reference F
or Dummies
978-0-470-03738-6

Flash CS3 For Dummies
978-0-470-12100-9

Mac OS X Leopard For Dummies
978-0-470-05433-8

Macs For Dummies, 10th Edition
978-0-470-27817-8

Networking All-in-One Desk Reference
For Dummies, 3rd Edition
978-0-470-17915-4

Office 2007 All-in-One Desk Reference
For Dummies
978-0-471-78279-7

Search Engine Optimization For
Dummies, 2nd Edition
978-0-471-97998-2

Second Life For Dummies
978-0-470-18025-9

The Internet For Dummies, 11th Edition
978-0-470-12174-0

Visual Studio 2008 All-In-One Desk
Reference For Dummies
978-0-470-19108-8

Web Analytics For Dummies
978-0-470-09824-0

Windows XP For Dummies, 2nd Edition
978-0-7645-7326-2

13902_p4